Collection Editor: Jennifer Grünwald
Associate Editor: Sarah Brunstad
Associate Managing Editor: Alex Starbuck
Editor, Special Projects: Mark D. Beazley
VP, Production & Special Projects: Jeff Youngquist
SVP Print, Sales & Marketing: David Gabriel

Editor in Chief: Axel Alonso
Chief Creative Officer: Joe Quesada
Publisher: Dan Buckley
Executive Producer: Alan Fine

SPIDER-WOMAN: SHIFTING GEARS VOL. 1 — BABY TALK. Contains material originally published in magazine form as SPIDER-WOMAN #1-5 and AMAZING SPIDER-MAN #1. First printing 2016. ISBN# 978-0-7851-9622-8. Published by MARVEL WORLDWIDE, INC., a subsidiary of MARVEL ENTERTAINMENT, LLC. OFFICE OF PUBLICATION: 135 West 50th Street, New York, NY 10020. **Printed in Canada.** ALAN FINE, President, Marvel Entertainment; DAN BUCKLEY, President, TV, Publishing & Brand Management; JOE QUESADA, Chief Creative Officer; TOM BREVOORT, SVP of Publishing; DAVID BOGART, SVP of Business Affairs & Operations, Publishing & Partnership; C.B. CEBULSKI, VP of Brand Management & Development, Asia; DAVID GABRIEL, SVP of Sales & Marketing, Publishing; JEFF YOUNGQUIST, VP of Production & Special Projects; DAN CARR, Executive Director of Publishing Technology; ALEX MORALES, Director of Publishing Operations; SUSAN CRESPI, Production Manager; STAN LEE, Chairman Emeritus. For information regarding advertising in Marvel Comics or on Marvel.com, please contact Vit DeBellis, Integrated Sales Manager, at vdebellis@marvel.com. For Marvel subscription inquiries, please call 888-511-5480. **Manufactured between 4/8/2016 and 5/16/2016 by SOLISCO PRINTERS, SCOTT, QC, CANADA.**

10 9 8 7 6 5 4 3 2 1

PREVIOUSLY

Forget what you've heard — Jessica Drew is the world's greatest spider-themed superspy.

As an infant, Jessica fell fataly ill; in an effort to save her life, her scientist father injected her with a serum of spider blood. The concoction cured her, but also gifted her with adhesive fingertips and toes, enhanced speed and agility and the ability to fire biokinetic "venom blasts."

She's been an Avenger, an agent of Hydra and a super-spy for the government, but she's hung up her holster and is returning to normal life with a little help from her pals Ben Urich (ace reporter for the *Daily Bugle*) and Roger Gocking (ace guy in a porcupine costume).

But what's "normal" for a pregnant super hero? She may be a mom-to-be, but she's still Spider-Woman!

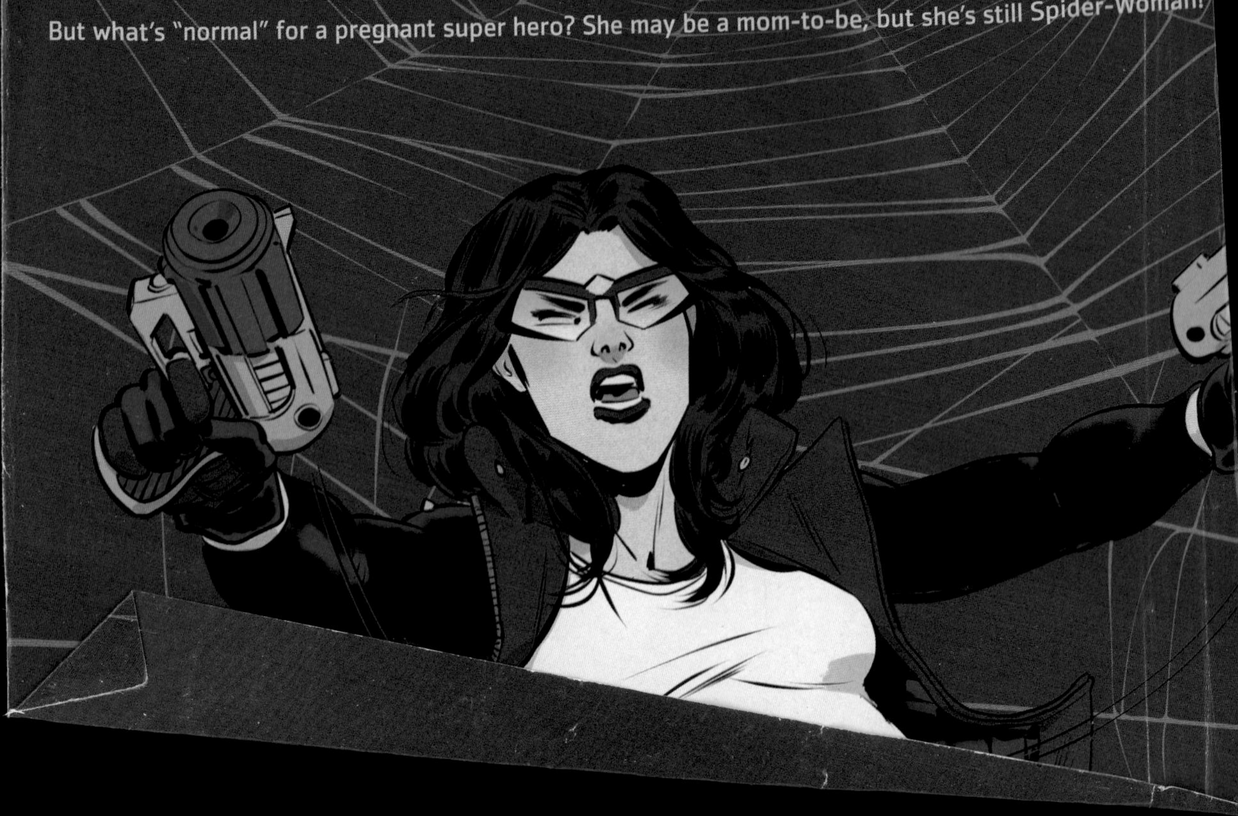

SPIDER-WOMAN
SHIFTING GEARS

BABY TALK

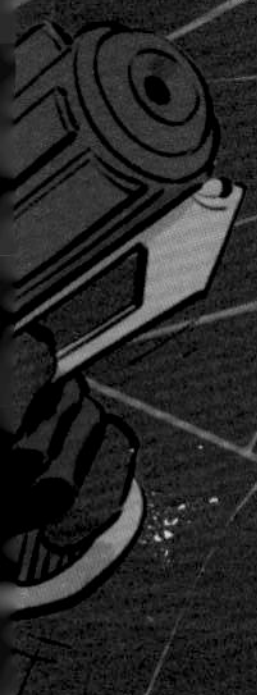

WRITER
DENNIS HOPELESS

PENCILER
JAVIER RODRIGUEZ

INKER
ALVARO LOPEZ

COLORISTS
JAVIER RODRIGUEZ (#1-2 & "WHAT TO EXPECT")
& **RACHELLE ROSENBERG** (#3-5)

LETTERER
VC'S TRAVIS LANHAM

COVER ART
JAVIER RODRIGUEZ
WITH **ALVARO LOPEZ** (#1)

EDITOR
DEVIN LEWIS

SENIOR EDITOR
NICK LOWE

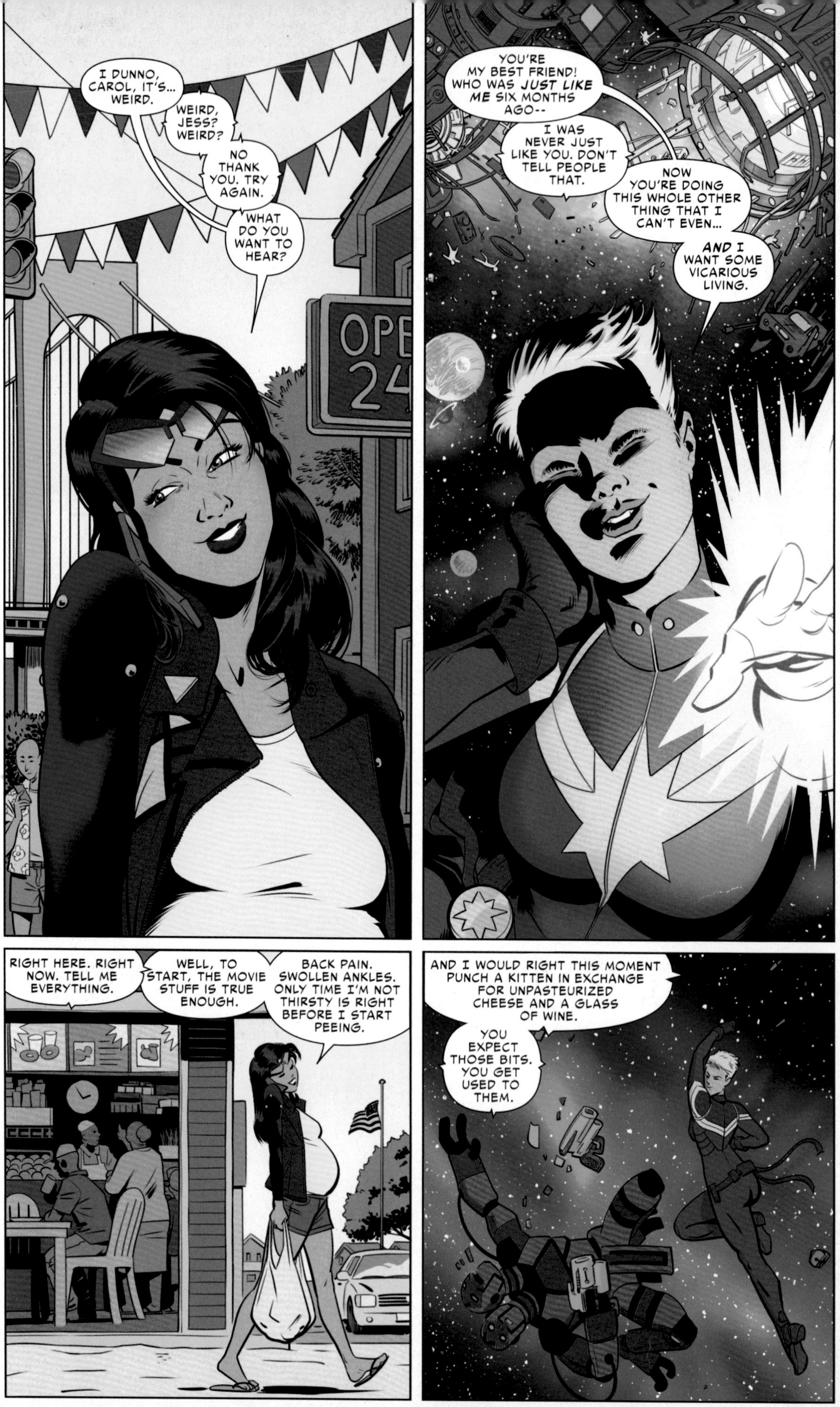
I DUNNO, CAROL, IT'S... WEIRD.
WEIRD, JESS? WEIRD?
NO THANK YOU. TRY AGAIN.
WHAT DO YOU WANT TO HEAR?
OPE
24
YOU'RE MY BEST FRIEND! WHO WAS *JUST LIKE ME* SIX MONTHS AGO--
I WAS NEVER JUST LIKE YOU. DON'T TELL PEOPLE THAT.
NOW YOU'RE DOING THIS WHOLE OTHER THING THAT I CAN'T EVEN...
AND I WANT SOME VICARIOUS LIVING.
RIGHT HERE. RIGHT NOW. TELL ME EVERYTHING.
WELL, TO START, THE MOVIE STUFF IS TRUE ENOUGH.
BACK PAIN. SWOLLEN ANKLES. ONLY TIME I'M NOT THIRSTY IS RIGHT BEFORE I START PEEING.
AND I WOULD RIGHT THIS MOMENT PUNCH A KITTEN IN EXCHANGE FOR UNPASTEURIZED CHEESE AND A GLASS OF WINE.
YOU EXPECT THOSE BITS. YOU GET USED TO THEM.

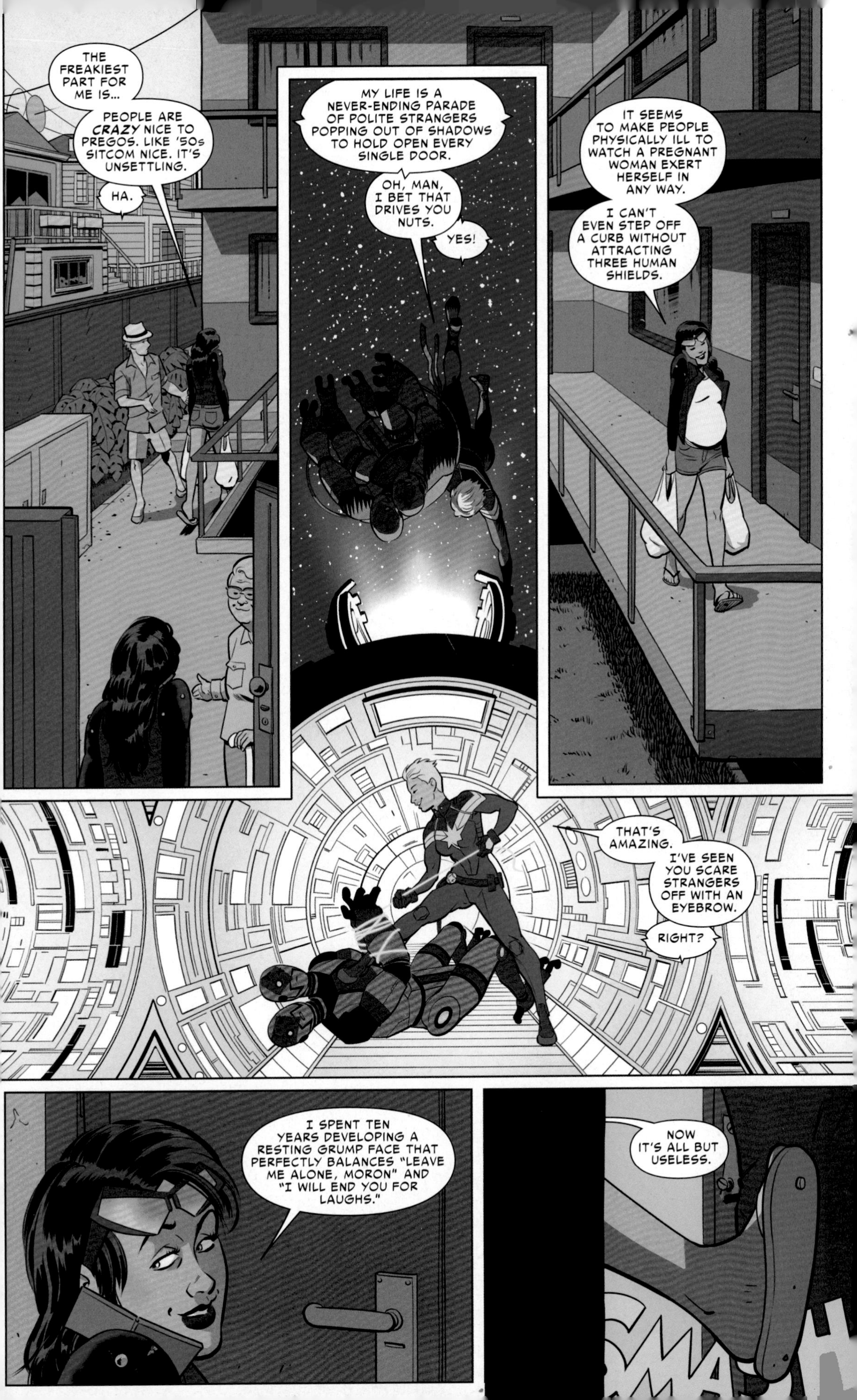
THE FREAKIEST PART FOR ME IS...
PEOPLE ARE CRAZY NICE TO PREGOS. LIKE '50s SITCOM NICE. IT'S UNSETTLING.
HA.
MY LIFE IS A NEVER-ENDING PARADE OF POLITE STRANGERS POPPING OUT OF SHADOWS TO HOLD OPEN EVERY SINGLE DOOR.
OH, MAN, I BET THAT DRIVES YOU NUTS.
YES!
IT SEEMS TO MAKE PEOPLE PHYSICALLY ILL TO WATCH A PREGNANT WOMAN EXERT HERSELF IN ANY WAY.
I CAN'T EVEN STEP OFF A CURB WITHOUT ATTRACTING THREE HUMAN SHIELDS.
THAT'S AMAZING.
I'VE SEEN YOU SCARE STRANGERS OFF WITH AN EYEBROW.
RIGHT?
I SPENT TEN YEARS DEVELOPING A RESTING GRUMP FACE THAT PERFECTLY BALANCES "LEAVE ME ALONE, MORON" AND "I WILL END YOU FOR LAUGHS."
NOW IT'S ALL BUT USELESS.

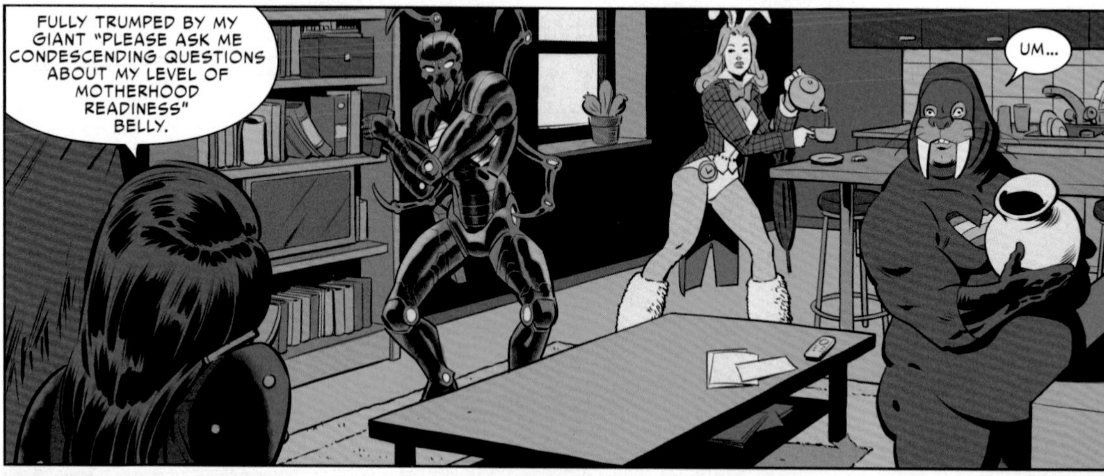
FULLY TRUMPED BY MY GIANT "PLEASE ASK ME CONDESCENDING QUESTIONS ABOUT MY LEVEL OF MOTHERHOOD READINESS" BELLY.
UM...

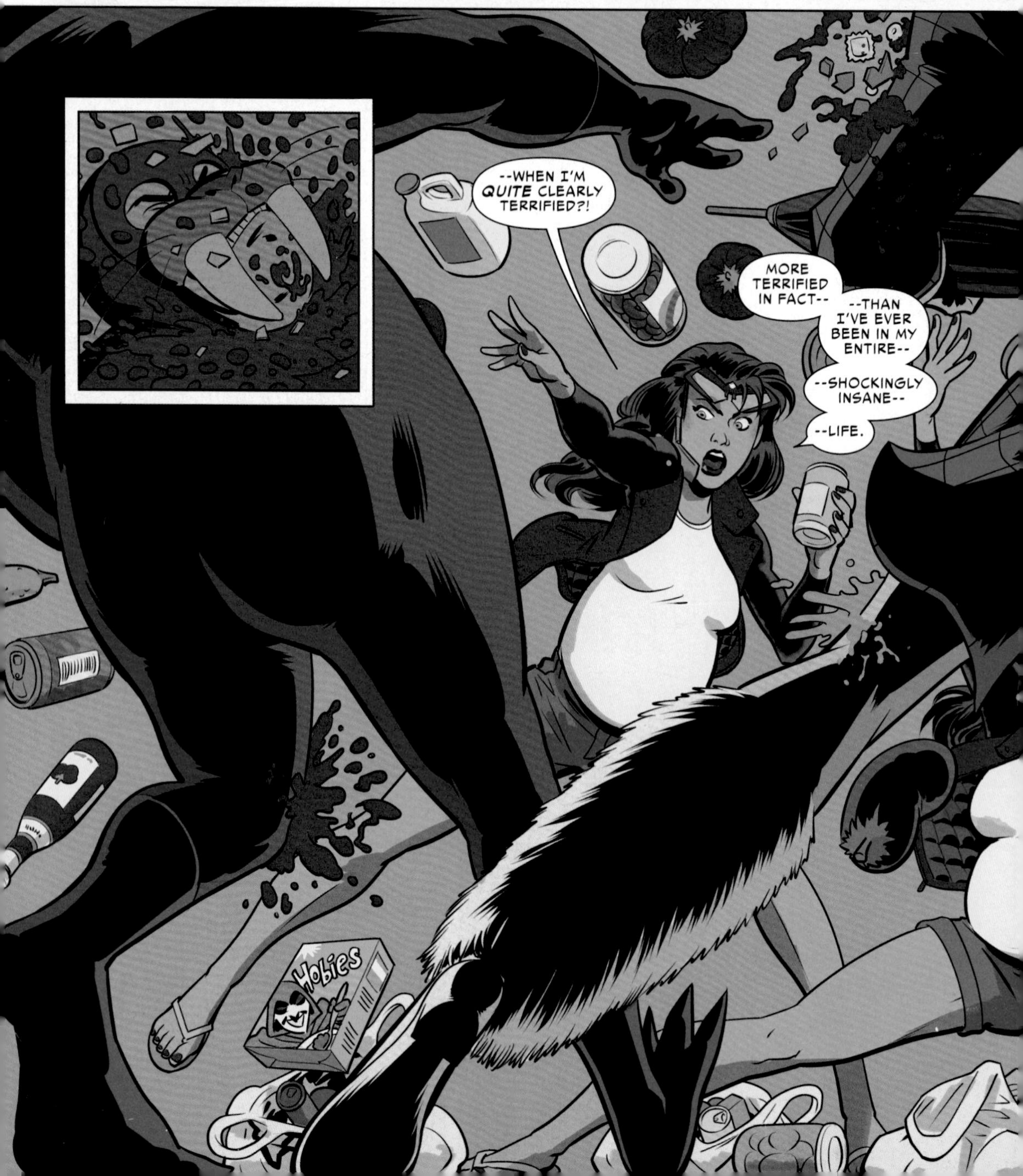
--WHEN I'M QUITE CLEARLY TERRIFIED?!
MORE TERRIFIED IN FACT--
--THAN I'VE EVER BEEN IN MY ENTIRE--
--SHOCKINGLY INSANE--
--LIFE.
HOBIES

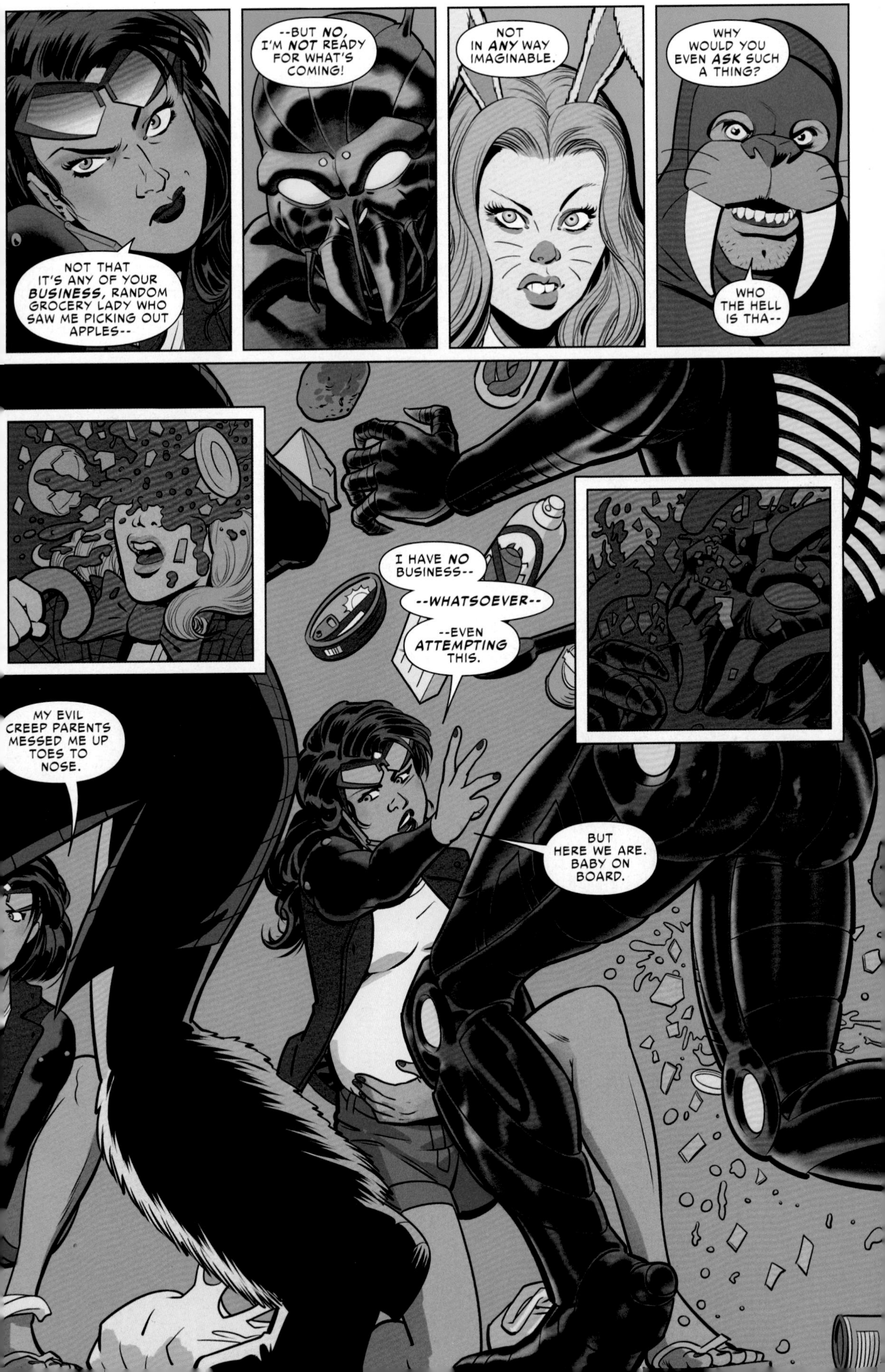

NOT THAT IT'S ANY OF YOUR BUSINESS, RANDOM GROCERY LADY WHO SAW ME PICKING OUT APPLES--
--BUT NO, I'M NOT READY FOR WHAT'S COMING!
NOT IN ANY WAY IMAGINABLE.
WHY WOULD YOU EVEN ASK SUCH A THING?
WHO THE HELL IS THA--
I HAVE NO BUSINESS--
--WHATSOEVER--
--EVEN ATTEMPTING THIS.
MY EVIL CREEP PARENTS MESSED ME UP TOES TO NOSE.
BUT HERE WE ARE. BABY ON BOARD.

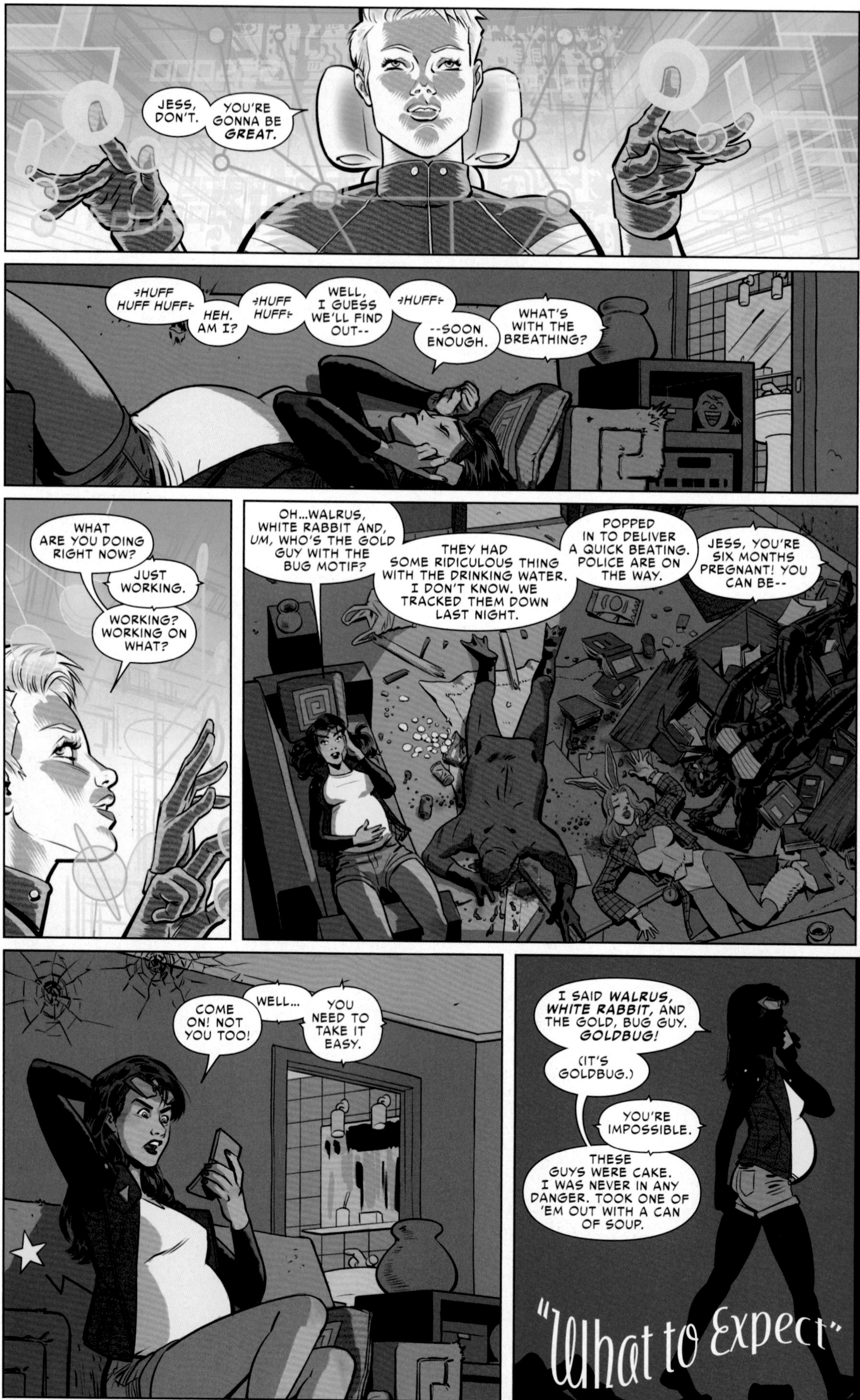
JESS, DON'T.
YOU'RE GONNA BE GREAT.
HUFF HUFF HUFF
HEH. AM I?
HUFF HUFF
WELL, I GUESS WE'LL FIND OUT--
HUFF
--SOON ENOUGH.
WHAT'S WITH THE BREATHING?
WHAT ARE YOU DOING RIGHT NOW?
JUST WORKING.
WORKING? WORKING ON WHAT?
OH...WALRUS, WHITE RABBIT AND, UM, WHO'S THE GOLD GUY WITH THE BUG MOTIF?
THEY HAD SOME RIDICULOUS THING WITH THE DRINKING WATER. I DON'T KNOW. WE TRACKED THEM DOWN LAST NIGHT.
POPPED IN TO DELIVER A QUICK BEATING. POLICE ARE ON THE WAY.
JESS, YOU'RE SIX MONTHS PREGNANT! YOU CAN BE--
COME ON! NOT YOU TOO!
WELL...
YOU NEED TO TAKE IT EASY.
I SAID WALRUS, WHITE RABBIT, AND THE GOLD, BUG GUY. GOLDBUG!
(IT'S GOLDBUG.)
YOU'RE IMPOSSIBLE.
THESE GUYS WERE CAKE. I WAS NEVER IN ANY DANGER. TOOK ONE OF 'EM OUT WITH A CAN OF SOUP.
"What to Expect"

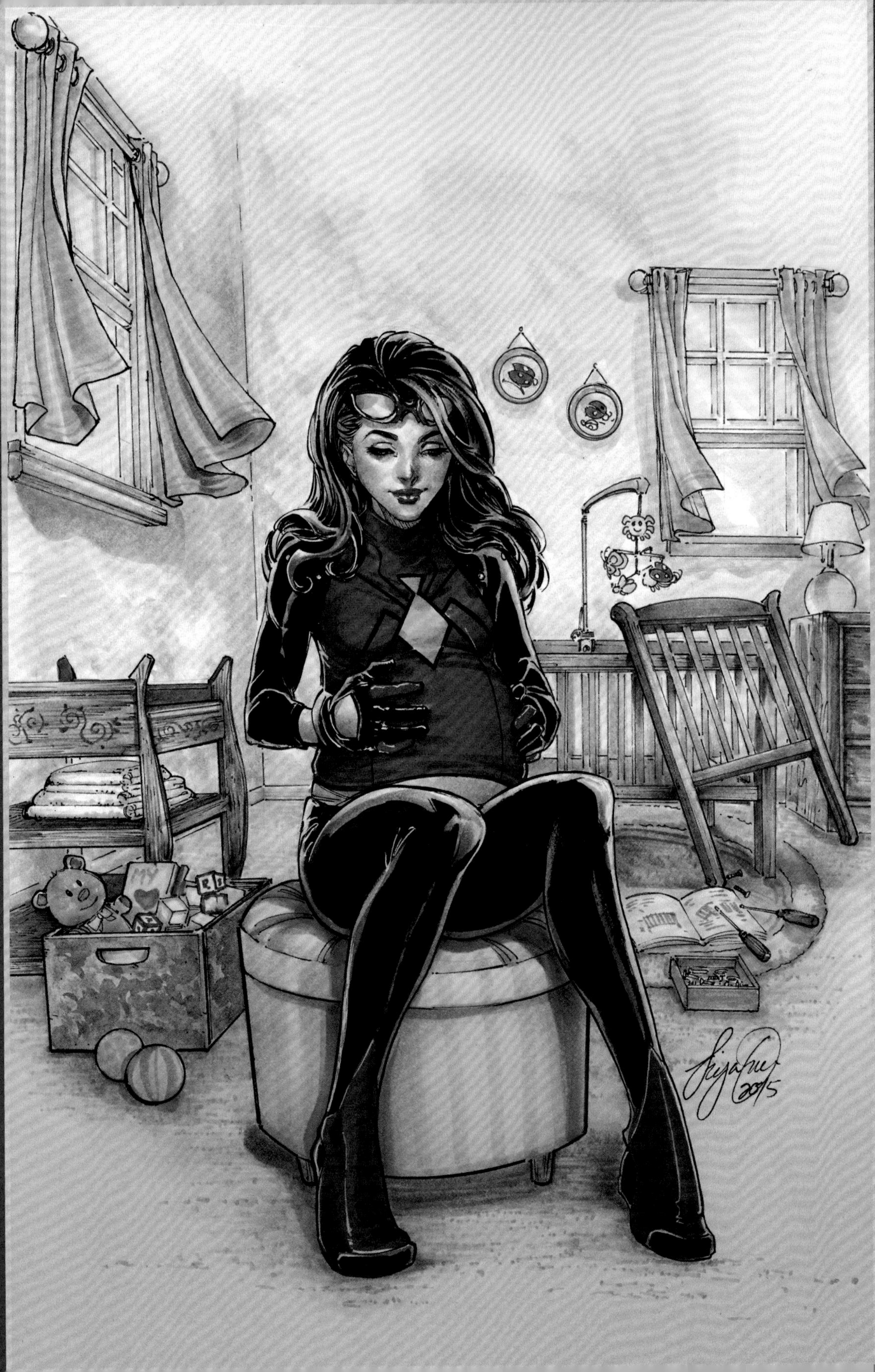
MY

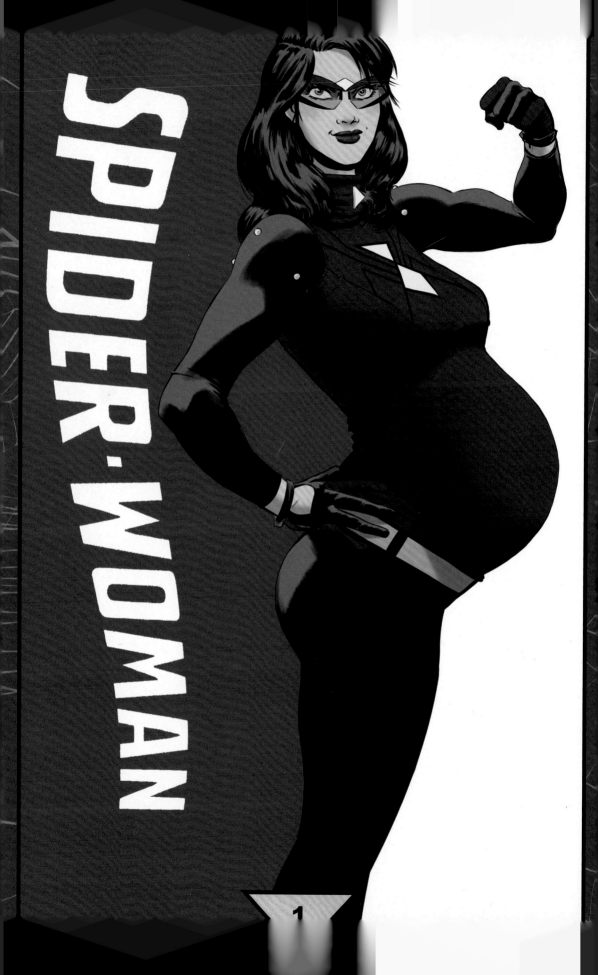

SPIDER-WOMAN

1

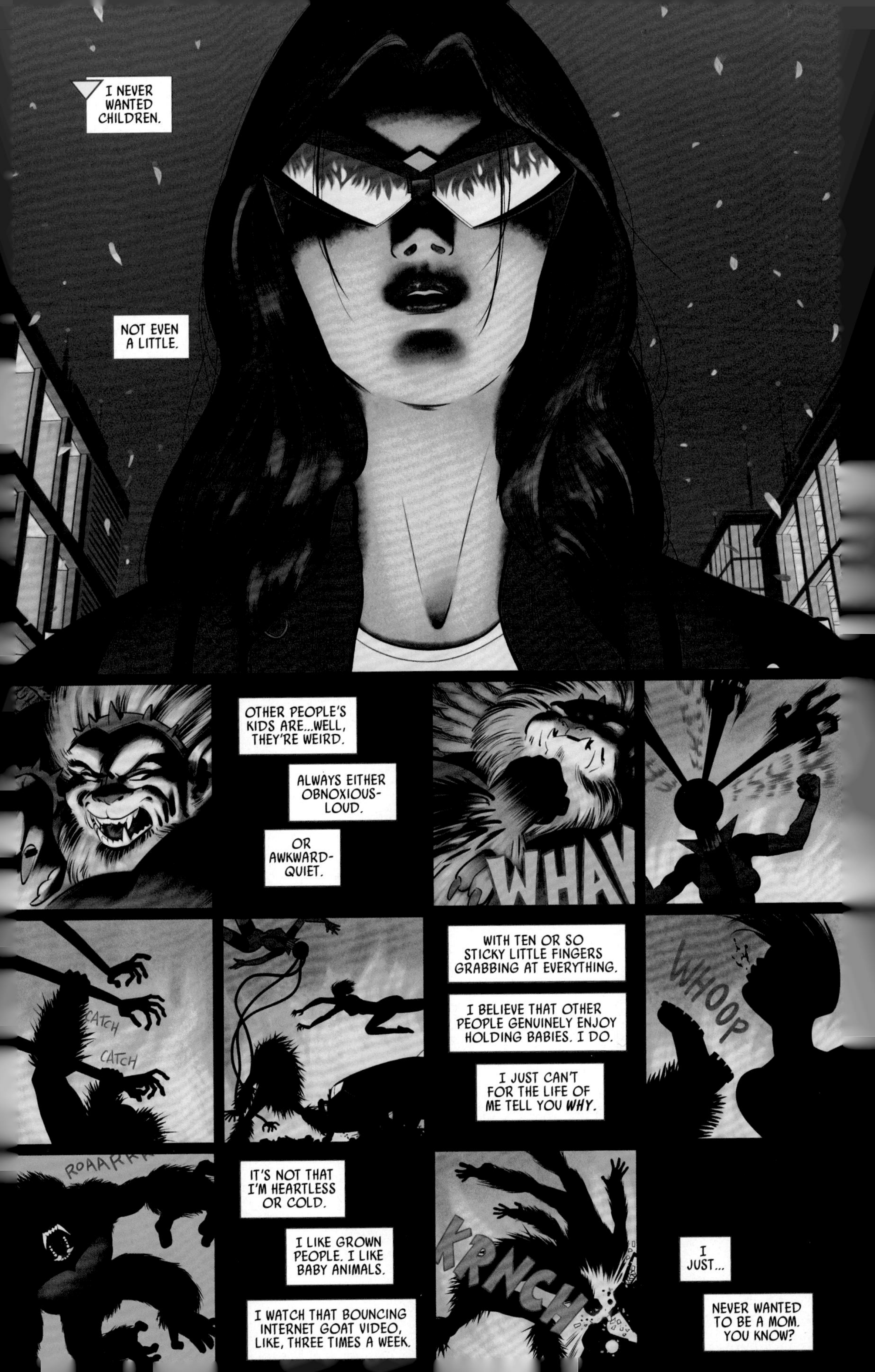
I NEVER WANTED CHILDREN.
NOT EVEN A LITTLE.
OTHER PEOPLE'S KIDS ARE...WELL, THEY'RE WEIRD.
ALWAYS EITHER OBNOXIOUS-LOUD.
OR AWKWARD-QUIET.
WHAM
CATCH
CATCH
WITH TEN OR SO STICKY LITTLE FINGERS GRABBING AT EVERYTHING.
I BELIEVE THAT OTHER PEOPLE GENUINELY ENJOY HOLDING BABIES. I DO.
I JUST CAN'T FOR THE LIFE OF ME TELL YOU *WHY*.
WHOOP
IT'S NOT THAT I'M HEARTLESS OR COLD.
I LIKE GROWN PEOPLE. I LIKE BABY ANIMALS.
I WATCH THAT BOUNCING INTERNET GOAT VIDEO, LIKE, THREE TIMES A WEEK.
KRNCH
I JUST...
NEVER WANTED TO BE A MOM. YOU KNOW?

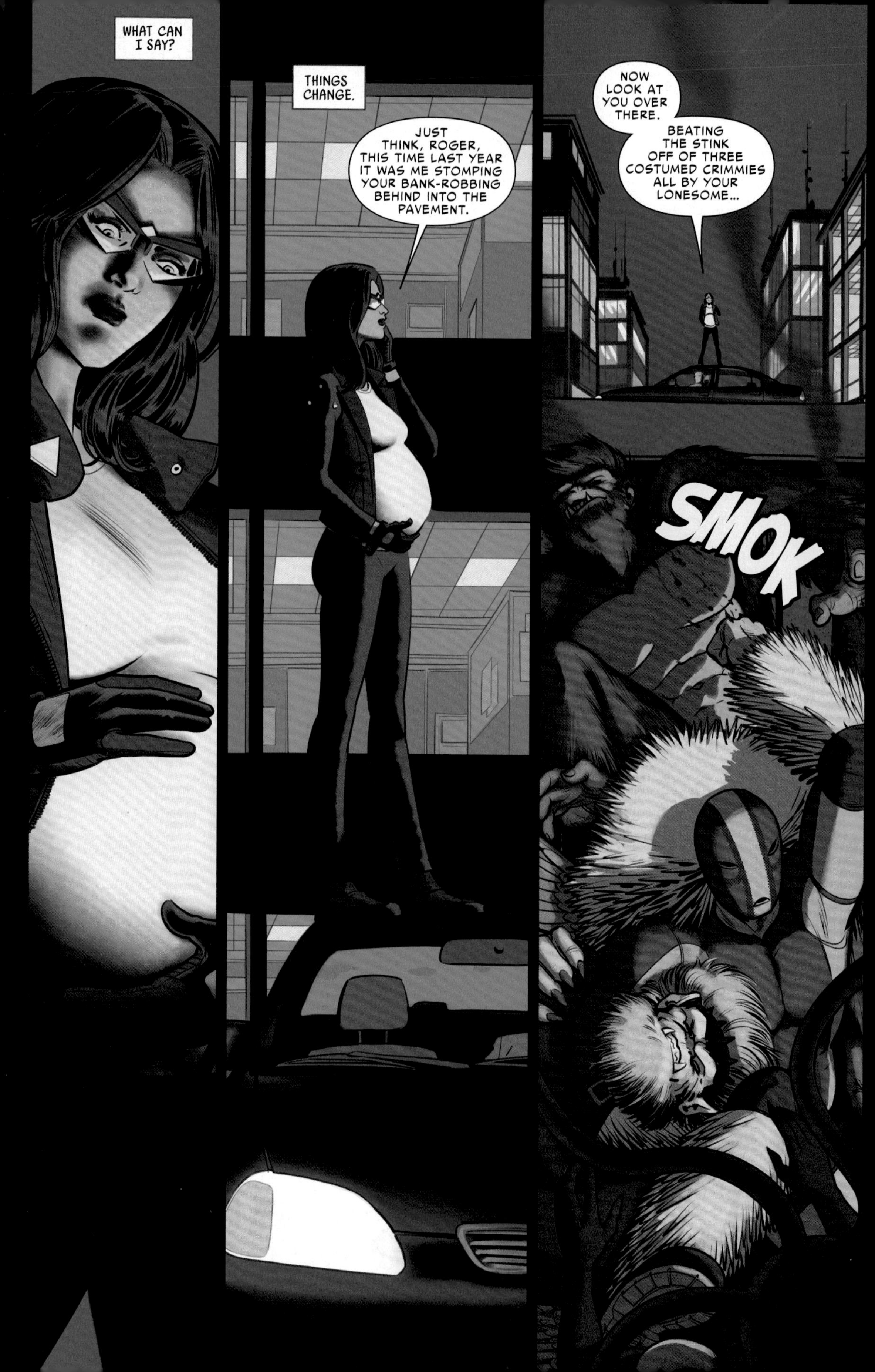

WHAT CAN I SAY?
THINGS CHANGE.
JUST THINK, ROGER, THIS TIME LAST YEAR IT WAS ME STOMPING YOUR BANK-ROBBING BEHIND INTO THE PAVEMENT.
NOW LOOK AT YOU OVER THERE.
BEATING THE STINK OFF OF THREE COSTUMED CRIMMIES ALL BY YOUR LONESOME...
SMOK

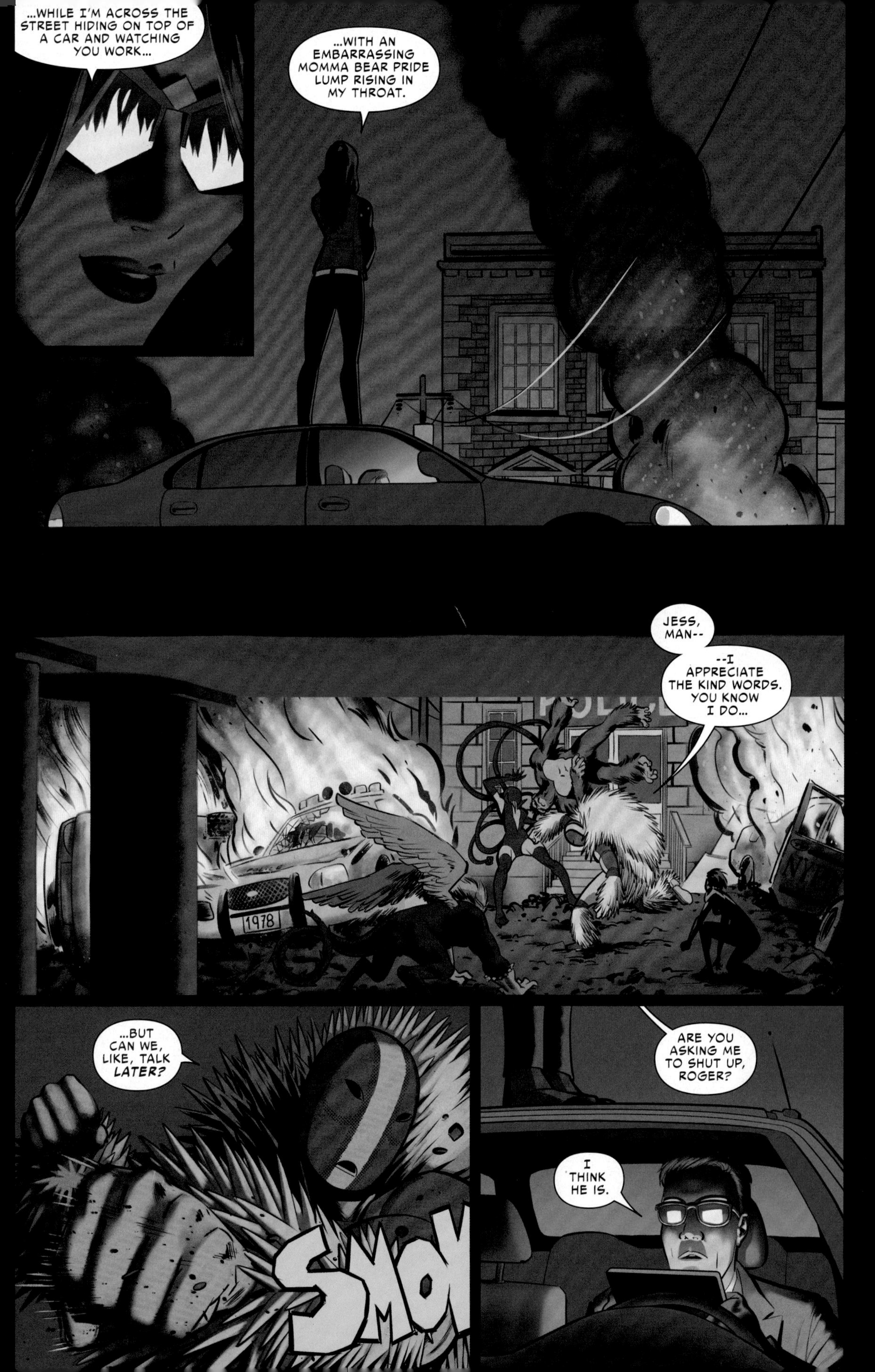
...WHILE I'M ACROSS THE STREET HIDING ON TOP OF A CAR AND WATCHING YOU WORK...
...WITH AN EMBARRASSING MOMMA BEAR PRIDE LUMP RISING IN MY THROAT.
JESS, MAN--
--I APPRECIATE THE KIND WORDS. YOU KNOW I DO...
1978
...BUT CAN WE, LIKE, TALK *LATER?*
SMOV
ARE YOU ASKING ME TO SHUT UP, ROGER?
I THINK HE IS.

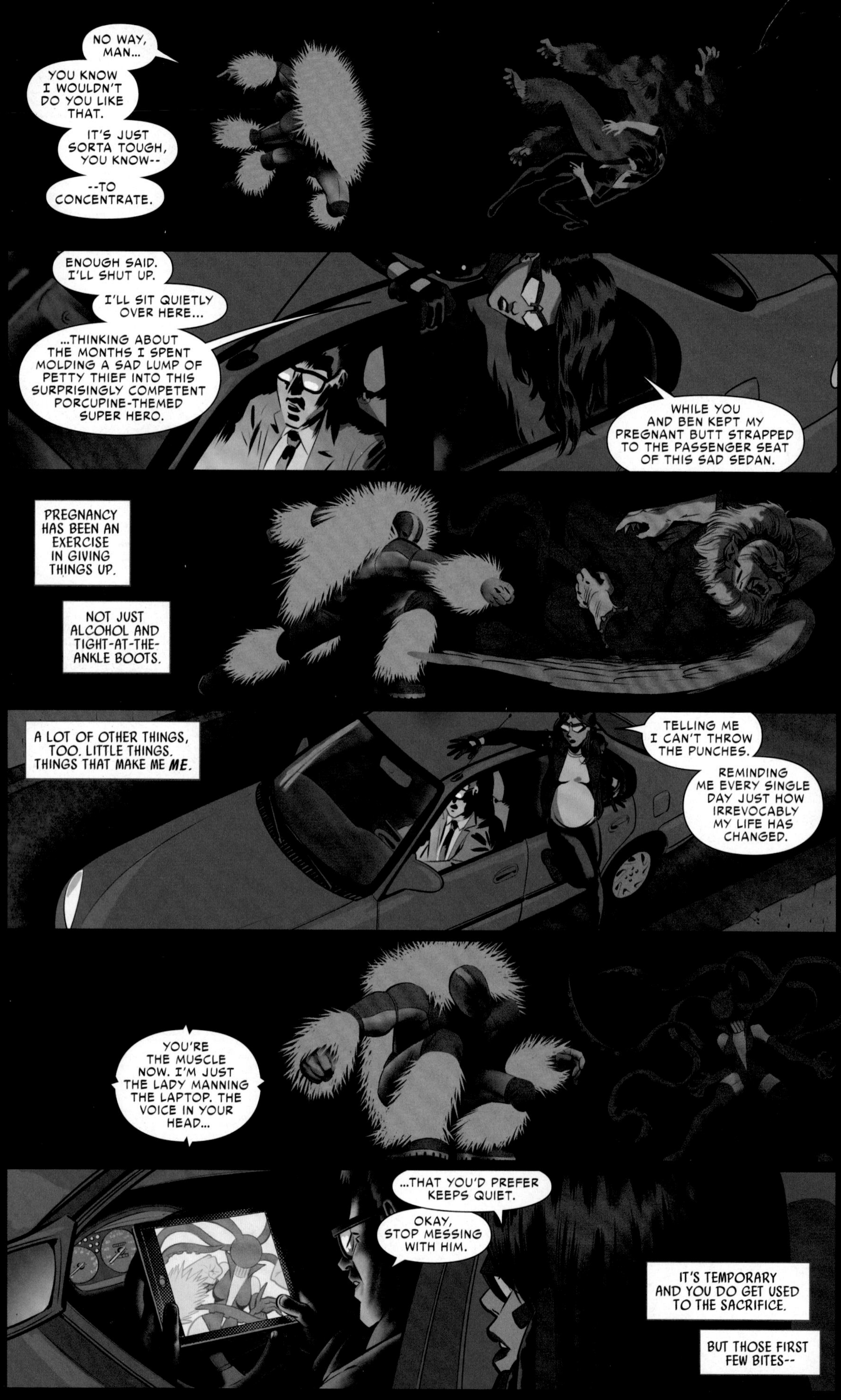
NO WAY, MAN...
YOU KNOW I WOULDN'T DO YOU LIKE THAT.
IT'S JUST SORTA TOUGH, YOU KNOW--
--TO CONCENTRATE.
ENOUGH SAID. I'LL SHUT UP.
I'LL SIT QUIETLY OVER HERE...
...THINKING ABOUT THE MONTHS I SPENT MOLDING A SAD LUMP OF PETTY THIEF INTO THIS SURPRISINGLY COMPETENT PORCUPINE-THEMED SUPER HERO.
WHILE YOU AND BEN KEPT MY PREGNANT BUTT STRAPPED TO THE PASSENGER SEAT OF THIS SAD SEDAN.
PREGNANCY HAS BEEN AN EXERCISE IN GIVING THINGS UP.
NOT JUST ALCOHOL AND TIGHT-AT-THE-ANKLE BOOTS.
A LOT OF OTHER THINGS, TOO. LITTLE THINGS. THINGS THAT MAKE ME *ME*.
TELLING ME I CAN'T THROW THE PUNCHES.
REMINDING ME EVERY SINGLE DAY JUST HOW IRREVOCABLY MY LIFE HAS CHANGED.
YOU'RE THE MUSCLE NOW. I'M JUST THE LADY MANNING THE LAPTOP. THE VOICE IN YOUR HEAD...
...THAT YOU'D PREFER KEEPS QUIET.
OKAY, STOP MESSING WITH HIM.
IT'S TEMPORARY AND YOU DO GET USED TO THE SACRIFICE.
BUT THOSE FIRST FEW BITES--

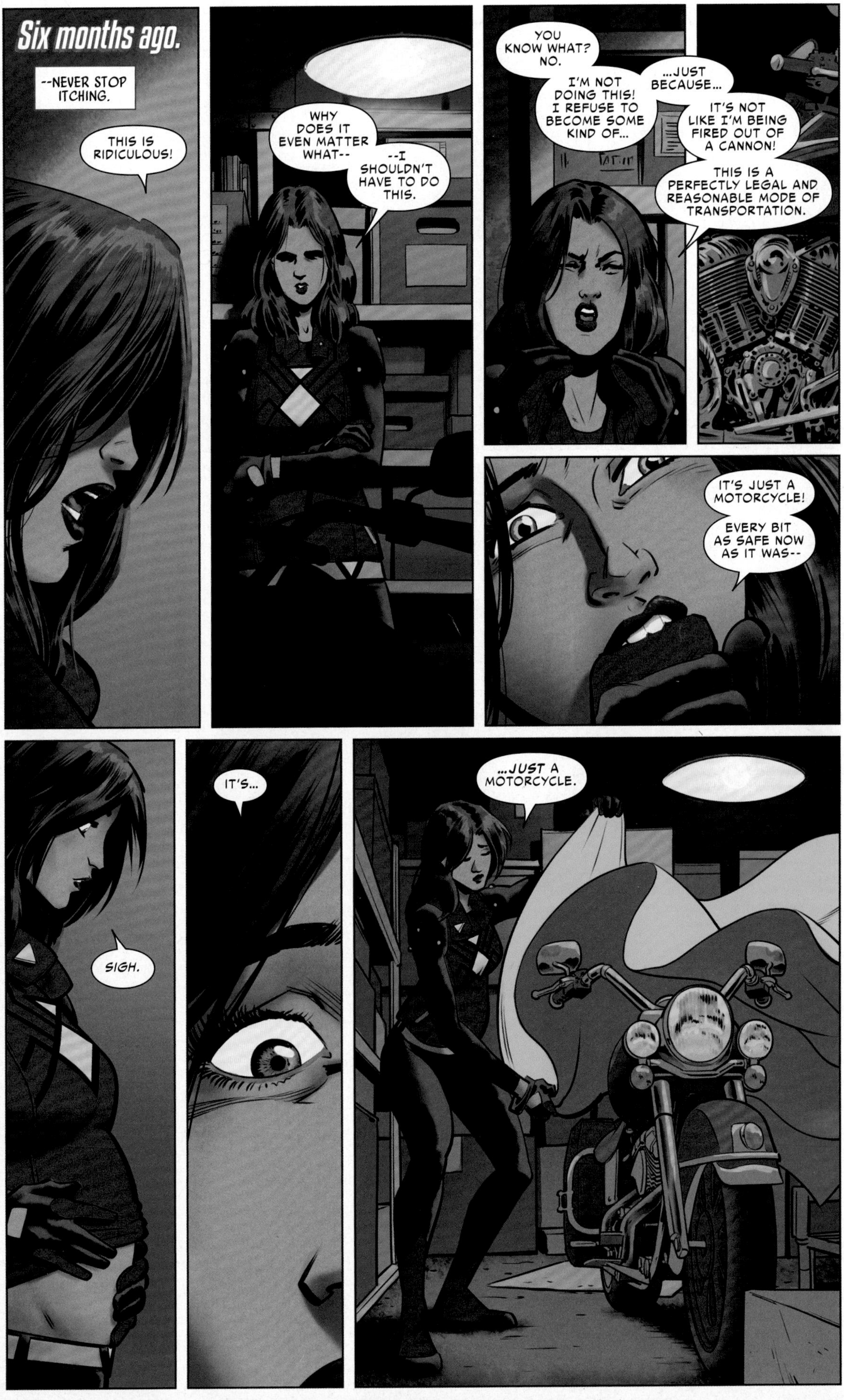
Six months ago.
--NEVER STOP ITCHING.
THIS IS RIDICULOUS!
WHY DOES IT EVEN MATTER WHAT--
--I SHOULDN'T HAVE TO DO THIS.
YOU KNOW WHAT? NO.
I'M NOT DOING THIS! I REFUSE TO BECOME SOME KIND OF...
...JUST BECAUSE...
IT'S NOT LIKE I'M BEING FIRED OUT OF A CANNON!
THIS IS A PERFECTLY LEGAL AND REASONABLE MODE OF TRANSPORTATION.
IT'S JUST A MOTORCYCLE!
EVERY BIT AS SAFE NOW AS IT WAS--
SIGH.
IT'S...
...JUST A MOTORCYCLE.

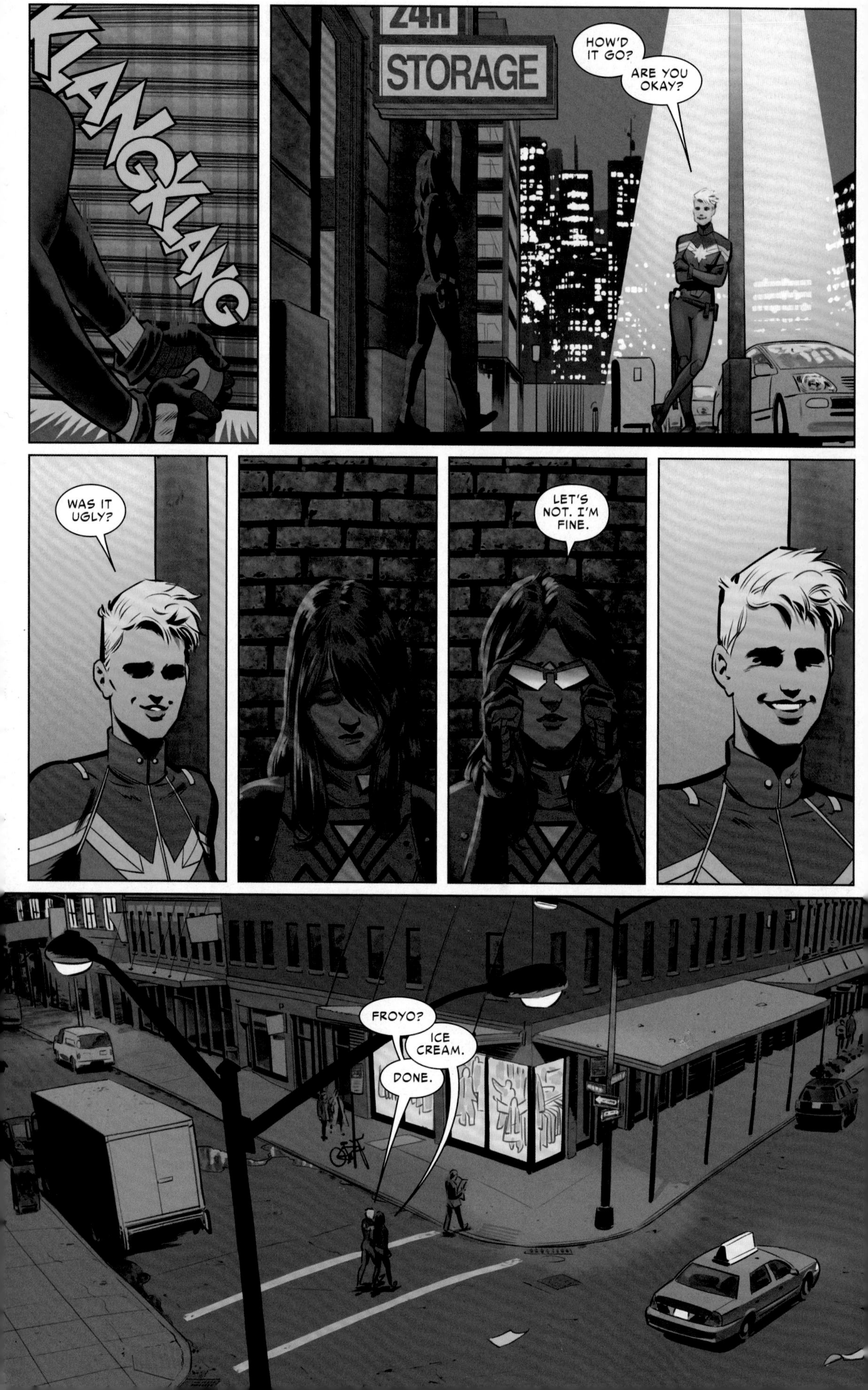
KLANGKLANG
STORAGE
HOW'D IT GO?
ARE YOU OKAY?
WAS IT UGLY?
LET'S NOT. I'M FINE.
FROYO?
ICE CREAM.
DONE.

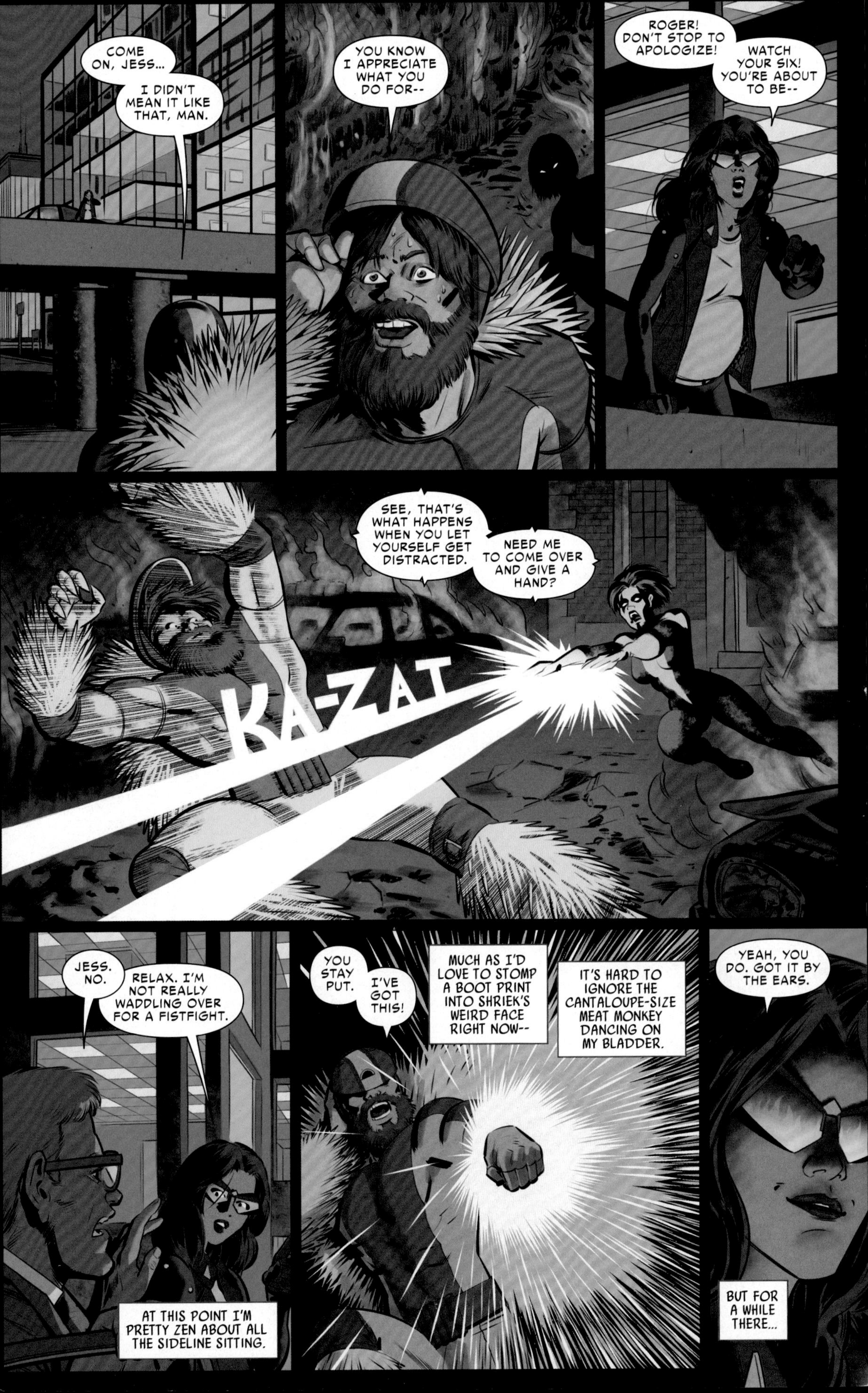
COME ON, JESS...
I DIDN'T MEAN IT LIKE THAT, MAN.
YOU KNOW I APPRECIATE WHAT YOU DO FOR--
ROGER! DON'T STOP TO APOLOGIZE!
WATCH YOUR SIX! YOU'RE ABOUT TO BE--
SEE, THAT'S WHAT HAPPENS WHEN YOU LET YOURSELF GET DISTRACTED.
NEED ME TO COME OVER AND GIVE A HAND?
KA-ZAT
JESS. NO.
RELAX. I'M NOT REALLY WADDLING OVER FOR A FISTFIGHT.
AT THIS POINT I'M PRETTY ZEN ABOUT ALL THE SIDELINE SITTING.
YOU STAY PUT.
I'VE GOT THIS!
MUCH AS I'D LOVE TO STOMP A BOOT PRINT INTO SHRIEK'S WEIRD FACE RIGHT NOW--
IT'S HARD TO IGNORE THE CANTALOUPE-SIZE MEAT MONKEY DANCING ON MY BLADDER.
YEAH, YOU DO. GOT IT BY THE EARS.
BUT FOR A WHILE THERE...

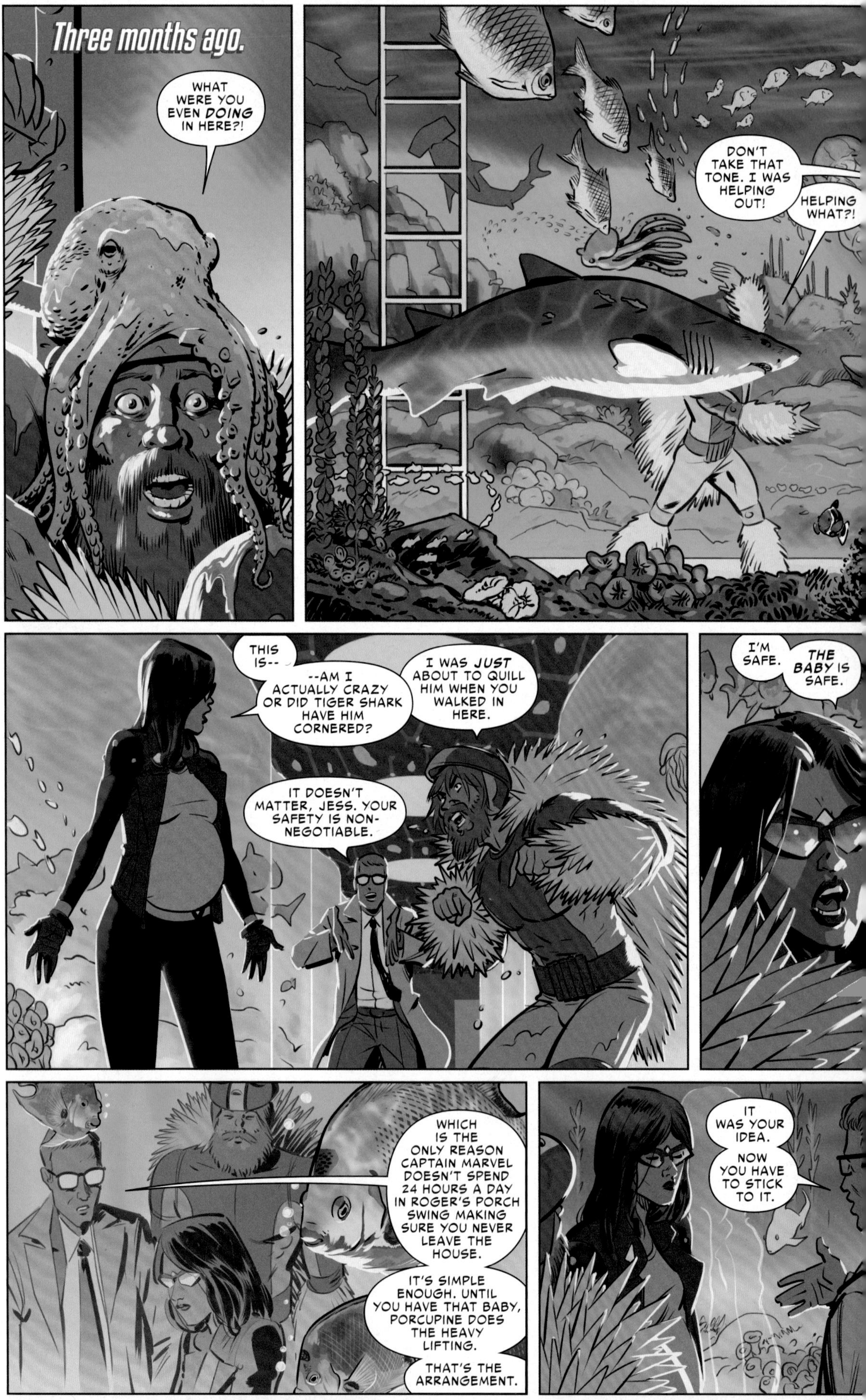
Three months ago.
WHAT WERE YOU EVEN DOING IN HERE?!
DON'T TAKE THAT TONE. I WAS HELPING OUT!
HELPING WHAT?!
THIS IS--
--AM I ACTUALLY CRAZY OR DID TIGER SHARK HAVE HIM CORNERED?
I WAS JUST ABOUT TO QUILL HIM WHEN YOU WALKED IN HERE.
IT DOESN'T MATTER, JESS. YOUR SAFETY IS NON-NEGOTIABLE.
I'M SAFE.
THE BABY IS SAFE.
WHICH IS THE ONLY REASON CAPTAIN MARVEL DOESN'T SPEND 24 HOURS A DAY IN ROGER'S PORCH SWING MAKING SURE YOU NEVER LEAVE THE HOUSE.
IT'S SIMPLE ENOUGH. UNTIL YOU HAVE THAT BABY, PORCUPINE DOES THE HEAVY LIFTING.
THAT'S THE ARRANGEMENT.
IT WAS YOUR IDEA.
NOW YOU HAVE TO STICK TO IT.

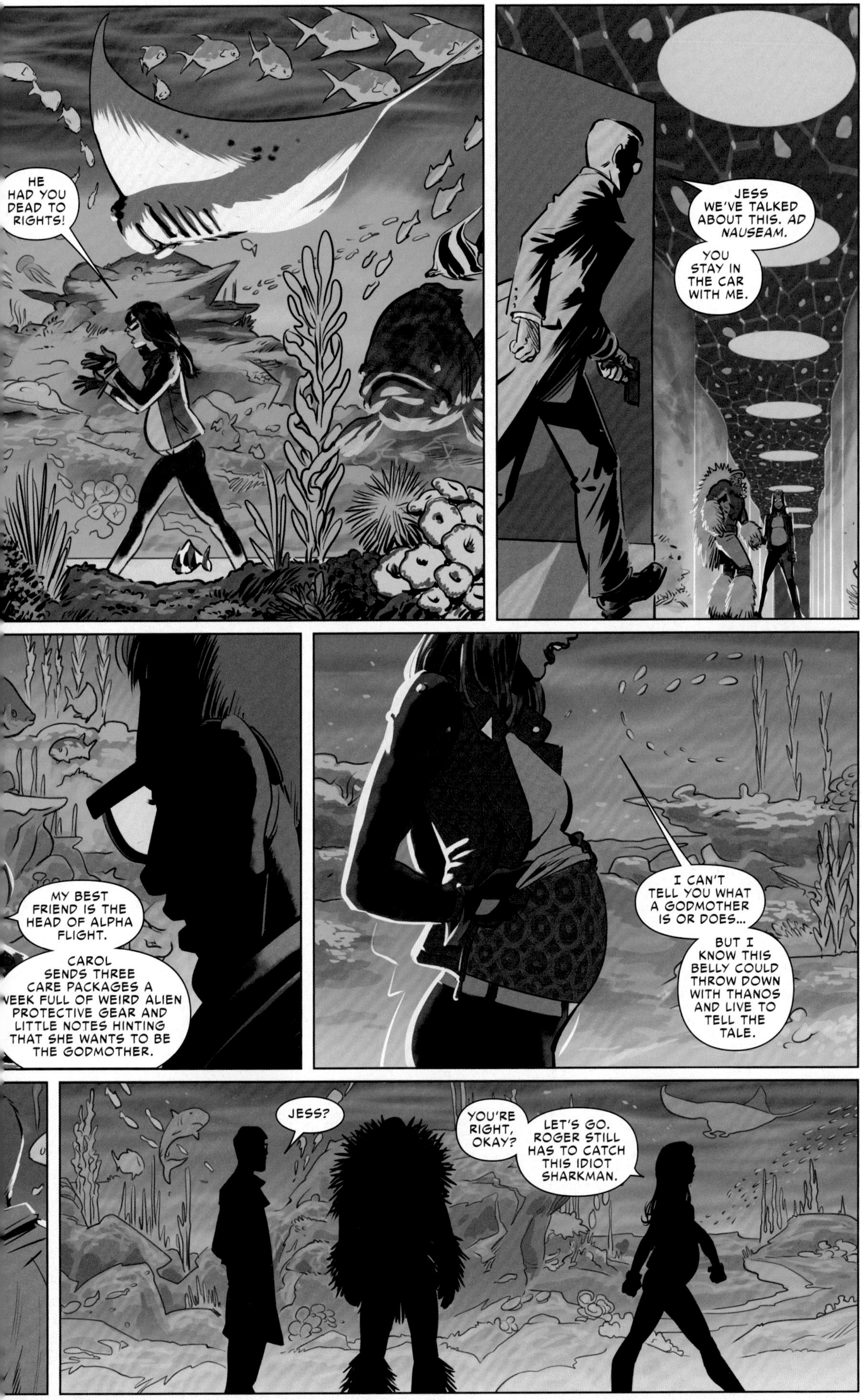

HE HAD YOU DEAD TO RIGHTS!
JESS WE'VE TALKED ABOUT THIS. AD *NAUSEAM.*
YOU STAY IN THE CAR WITH ME.
MY BEST FRIEND IS THE HEAD OF ALPHA FLIGHT.
CAROL SENDS THREE CARE PACKAGES A WEEK FULL OF WEIRD ALIEN PROTECTIVE GEAR AND LITTLE NOTES HINTING THAT SHE WANTS TO BE THE GODMOTHER.
I CAN'T TELL YOU WHAT A GODMOTHER IS OR DOES...
BUT I KNOW THIS BELLY COULD THROW DOWN WITH THANOS AND LIVE TO TELL THE TALE.
JESS?
YOU'RE RIGHT, OKAY?
LET'S GO. ROGER STILL HAS TO CATCH THIS IDIOT SHARKMAN.

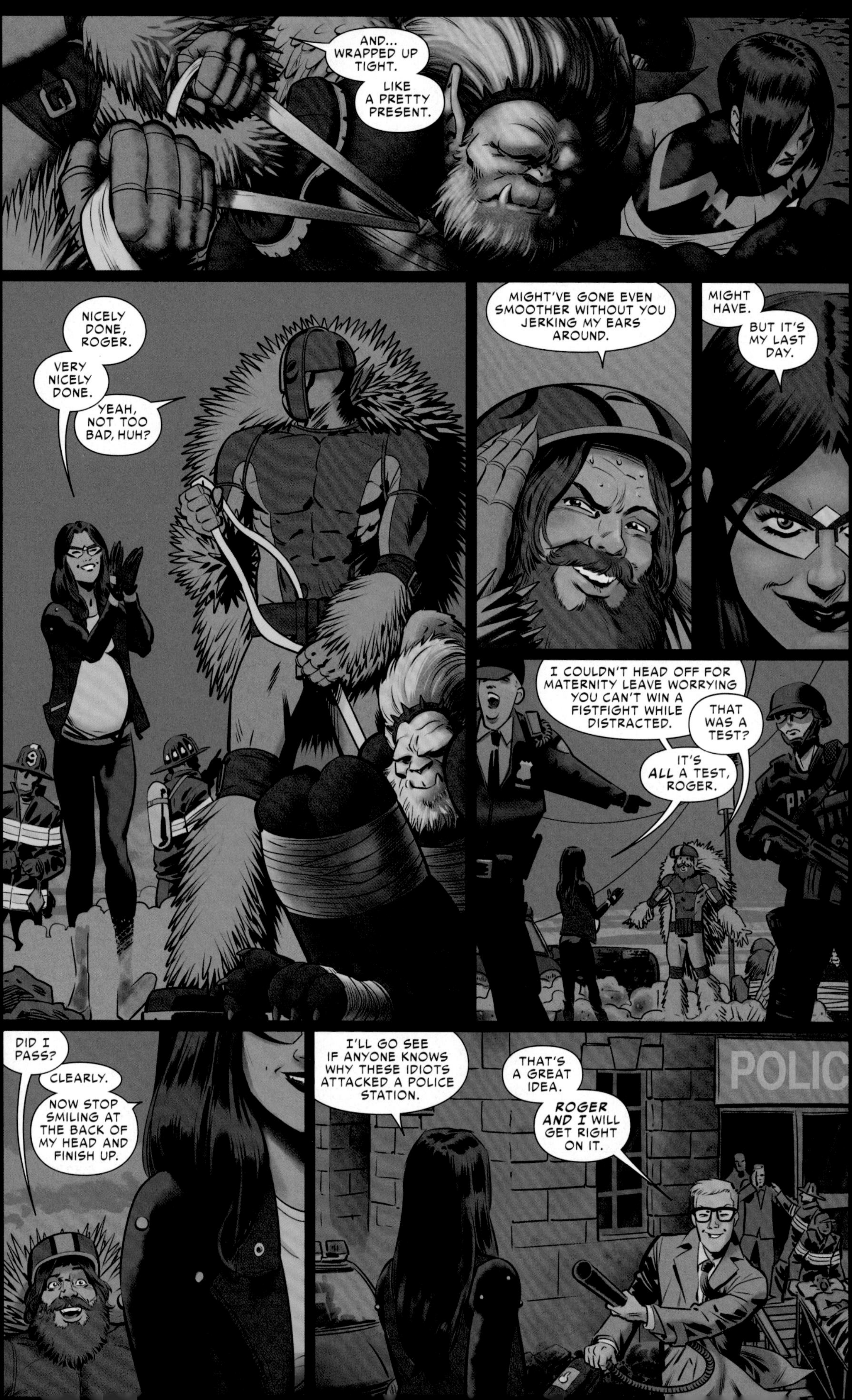
AND... WRAPPED UP TIGHT.
LIKE A PRETTY PRESENT.
NICELY DONE, ROGER.
VERY NICELY DONE.
YEAH, NOT TOO BAD, HUH?
MIGHT'VE GONE EVEN SMOOTHER WITHOUT YOU JERKING MY EARS AROUND.
MIGHT HAVE.
BUT IT'S MY LAST DAY.
I COULDN'T HEAD OFF FOR MATERNITY LEAVE WORRYING YOU CAN'T WIN A FISTFIGHT WHILE DISTRACTED.
THAT WAS A TEST?
IT'S ALL A TEST, ROGER.
DID I PASS?
CLEARLY.
NOW STOP SMILING AT THE BACK OF MY HEAD AND FINISH UP.
I'LL GO SEE IF ANYONE KNOWS WHY THESE IDIOTS ATTACKED A POLICE STATION.
THAT'S A GREAT IDEA.
ROGER AND I WILL GET RIGHT ON IT.
POLIC

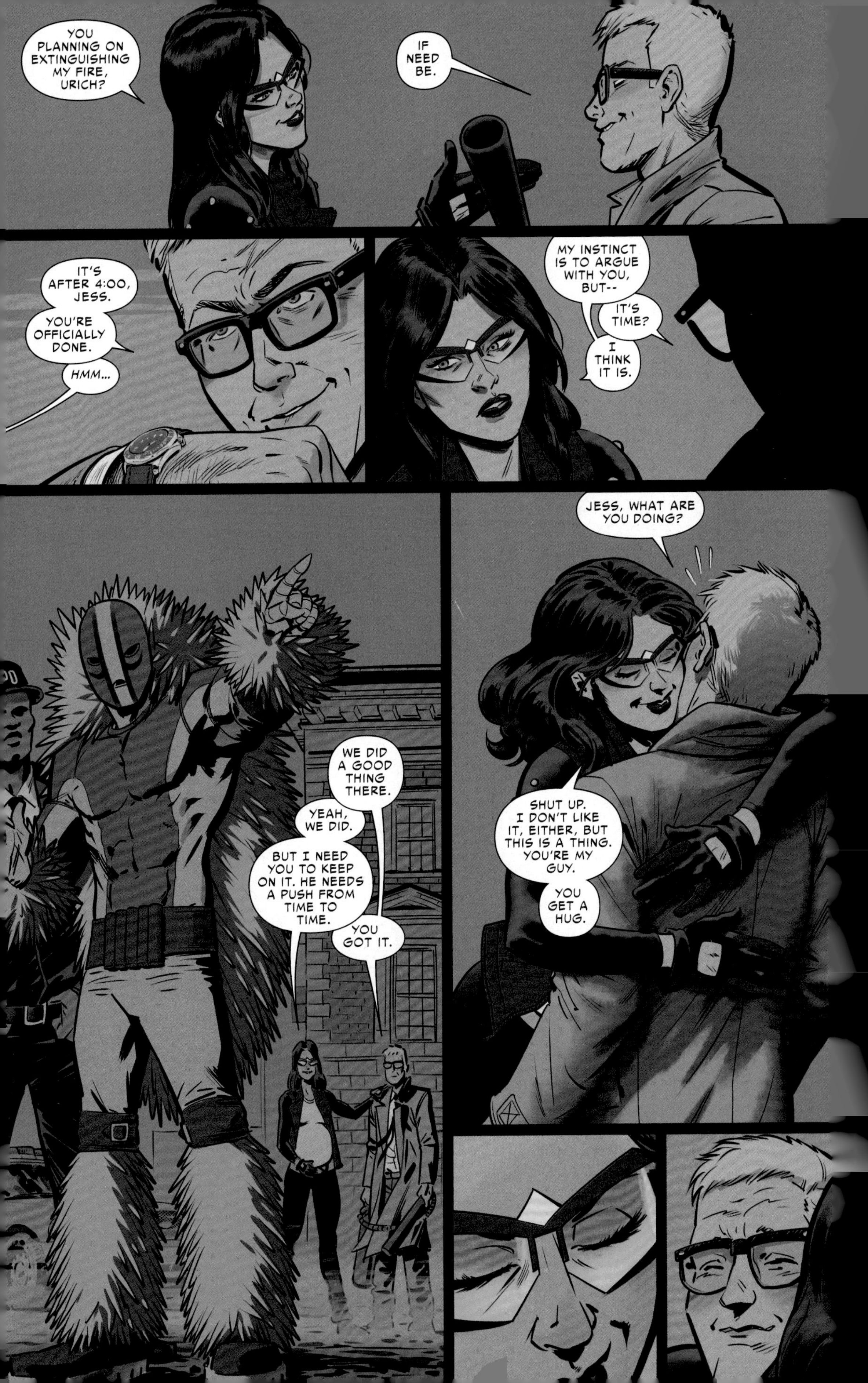
YOU PLANNING ON EXTINGUISHING MY FIRE, URICH?
IF NEED BE.
IT'S AFTER 4:00, JESS.
YOU'RE OFFICIALLY DONE.
HMM...
MY INSTINCT IS TO ARGUE WITH YOU, BUT--
IT'S TIME?
I THINK IT IS.
WE DID A GOOD THING THERE.
YEAH, WE DID.
BUT I NEED YOU TO KEEP ON IT. HE NEEDS A PUSH FROM TIME TO TIME.
YOU GOT IT.
JESS, WHAT ARE YOU DOING?
SHUT UP. I DON'T LIKE IT, EITHER, BUT THIS IS A THING. YOU'RE MY GUY.
YOU GET A HUG.

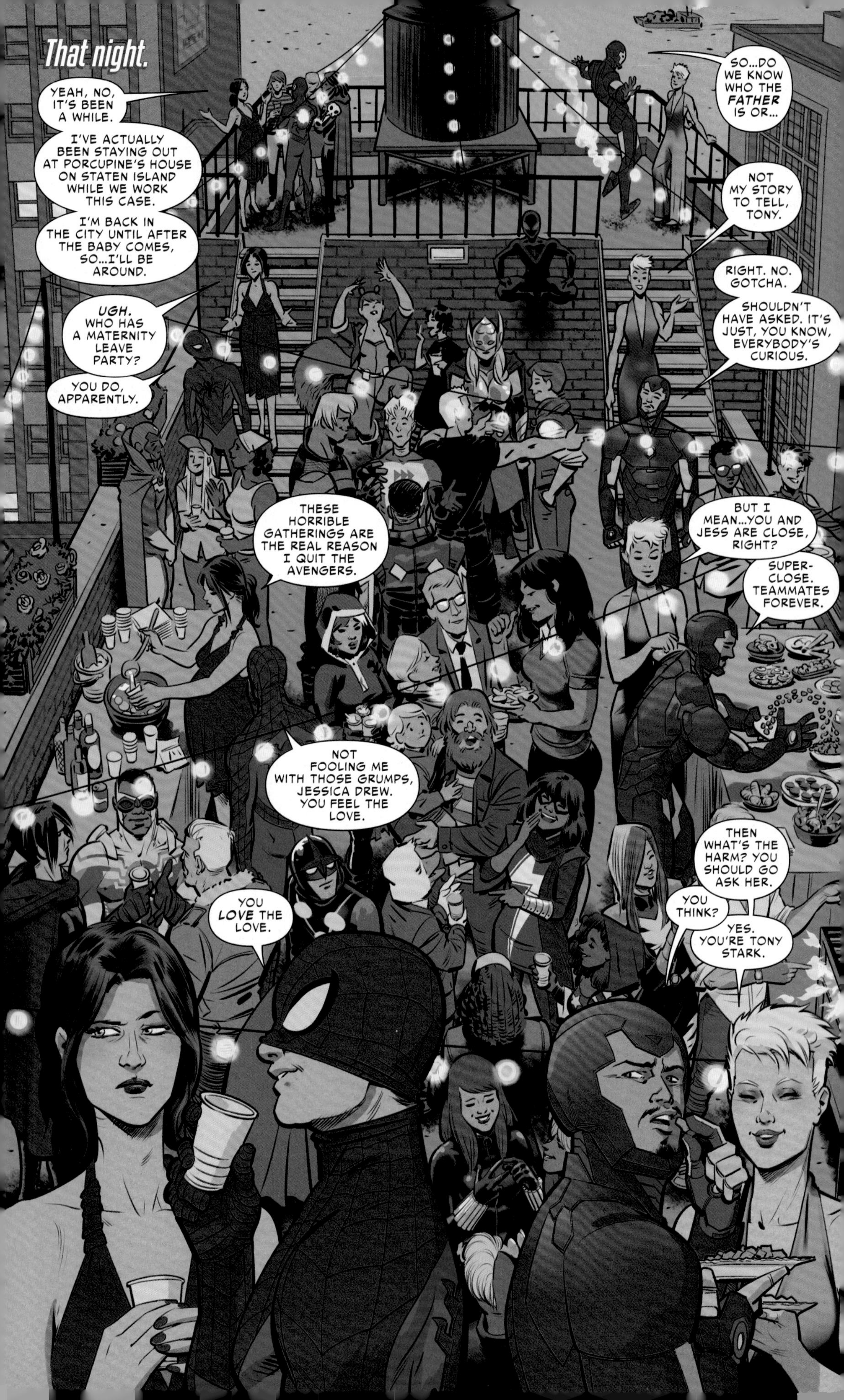
That night.
YEAH, NO, IT'S BEEN A WHILE.
I'VE ACTUALLY BEEN STAYING OUT AT PORCUPINE'S HOUSE ON STATEN ISLAND WHILE WE WORK THIS CASE.
I'M BACK IN THE CITY UNTIL AFTER THE BABY COMES, SO...I'LL BE AROUND.
UGH. WHO HAS A MATERNITY LEAVE PARTY?
YOU DO, APPARENTLY.
SO...DO WE KNOW WHO THE FATHER IS OR...
NOT MY STORY TO TELL, TONY.
RIGHT. NO. GOTCHA.
SHOULDN'T HAVE ASKED. IT'S JUST, YOU KNOW, EVERYBODY'S CURIOUS.
THESE HORRIBLE GATHERINGS ARE THE REAL REASON I QUIT THE AVENGERS.
BUT I MEAN...YOU AND JESS ARE CLOSE, RIGHT?
SUPER-CLOSE. TEAMMATES FOREVER.
NOT FOOLING ME WITH THOSE GRUMPS, JESSICA DREW. YOU FEEL THE LOVE.
YOU LOVE THE LOVE.
THEN WHAT'S THE HARM? YOU SHOULD GO ASK HER.
YOU THINK?
YES. YOU'RE TONY STARK.

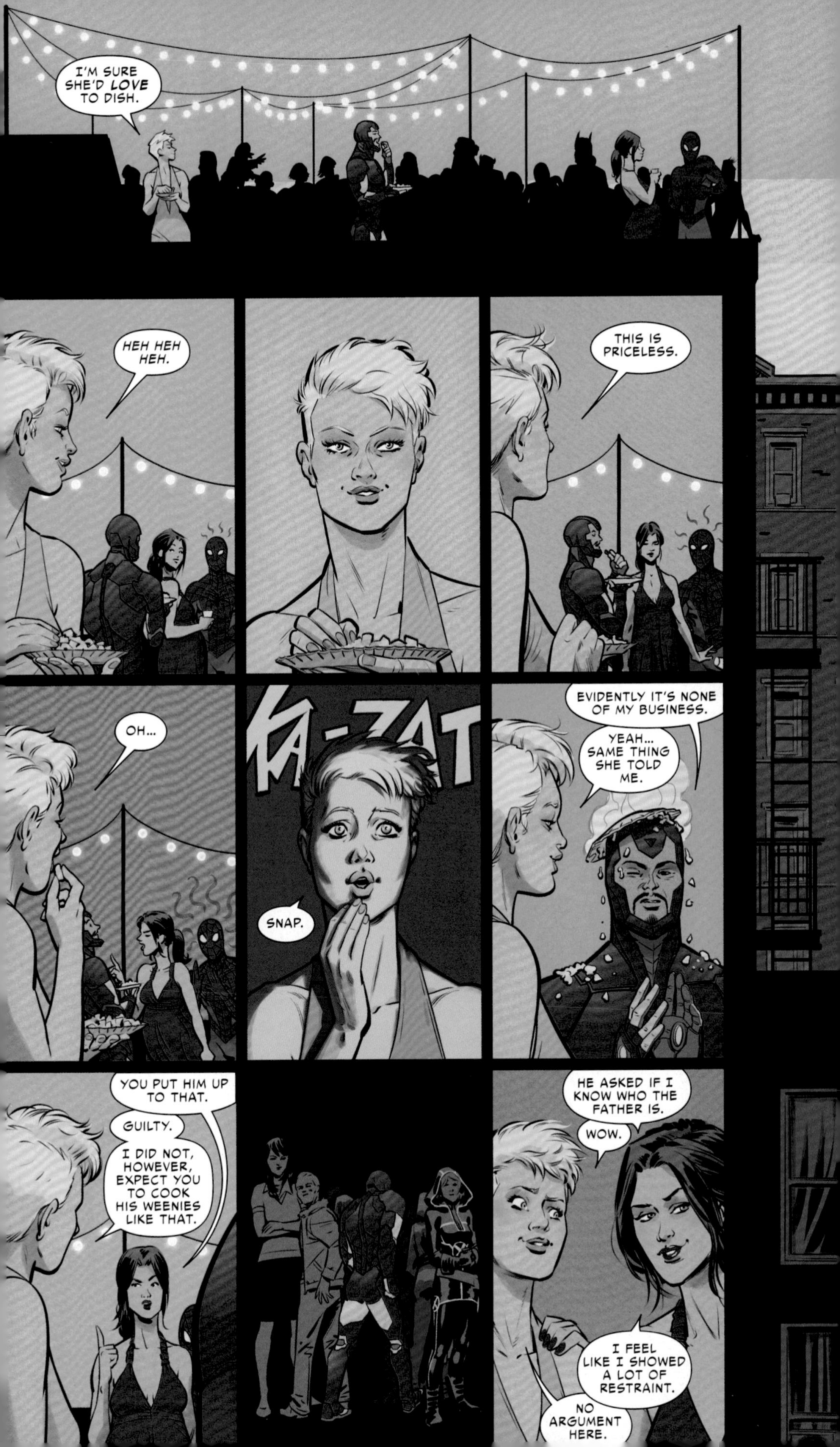
I'M SURE SHE'D LOVE TO DISH.
HEH HEH HEH.
THIS IS PRICELESS.
OH...
KA-ZAT
SNAP.
EVIDENTLY IT'S NONE OF MY BUSINESS.
YEAH... SAME THING SHE TOLD ME.
YOU PUT HIM UP TO THAT.
GUILTY.
I DID NOT, HOWEVER, EXPECT YOU TO COOK HIS WEENIES LIKE THAT.
HE ASKED IF I KNOW WHO THE FATHER IS.
WOW.
I FEEL LIKE I SHOWED A LOT OF RESTRAINT.
NO ARGUMENT HERE.

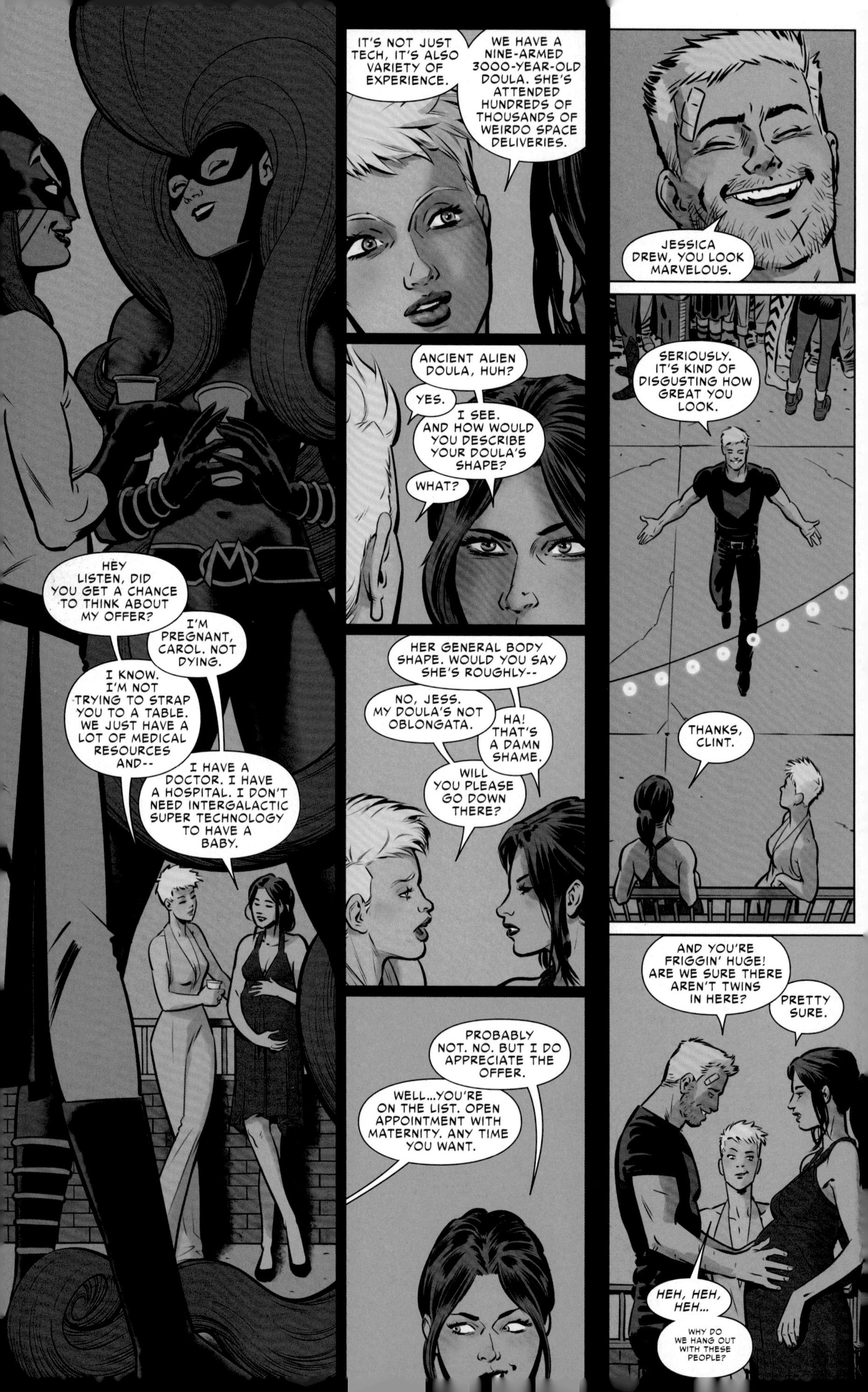
HEY LISTEN, DID YOU GET A CHANCE TO THINK ABOUT MY OFFER?
I'M PREGNANT, CAROL. NOT DYING.
I KNOW. I'M NOT TRYING TO STRAP YOU TO A TABLE. WE JUST HAVE A LOT OF MEDICAL RESOURCES AND--
I HAVE A DOCTOR. I HAVE A HOSPITAL. I DON'T NEED INTERGALACTIC SUPER TECHNOLOGY TO HAVE A BABY.
IT'S NOT JUST TECH, IT'S ALSO VARIETY OF EXPERIENCE.
WE HAVE A NINE-ARMED 3000-YEAR-OLD DOULA. SHE'S ATTENDED HUNDREDS OF THOUSANDS OF WEIRDO SPACE DELIVERIES.
ANCIENT ALIEN DOULA, HUH?
YES.
I SEE. AND HOW WOULD YOU DESCRIBE YOUR DOULA'S SHAPE?
WHAT?
HER GENERAL BODY SHAPE. WOULD YOU SAY SHE'S ROUGHLY--
NO, JESS. MY DOULA'S NOT OBLONGATA.
HA! THAT'S A DAMN SHAME.
WILL YOU PLEASE GO DOWN THERE?
PROBABLY NOT. NO. BUT I DO APPRECIATE THE OFFER.
WELL...YOU'RE ON THE LIST. OPEN APPOINTMENT WITH MATERNITY. ANY TIME YOU WANT.
JESSICA DREW, YOU LOOK MARVELOUS.
SERIOUSLY. IT'S KIND OF DISGUSTING HOW GREAT YOU LOOK.
THANKS, CLINT.
AND YOU'RE FRIGGIN' HUGE! ARE WE SURE THERE AREN'T TWINS IN HERE?
PRETTY SURE.
HEH, HEH, HEH...
WHY DO WE HANG OUT WITH THESE PEOPLE?

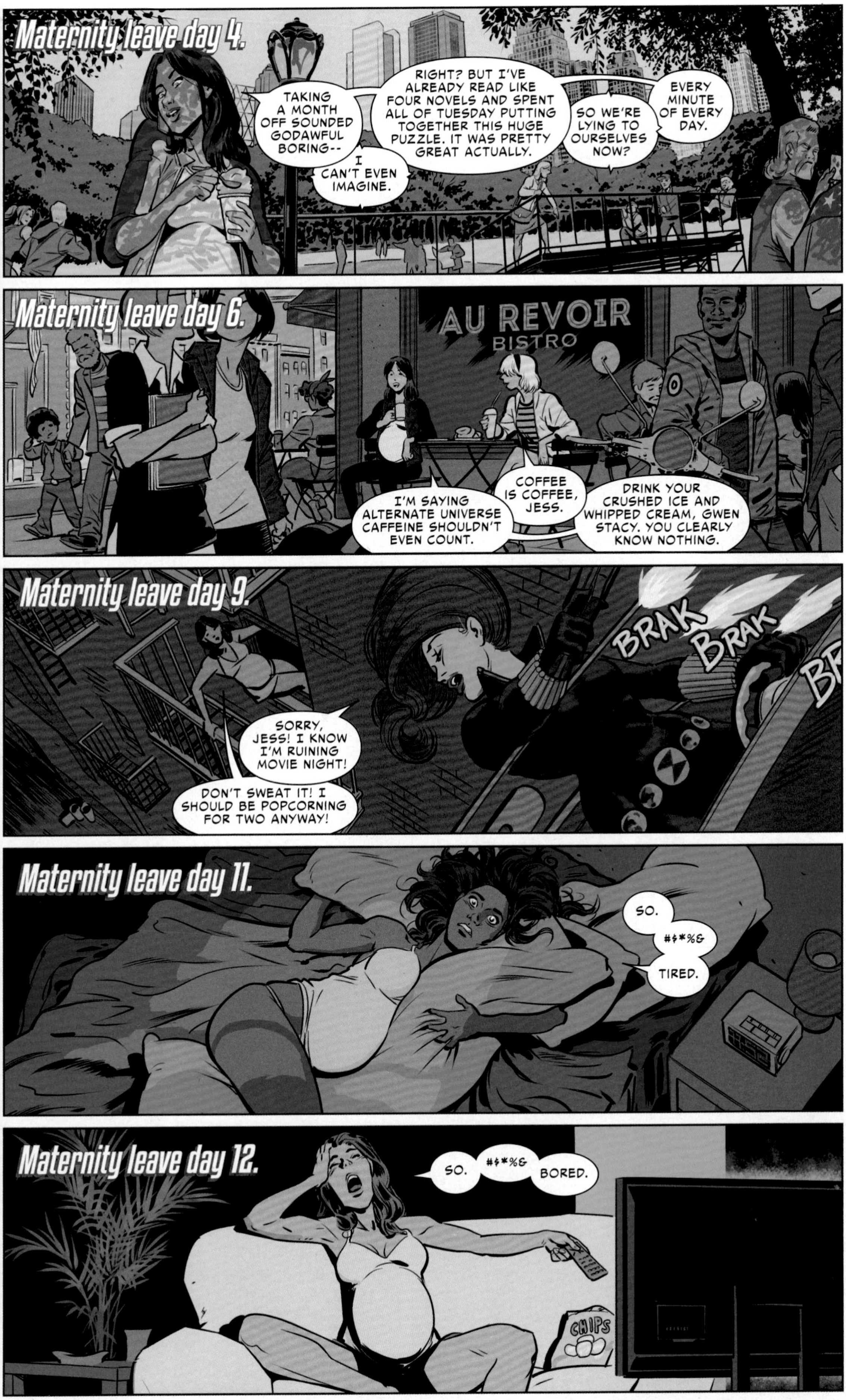
Maternity leave day 4.
TAKING A MONTH OFF SOUNDED GODAWFUL BORING--
I CAN'T EVEN IMAGINE.
RIGHT? BUT I'VE ALREADY READ LIKE FOUR NOVELS AND SPENT ALL OF TUESDAY PUTTING TOGETHER THIS HUGE PUZZLE. IT WAS PRETTY GREAT ACTUALLY.
SO WE'RE LYING TO OURSELVES NOW?
EVERY MINUTE OF EVERY DAY.
Maternity leave day 6.
AU REVOIR
BISTRO
I'M SAYING ALTERNATE UNIVERSE CAFFEINE SHOULDN'T EVEN COUNT.
COFFEE IS COFFEE, JESS.
DRINK YOUR CRUSHED ICE AND WHIPPED CREAM, GWEN STACY. YOU CLEARLY KNOW NOTHING.
Maternity leave day 9.
BRAK
BRAK
SORRY, JESS! I KNOW I'M RUINING MOVIE NIGHT!
DON'T SWEAT IT! I SHOULD BE POPCORNING FOR TWO ANYWAY!
Maternity leave day 11.
SO.
#$*%&
TIRED.
Maternity leave day 12.
SO.
#$*%&
BORED.
CHIPS

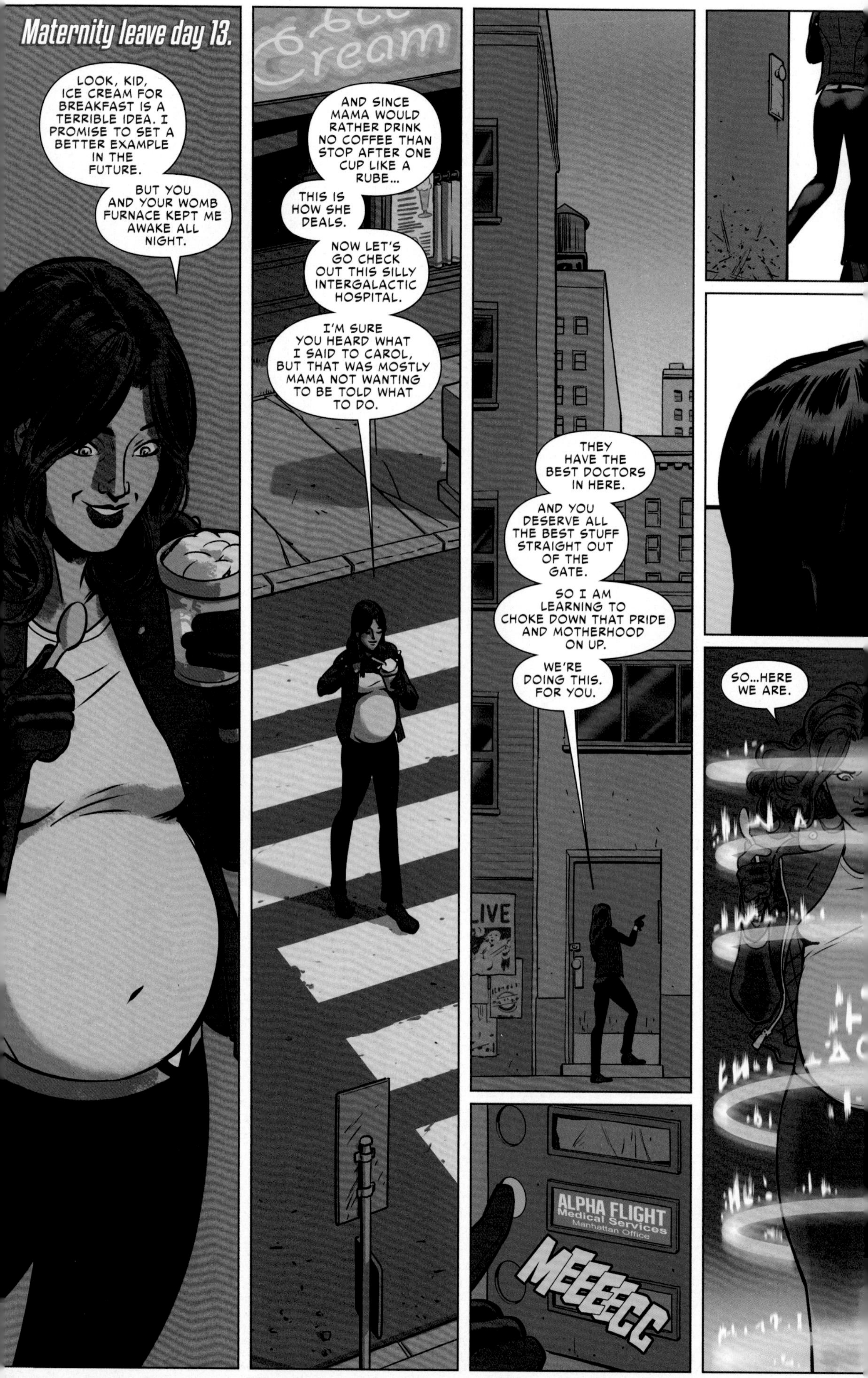
Maternity leave day 13.
LOOK, KID, ICE CREAM FOR BREAKFAST IS A TERRIBLE IDEA. I PROMISE TO SET A BETTER EXAMPLE IN THE FUTURE.
BUT YOU AND YOUR WOMB FURNACE KEPT ME AWAKE ALL NIGHT.
Ice Cream
AND SINCE MAMA WOULD RATHER DRINK NO COFFEE THAN STOP AFTER ONE CUP LIKE A RUBE...
THIS IS HOW SHE DEALS.
NOW LET'S GO CHECK OUT THIS SILLY INTERGALACTIC HOSPITAL.
I'M SURE YOU HEARD WHAT I SAID TO CAROL, BUT THAT WAS MOSTLY MAMA NOT WANTING TO BE TOLD WHAT TO DO.
THEY HAVE THE BEST DOCTORS IN HERE.
AND YOU DESERVE ALL THE BEST STUFF STRAIGHT OUT OF THE GATE.
SO I AM LEARNING TO CHOKE DOWN THAT PRIDE AND MOTHERHOOD ON UP.
WE'RE DOING THIS. FOR YOU.
LIVE
ALPHA FLIGHT
Medical Services
Manhattan Office
MEEEECC
SO...HERE WE ARE.

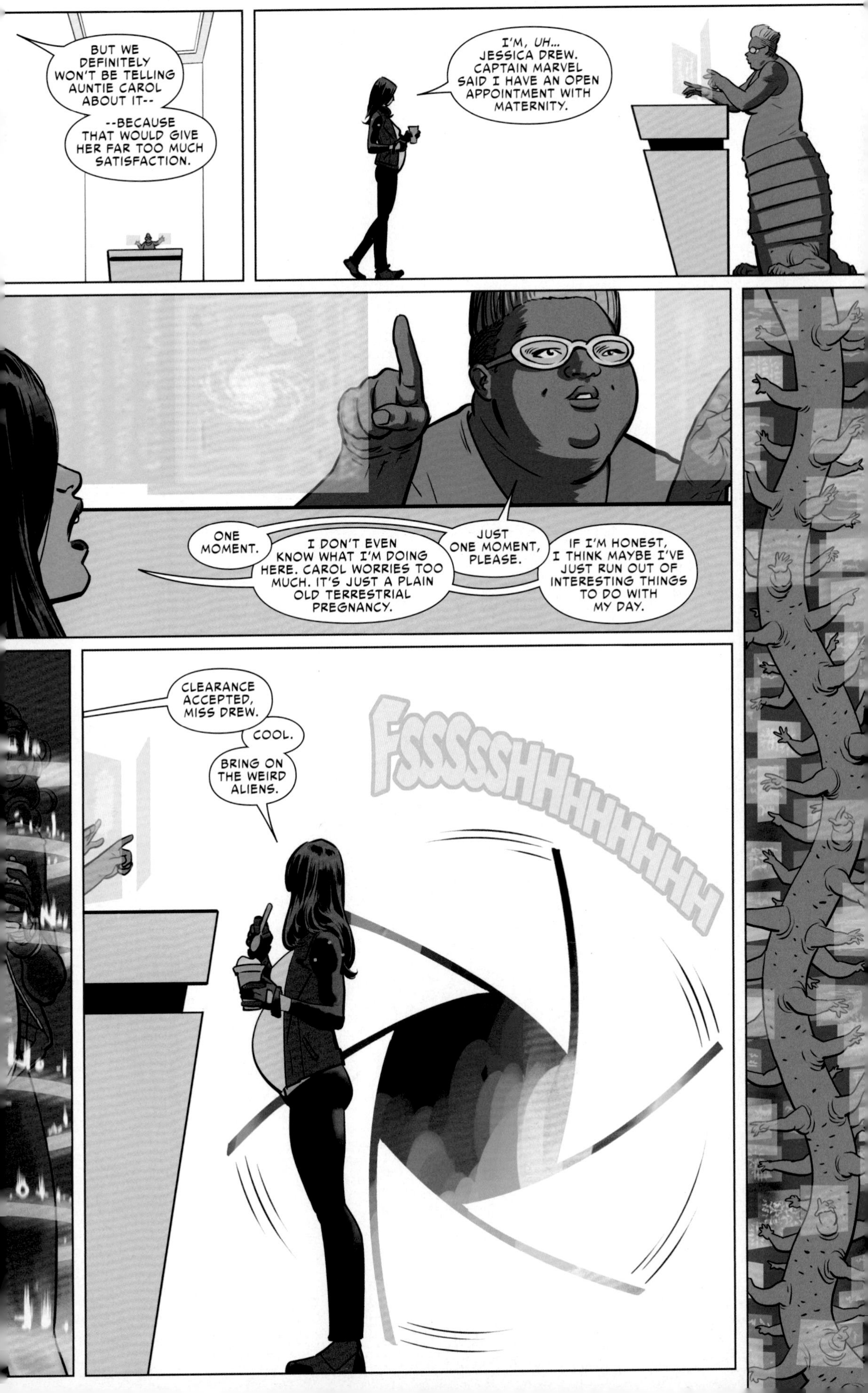

BUT WE DEFINITELY WON'T BE TELLING AUNTIE CAROL ABOUT IT--
--BECAUSE THAT WOULD GIVE HER FAR TOO MUCH SATISFACTION.
I'M, *UH*... JESSICA DREW. CAPTAIN MARVEL SAID I HAVE AN OPEN APPOINTMENT WITH MATERNITY.
ONE MOMENT.
I DON'T EVEN KNOW WHAT I'M DOING HERE. CAROL WORRIES TOO MUCH. IT'S JUST A PLAIN OLD TERRESTRIAL PREGNANCY.
JUST ONE MOMENT, PLEASE.
IF I'M HONEST, I THINK MAYBE I'VE JUST RUN OUT OF INTERESTING THINGS TO DO WITH MY DAY.
CLEARANCE ACCEPTED, MISS DREW.
COOL.
BRING ON THE WEIRD ALIENS.
FSSSSSHHHHHHHHH

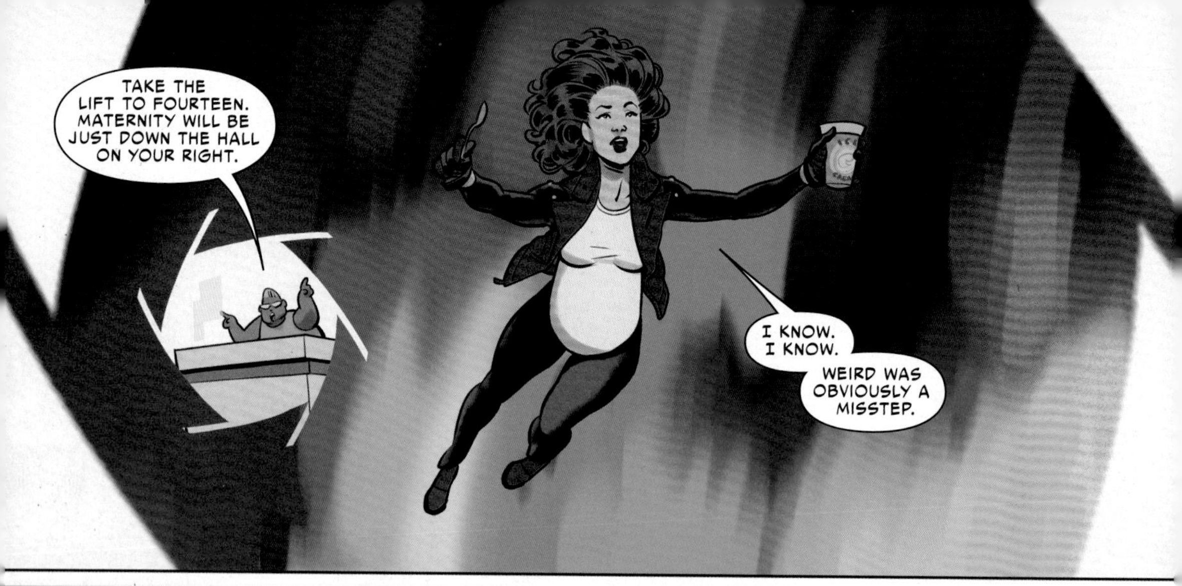
TAKE THE LIFT TO FOURTEEN. MATERNITY WILL BE JUST DOWN THE HALL ON YOUR RIGHT.
I KNOW. I KNOW.
WEIRD WAS OBVIOUSLY A MISSTEP.

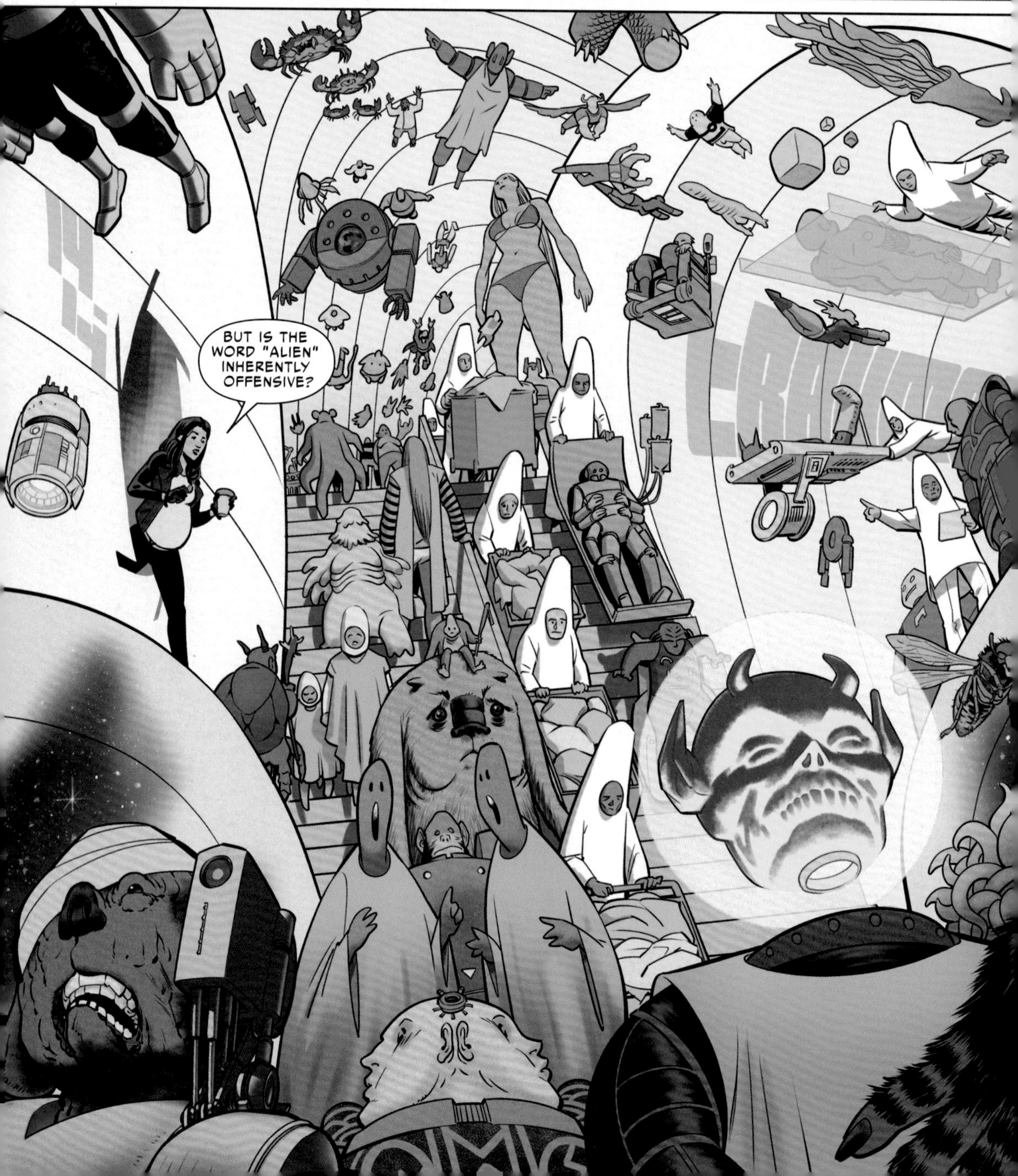
BUT IS THE WORD "ALIEN" INHERENTLY OFFENSIVE?

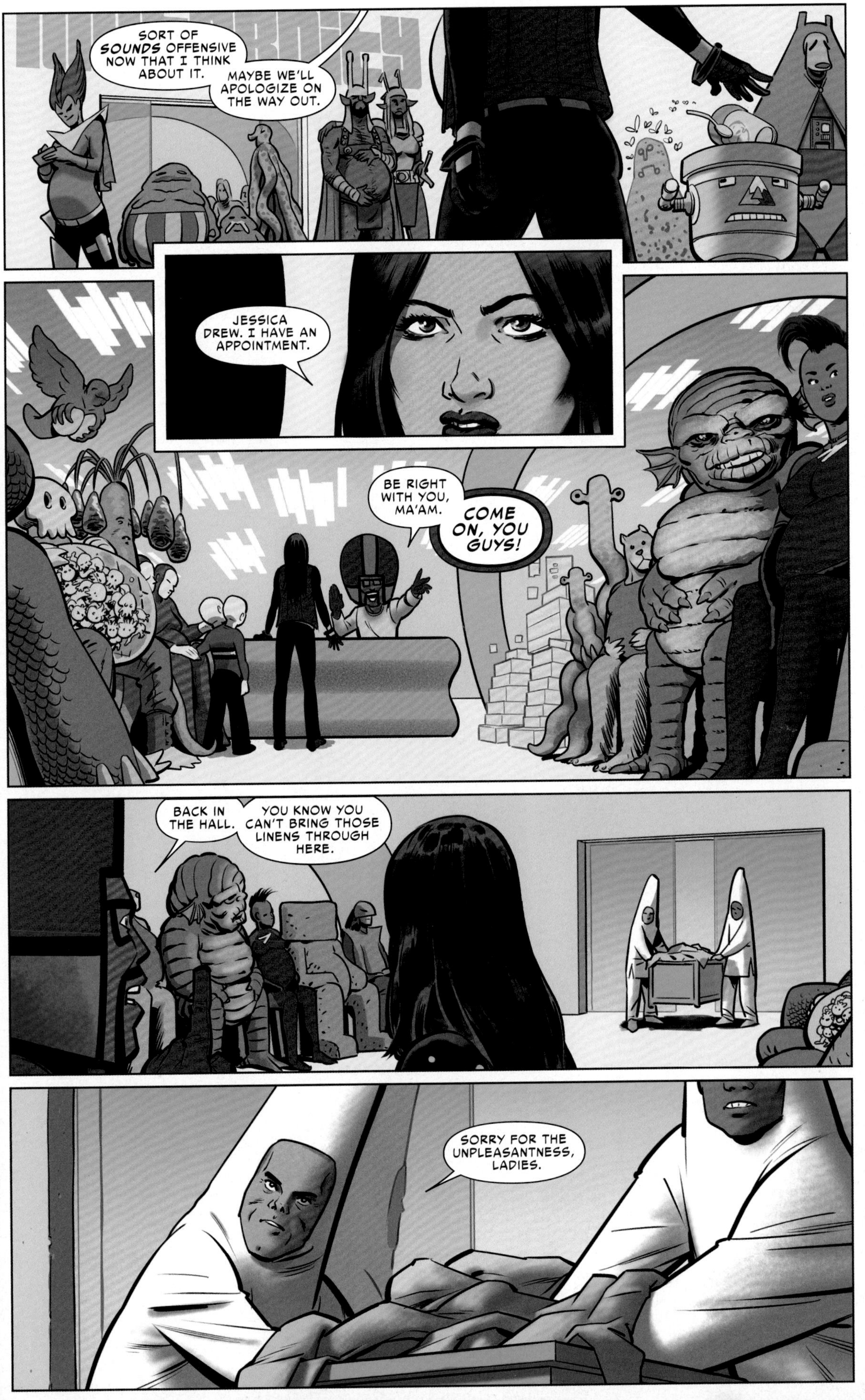
SORT OF SOUNDS OFFENSIVE NOW THAT I THINK ABOUT IT.
MAYBE WE'LL APOLOGIZE ON THE WAY OUT.
JESSICA DREW. I HAVE AN APPOINTMENT.
BE RIGHT WITH YOU, MA'AM.
COME ON, YOU GUYS!
BACK IN THE HALL.
YOU KNOW YOU CAN'T BRING THOSE LINENS THROUGH HERE.
SORRY FOR THE UNPLEASANTNESS, LADIES.

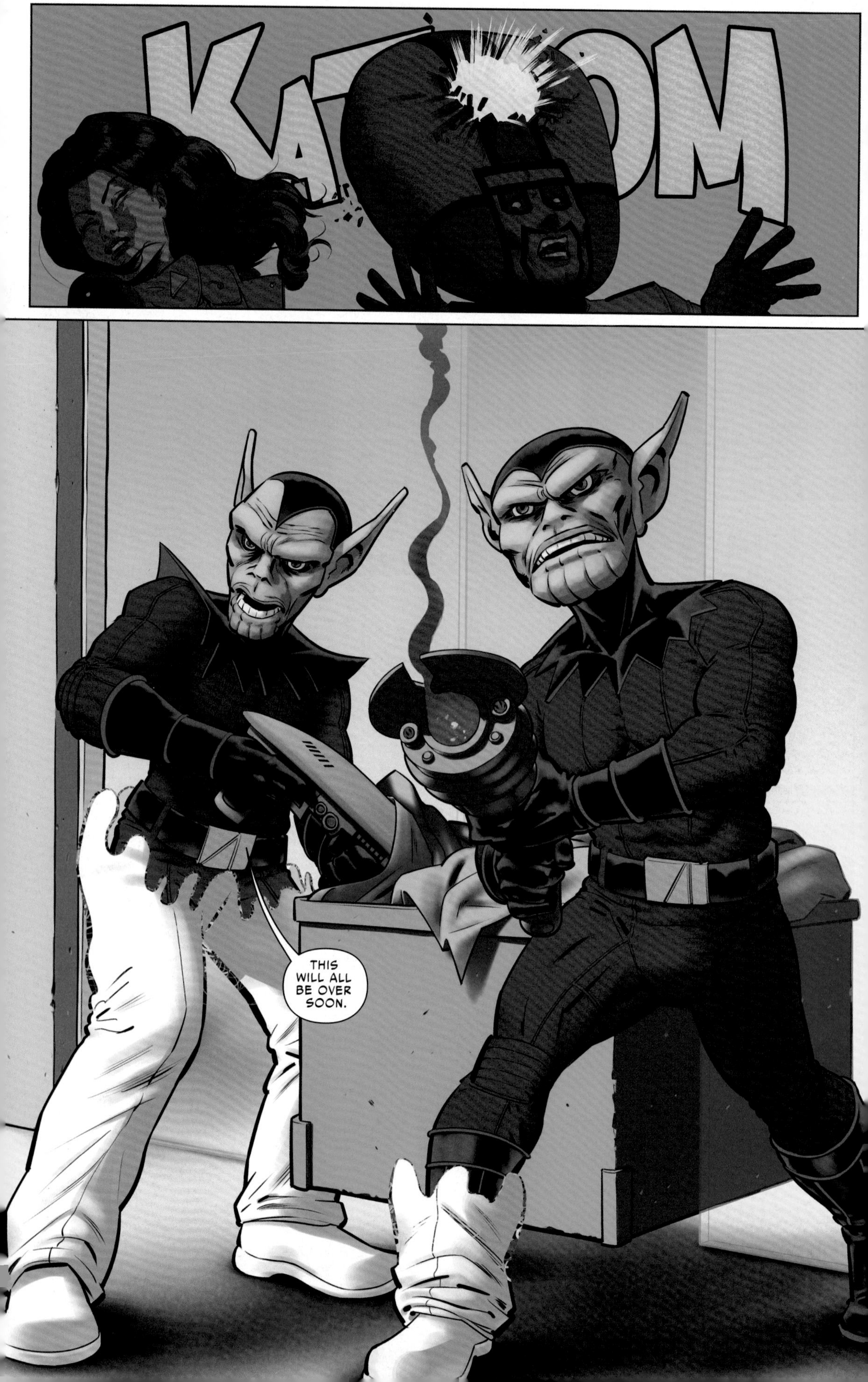
KA-BOOM
THIS WILL ALL BE OVER SOON.

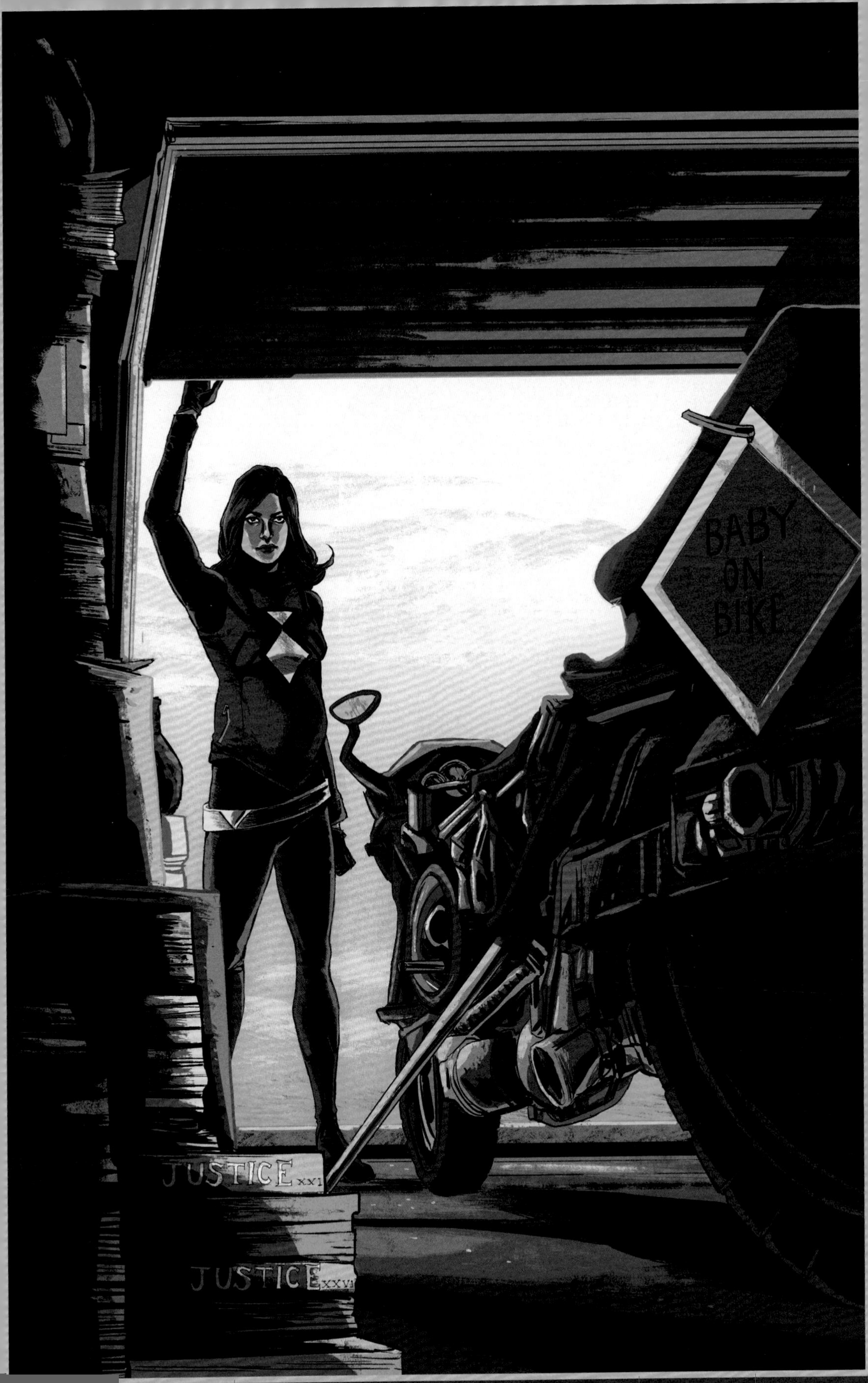
BABY ON BIKE
JUSTICE XXI
JUSTICE

[redacted]**ANT** BY MING DOYLE

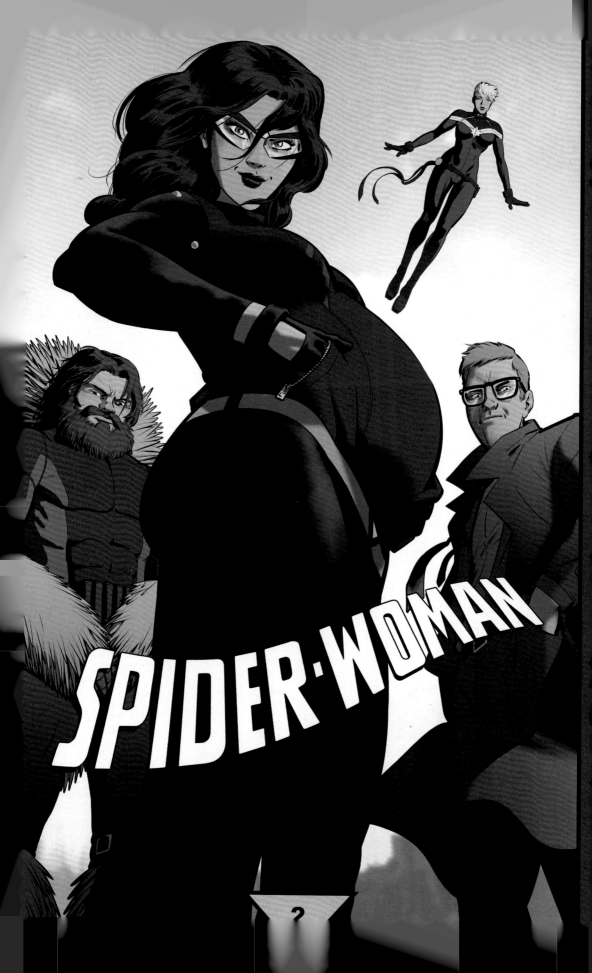

SPIDER-WOMAN

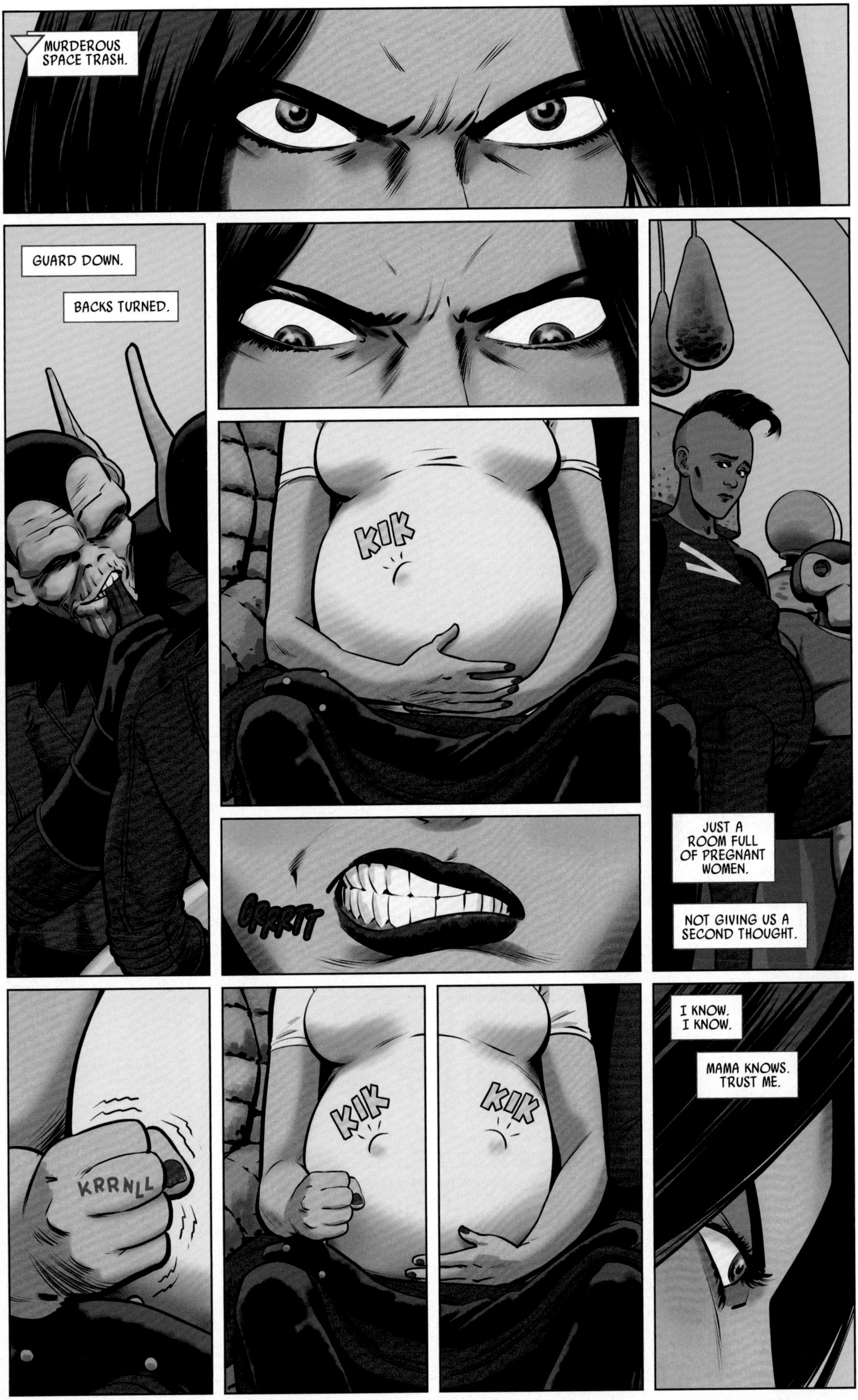
MURDEROUS SPACE TRASH.
GUARD DOWN.
BACKS TURNED.
KIK
GRRRTT
JUST A ROOM FULL OF PREGNANT WOMEN.
NOT GIVING US A SECOND THOUGHT.
KRRNLL
KIK
KIK
I KNOW. I KNOW.
MAMA KNOWS. TRUST ME.

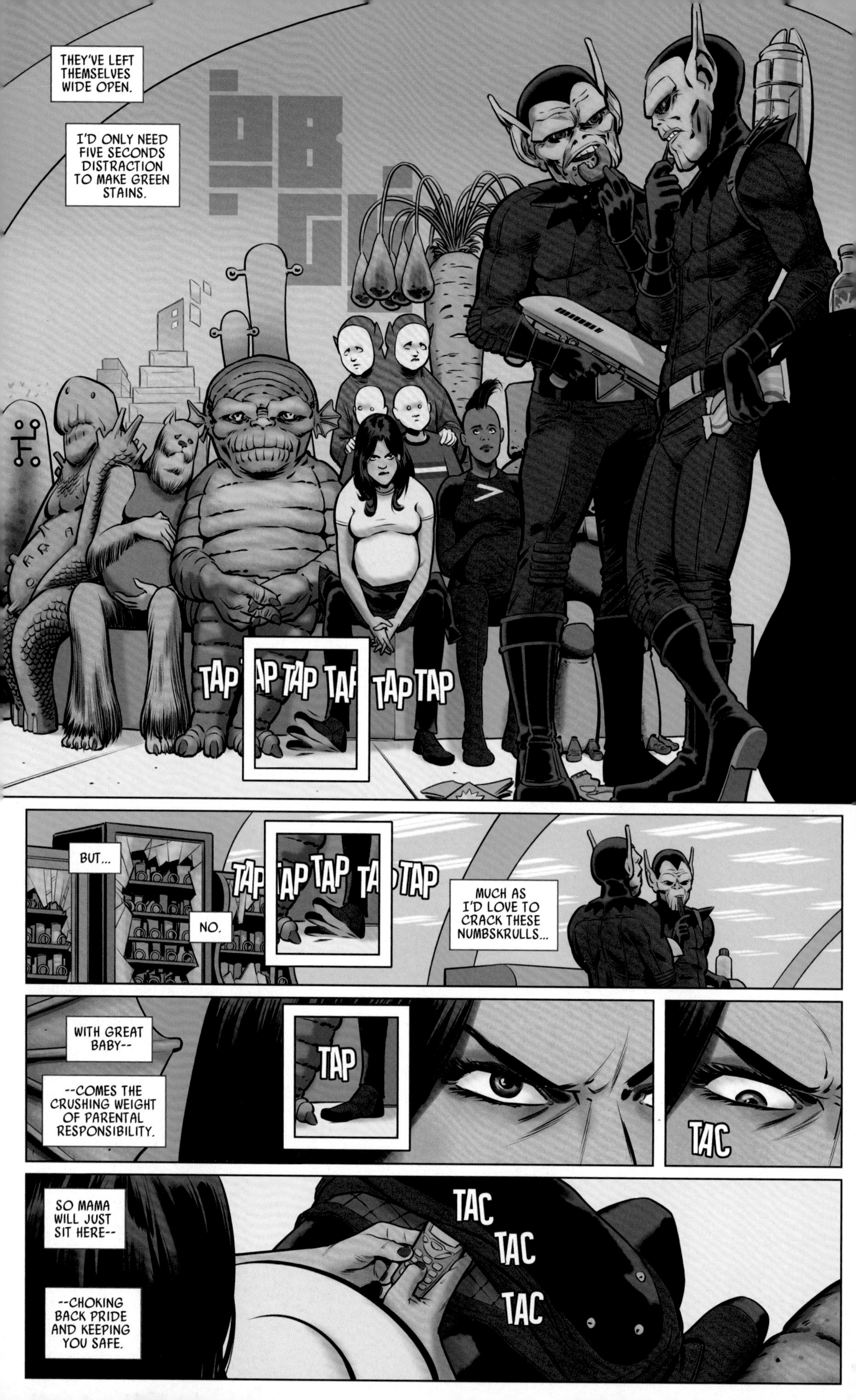
THEY'VE LEFT THEMSELVES WIDE OPEN.
I'D ONLY NEED FIVE SECONDS DISTRACTION TO MAKE GREEN STAINS.
TAP TAP TAP TAP TAP TAP
BUT...
NO.
TAP TAP TAP TA TAP
MUCH AS I'D LOVE TO CRACK THESE NUMBSKRULLS...
WITH GREAT BABY--
--COMES THE CRUSHING WEIGHT OF PARENTAL RESPONSIBILITY.
TAP
TAC
SO MAMA WILL JUST SIT HERE--
TAC
TAC
TAC
--CHOKING BACK PRIDE AND KEEPING YOU SAFE.

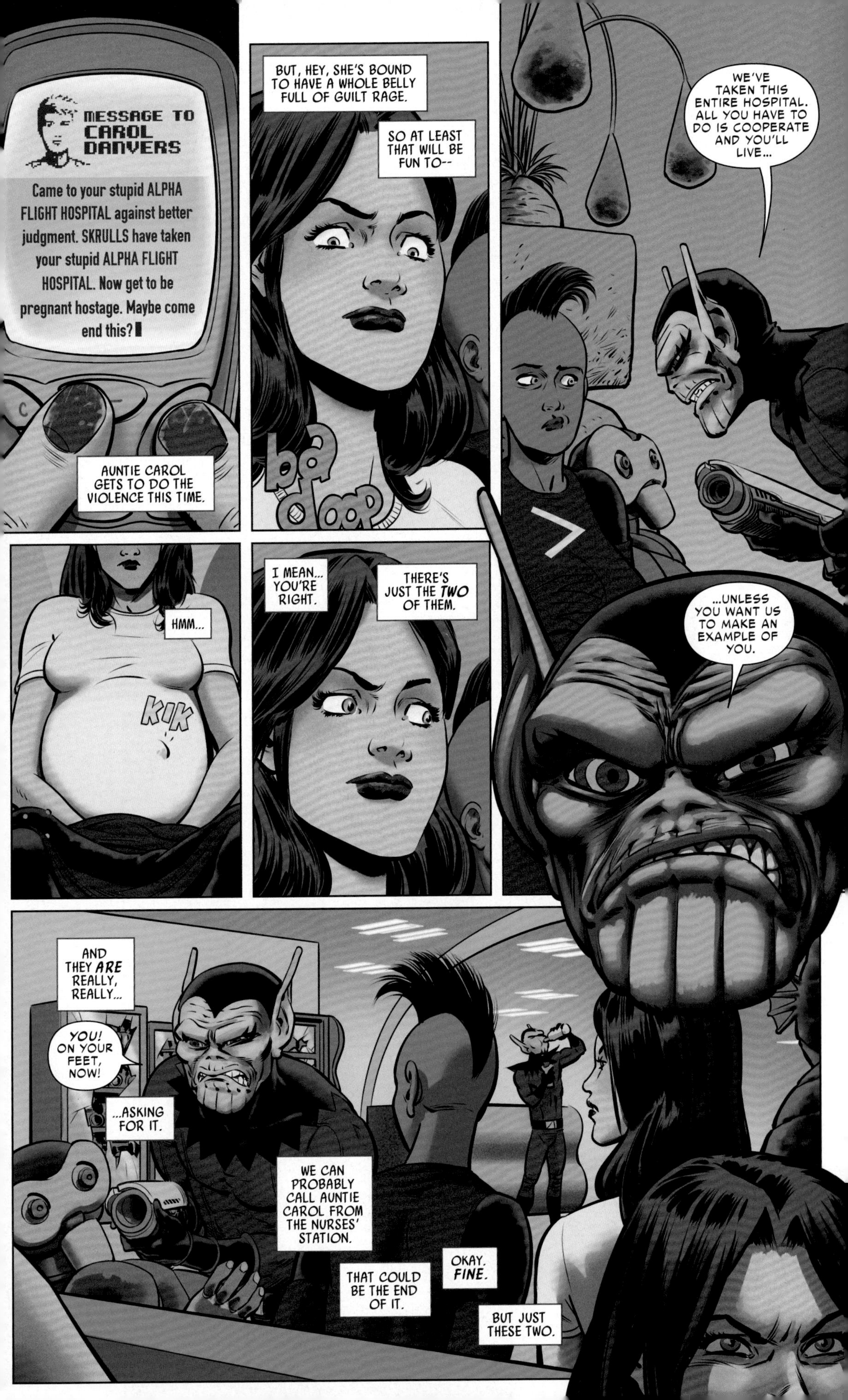
MESSAGE TO CAROL DANVERS
Came to your stupid ALPHA FLIGHT HOSPITAL against better judgment. SKRULLS have taken your stupid ALPHA FLIGHT HOSPITAL. Now get to be pregnant hostage. Maybe come end this?
AUNTIE CAROL GETS TO DO THE VIOLENCE THIS TIME.
BUT, HEY, SHE'S BOUND TO HAVE A WHOLE BELLY FULL OF GUILT RAGE.
SO AT LEAST THAT WILL BE FUN TO--
ba doop
WE'VE TAKEN THIS ENTIRE HOSPITAL. ALL YOU HAVE TO DO IS COOPERATE AND YOU'LL LIVE...
HMM...
KIK
I MEAN... YOU'RE RIGHT.
THERE'S JUST THE TWO OF THEM.
...UNLESS YOU WANT US TO MAKE AN EXAMPLE OF YOU.
AND THEY ARE REALLY, REALLY...
YOU! ON YOUR FEET, NOW!
...ASKING FOR IT.
WE CAN PROBABLY CALL AUNTIE CAROL FROM THE NURSES' STATION.
THAT COULD BE THE END OF IT.
OKAY. FINE.
BUT JUST THESE TWO.

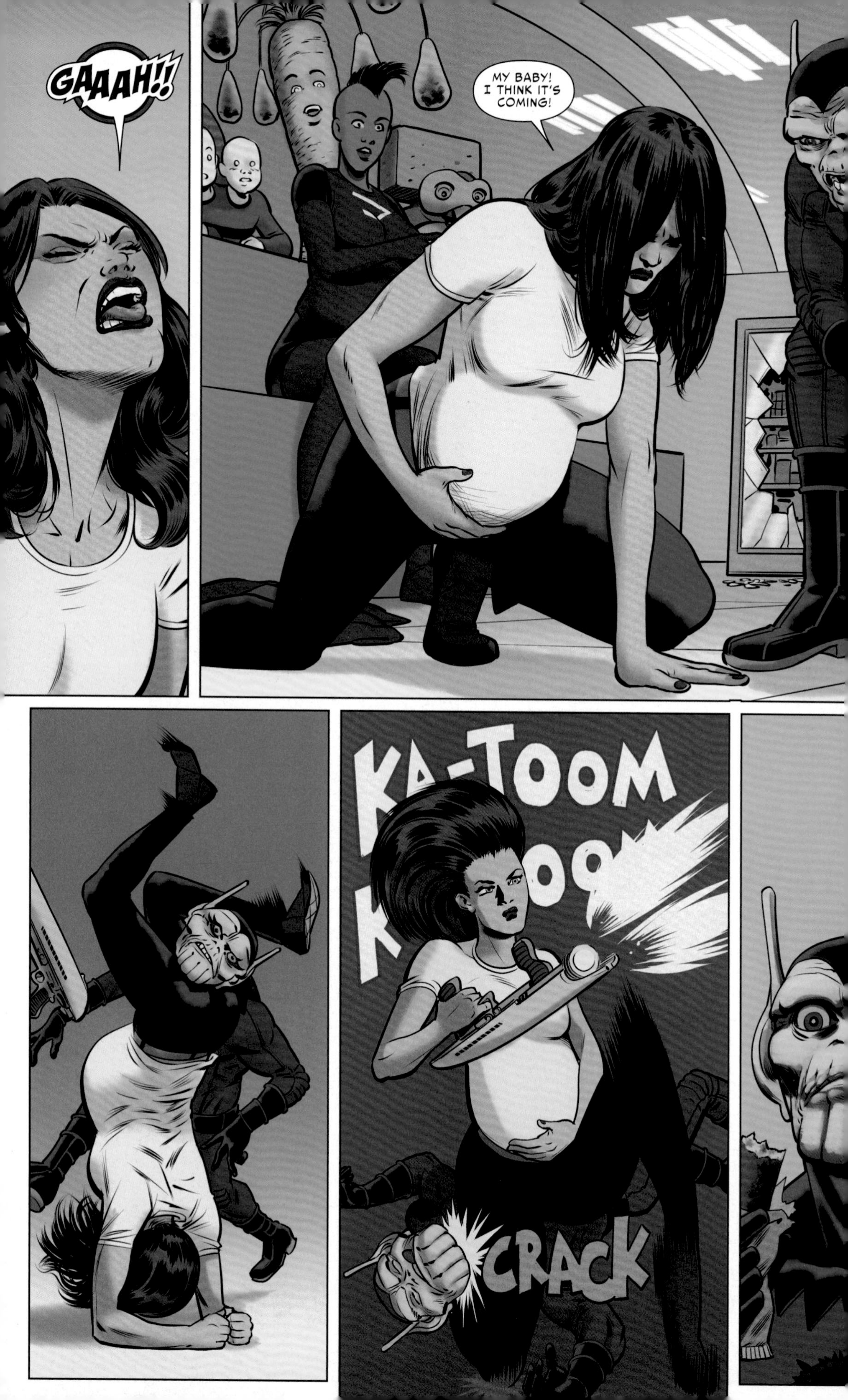
GAAAH!!
MY BABY! I THINK IT'S COMING!
KA-TOOM
KOOO
CRACK

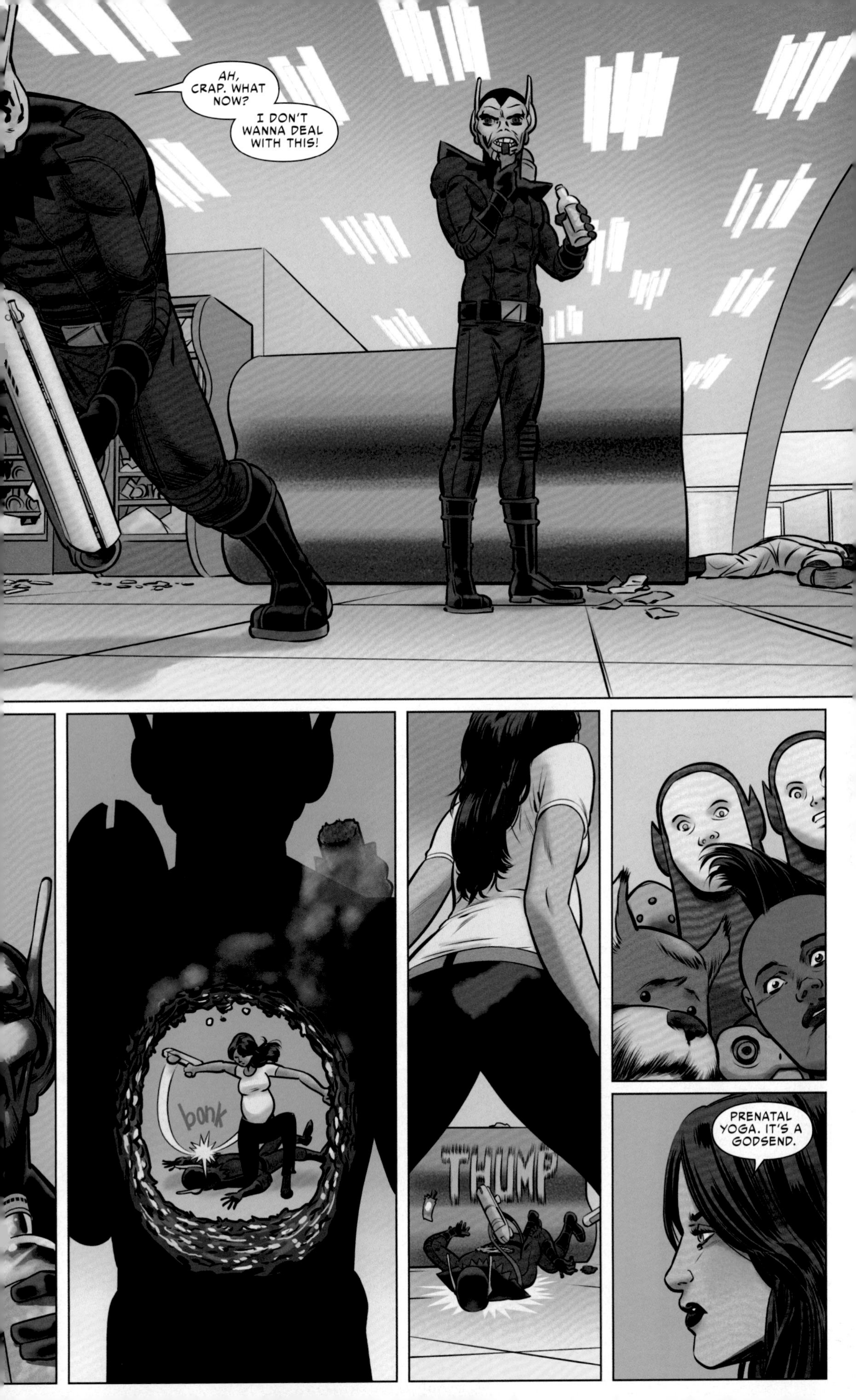
AH, CRAP. WHAT NOW?
I DON'T WANNA DEAL WITH THIS!
bonk
THUMP
PRENATAL YOGA. IT'S A GODSEND.

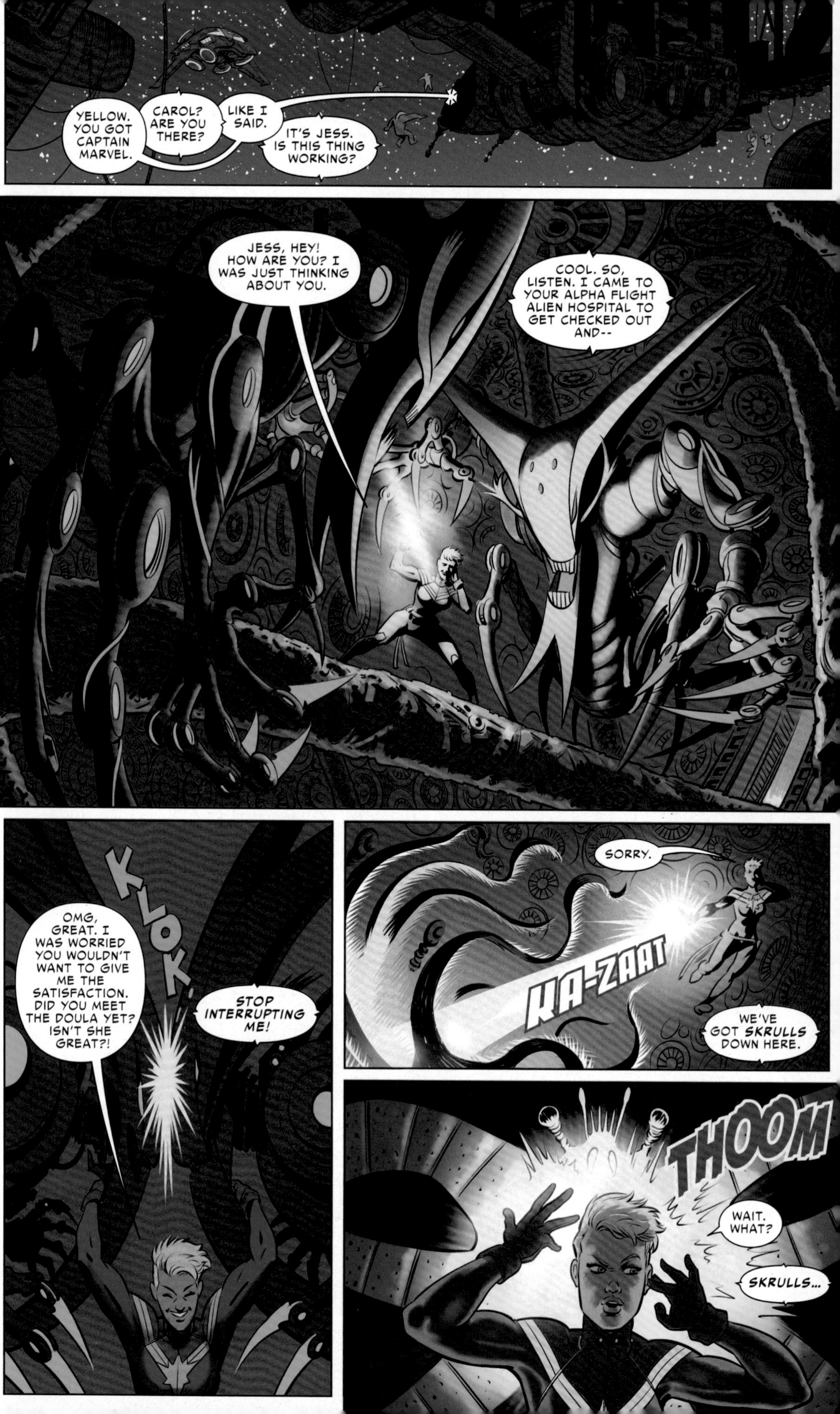

YELLOW. YOU GOT CAPTAIN MARVEL.
CAROL? ARE YOU THERE?
LIKE I SAID.
IT'S JESS. IS THIS THING WORKING?
JESS, HEY! HOW ARE YOU? I WAS JUST THINKING ABOUT YOU.
COOL. SO, LISTEN. I CAME TO YOUR ALPHA FLIGHT ALIEN HOSPITAL TO GET CHECKED OUT AND--
KLOK!
OMG, GREAT. I WAS WORRIED YOU WOULDN'T WANT TO GIVE ME THE SATISFACTION. DID YOU MEET THE DOULA YET? ISN'T SHE GREAT?!
STOP INTERRUPTING ME!
SORRY.
KA-ZAAT
WE'VE GOT SKRULLS DOWN HERE.
THOOM
WAIT. WHAT?
SKRULLS...

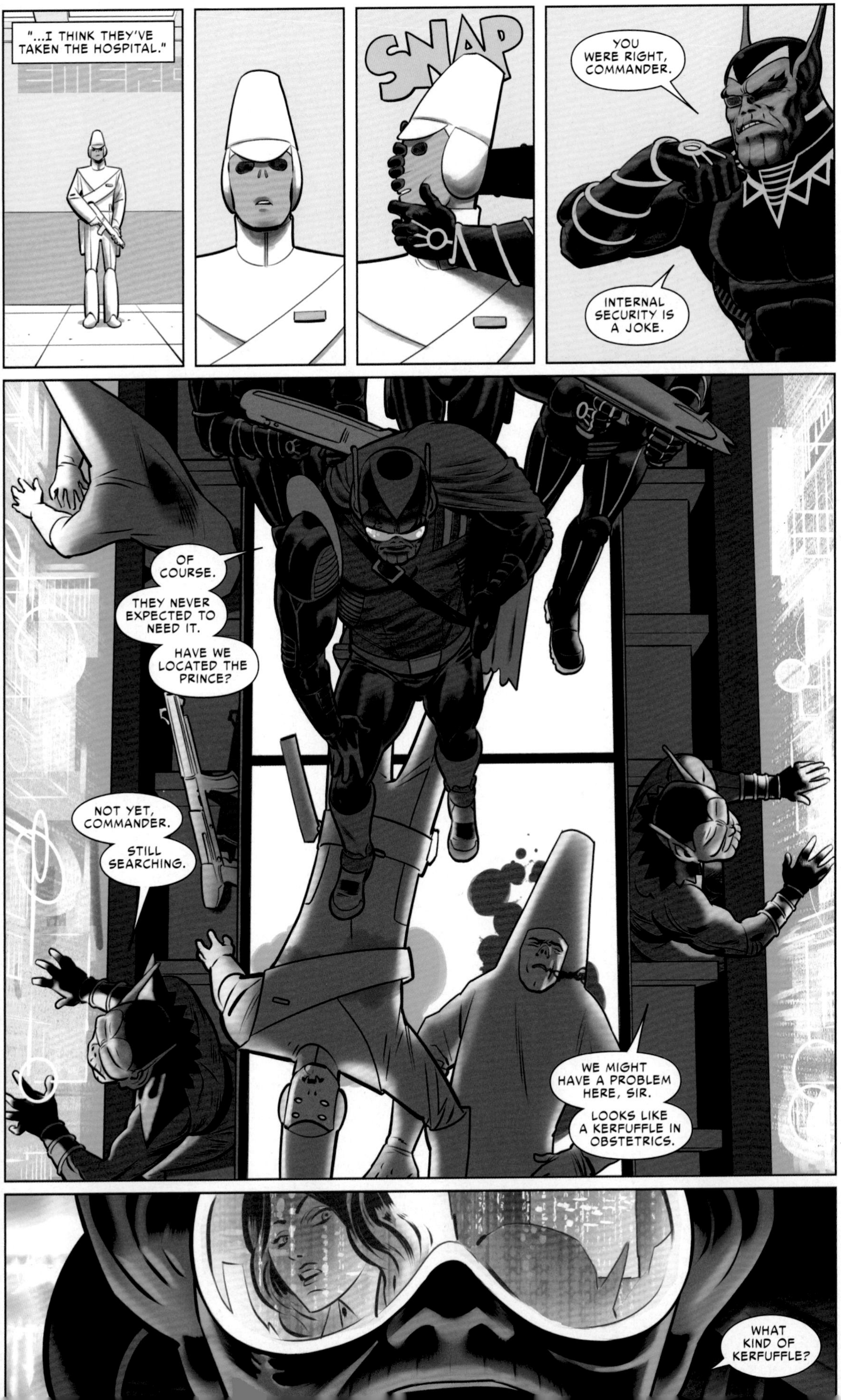
"...I THINK THEY'VE TAKEN THE HOSPITAL."
SNAP
YOU WERE RIGHT, COMMANDER.
INTERNAL SECURITY IS A JOKE.
OF COURSE.
THEY NEVER EXPECTED TO NEED IT.
HAVE WE LOCATED THE PRINCE?
NOT YET, COMMANDER.
STILL SEARCHING.
WE MIGHT HAVE A PROBLEM HERE, SIR.
LOOKS LIKE A KERFUFFLE IN OBSTETRICS.
WHAT KIND OF KERFUFFLE?

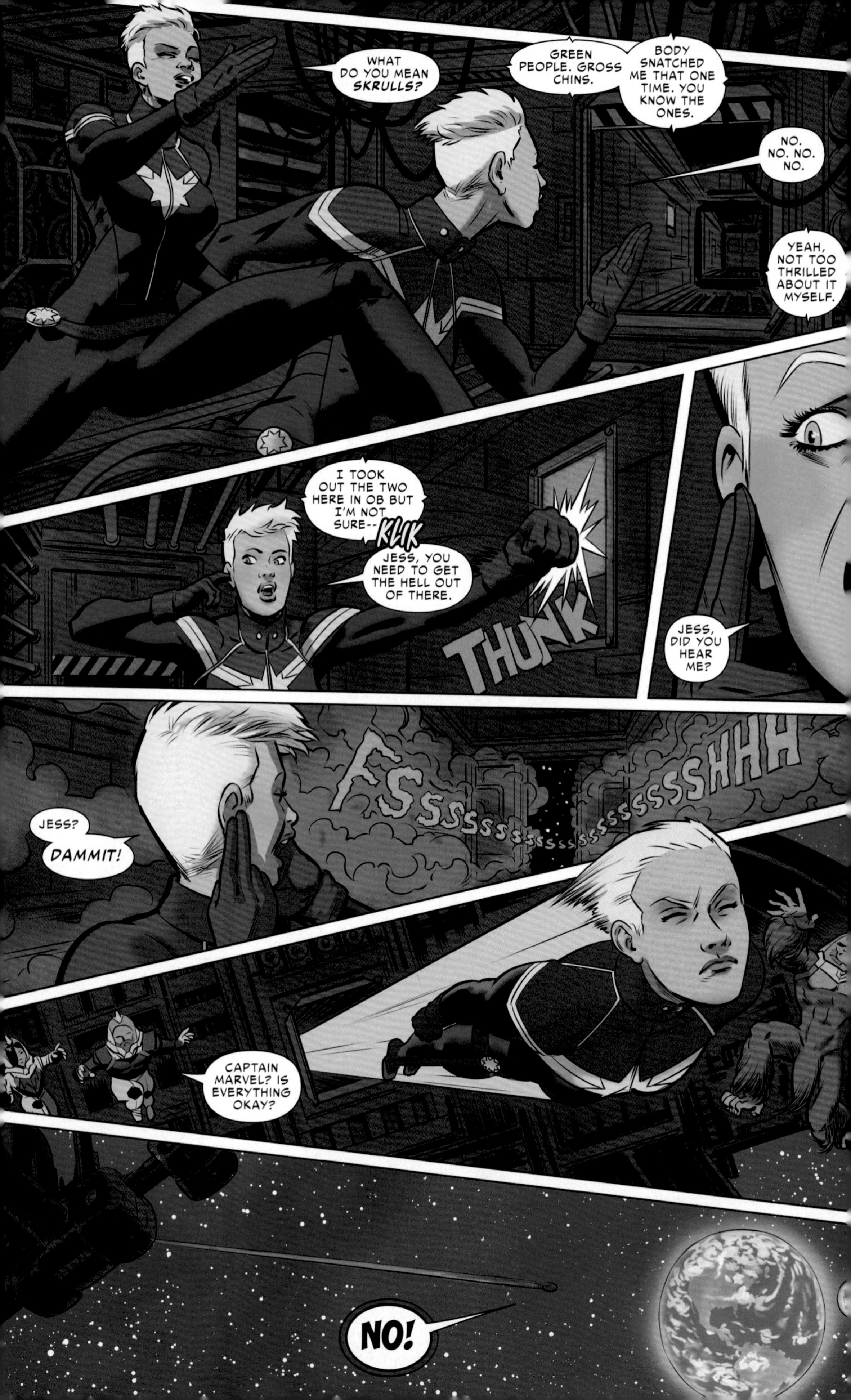
WHAT DO YOU MEAN SKRULLS?
GREEN PEOPLE. GROSS CHINS.
BODY SNATCHED ME THAT ONE TIME. YOU KNOW THE ONES.
NO. NO. NO. NO.
YEAH, NOT TOO THRILLED ABOUT IT MYSELF.
I TOOK OUT THE TWO HERE IN OB BUT I'M NOT SURE--
KLIK
JESS, YOU NEED TO GET THE HELL OUT OF THERE.
THUNK
JESS, DID YOU HEAR ME?
FSSSSSSSSSSSSSSSSSSSSHHH
JESS?
DAMMIT!
CAPTAIN MARVEL? IS EVERYTHING OKAY?
NO!

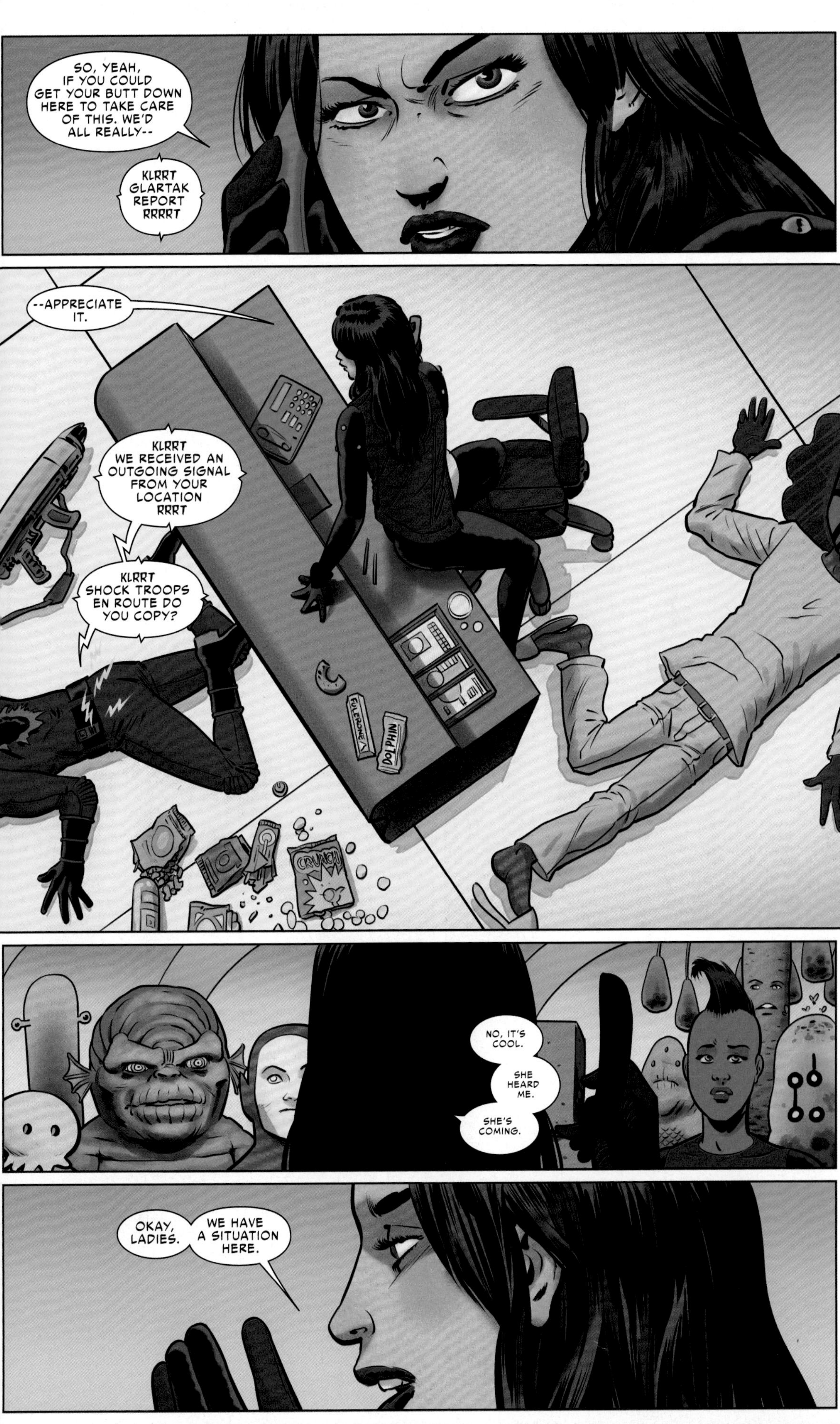
SO, YEAH, IF YOU COULD GET YOUR BUTT DOWN HERE TO TAKE CARE OF THIS. WE'D ALL REALLY--
KLRRT GLARTAK REPORT RRRRT
--APPRECIATE IT.
KLRRT WE RECEIVED AN OUTGOING SIGNAL FROM YOUR LOCATION RRRT
KLRRT SHOCK TROOPS EN ROUTE DO YOU COPY?
FULERONE
DOL'PHIN
CRUNCH
NO, IT'S COOL.
SHE HEARD ME.
SHE'S COMING.
OKAY, LADIES.
WE HAVE A SITUATION HERE.

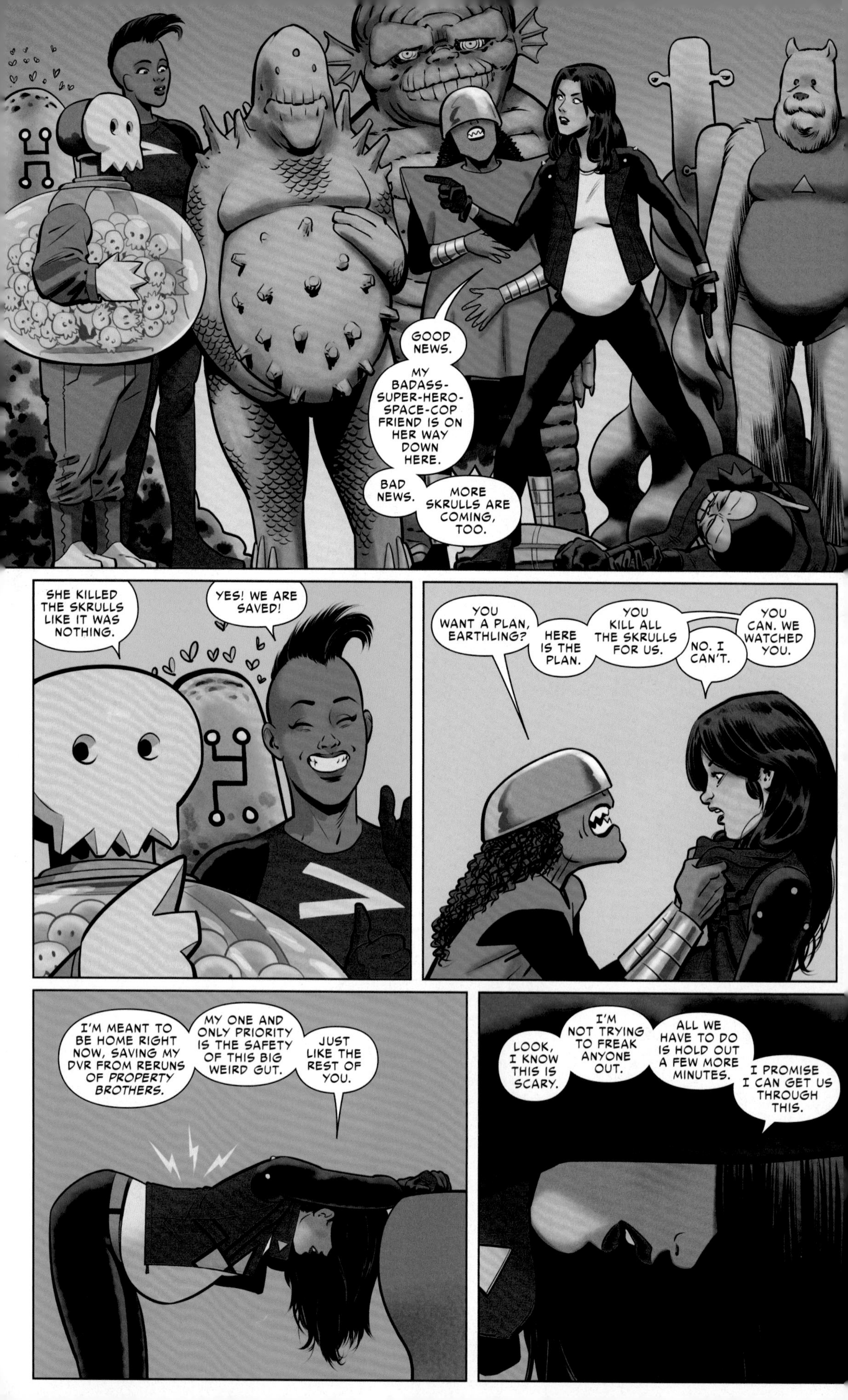
GOOD NEWS.
MY BADASS-SUPER-HERO-SPACE-COP FRIEND IS ON HER WAY DOWN HERE.
BAD NEWS.
MORE SKRULLS ARE COMING, TOO.
SHE KILLED THE SKRULLS LIKE IT WAS NOTHING.
YES! WE ARE SAVED!
YOU WANT A PLAN, EARTHLING?
HERE IS THE PLAN.
YOU KILL ALL THE SKRULLS FOR US.
NO. I CAN'T.
YOU CAN. WE WATCHED YOU.
I'M MEANT TO BE HOME RIGHT NOW, SAVING MY DVR FROM RERUNS OF *PROPERTY BROTHERS.*
MY ONE AND ONLY PRIORITY IS THE SAFETY OF THIS BIG WEIRD GUT.
JUST LIKE THE REST OF YOU.
LOOK, I KNOW THIS IS SCARY.
I'M NOT TRYING TO FREAK ANYONE OUT.
ALL WE HAVE TO DO IS HOLD OUT A FEW MORE MINUTES.
I PROMISE I CAN GET US THROUGH THIS.

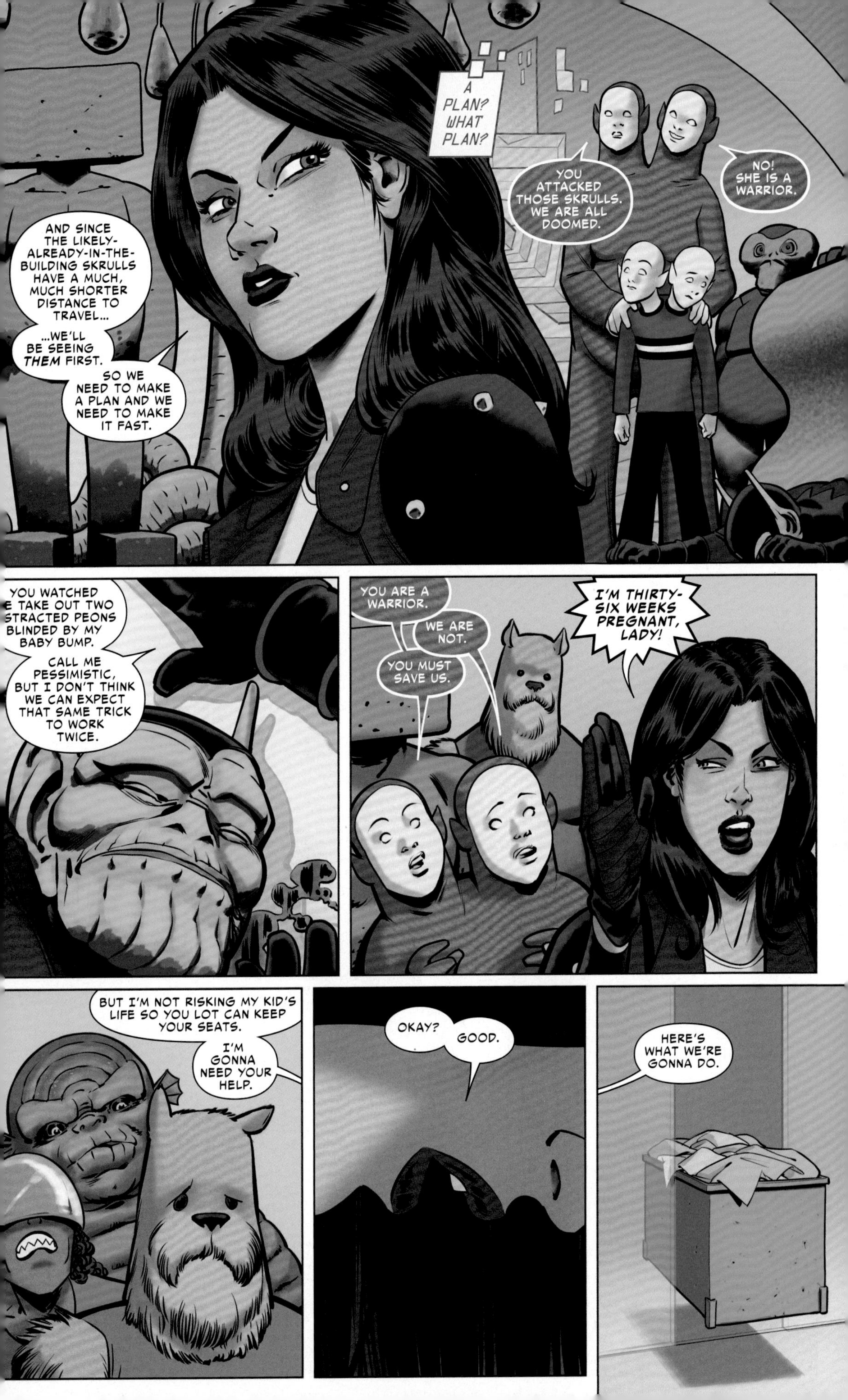
A PLAN? WHAT PLAN?
YOU ATTACKED THOSE SKRULLS. WE ARE ALL DOOMED.
NO! SHE IS A WARRIOR.
AND SINCE THE LIKELY-ALREADY-IN-THE-BUILDING SKRULLS HAVE A MUCH, MUCH SHORTER DISTANCE TO TRAVEL...
...WE'LL BE SEEING THEM FIRST.
SO WE NEED TO MAKE A PLAN AND WE NEED TO MAKE IT FAST.
YOU WATCHED E TAKE OUT TWO STRACTED PEONS BLINDED BY MY BABY BUMP.
CALL ME PESSIMISTIC, BUT I DON'T THINK WE CAN EXPECT THAT SAME TRICK TO WORK TWICE.
YOU ARE A WARRIOR.
WE ARE NOT.
YOU MUST SAVE US.
I'M THIRTY-SIX WEEKS PREGNANT, LADY!
BUT I'M NOT RISKING MY KID'S LIFE SO YOU LOT CAN KEEP YOUR SEATS.
I'M GONNA NEED YOUR HELP.
OKAY?
GOOD.
HERE'S WHAT WE'RE GONNA DO.

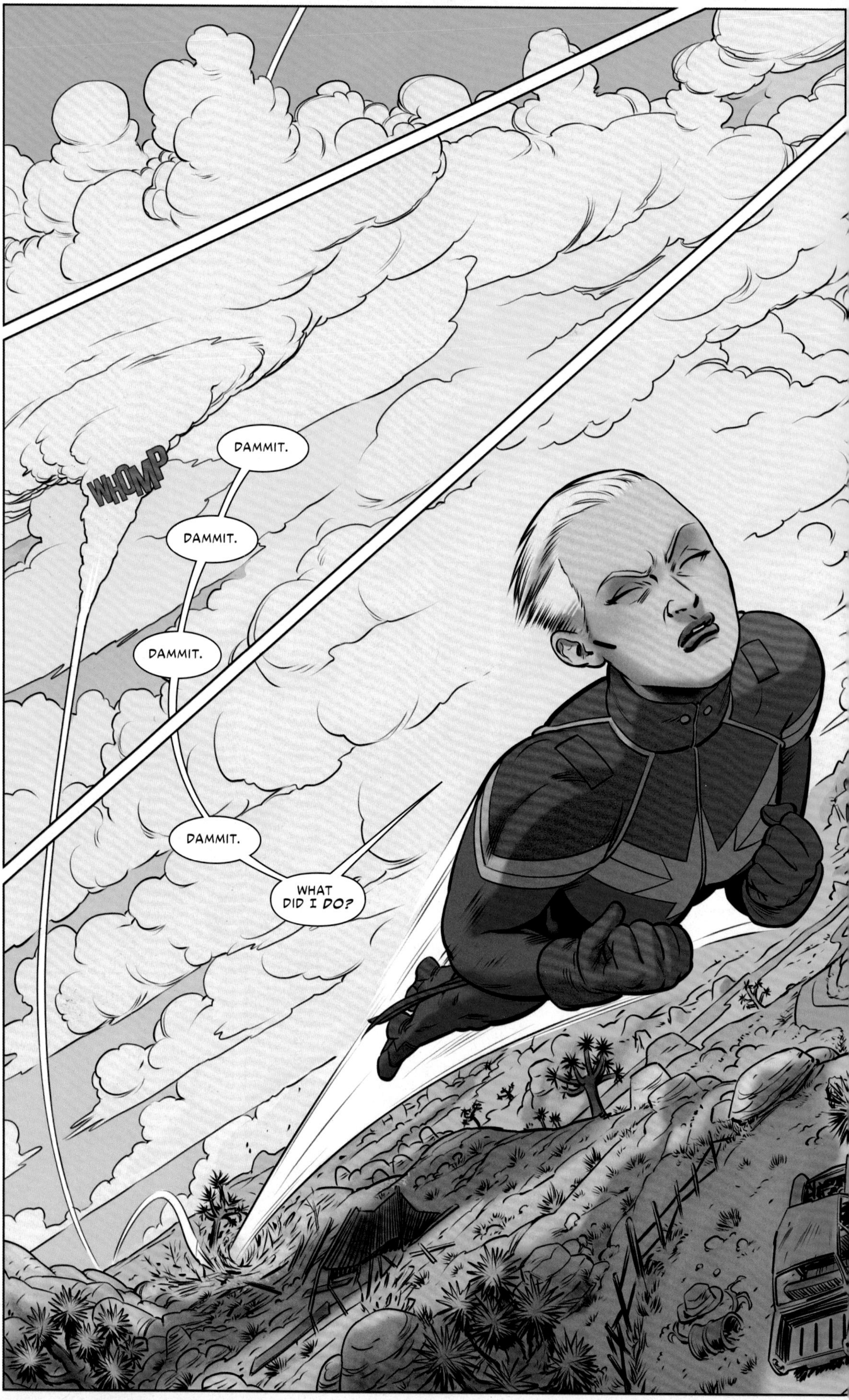
WHOMP
DAMMIT.
DAMMIT.
DAMMIT.
DAMMIT.
WHAT DID I DO?

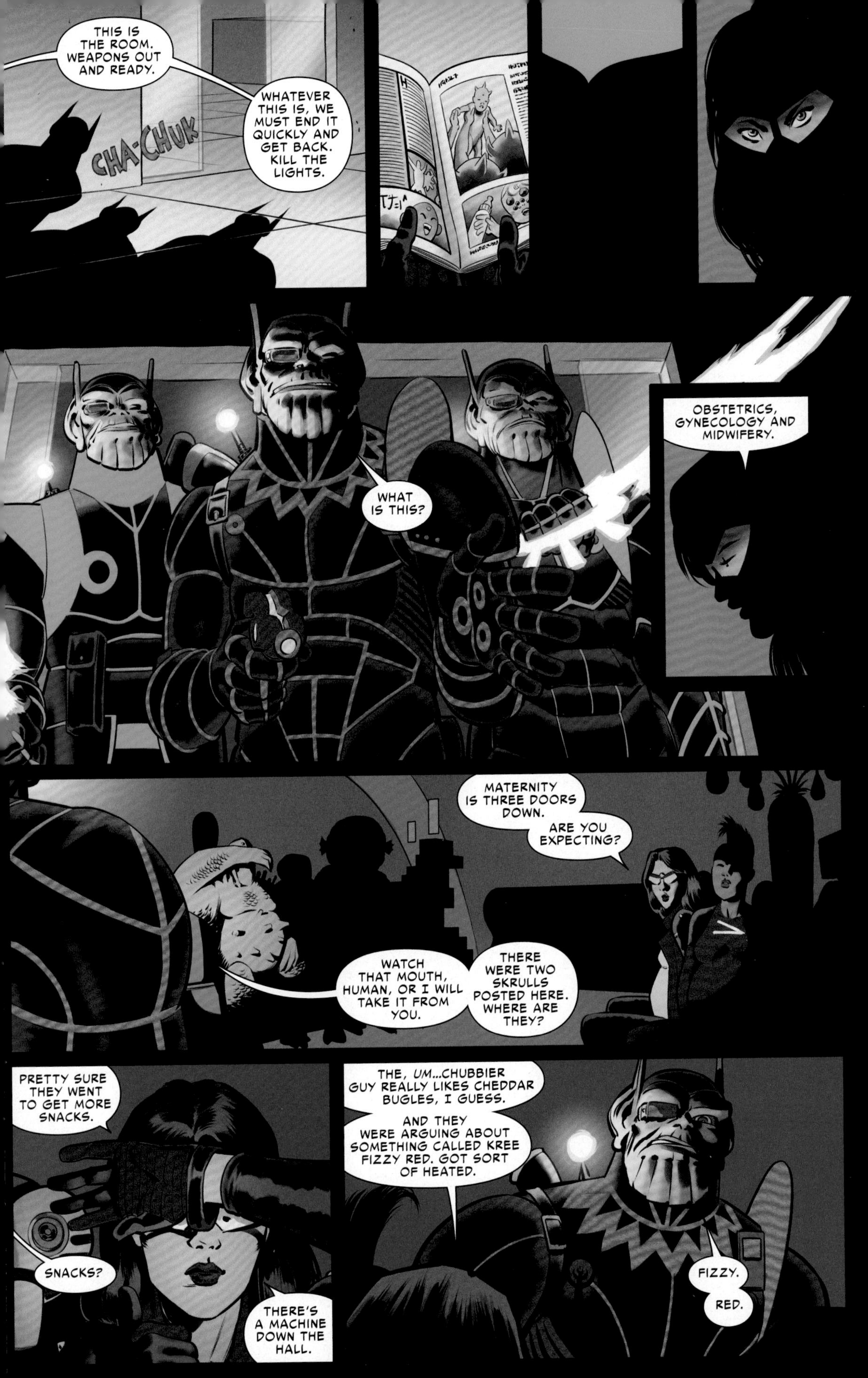
THIS IS THE ROOM. WEAPONS OUT AND READY.
CHA-CHUK
WHATEVER THIS IS, WE MUST END IT QUICKLY AND GET BACK. KILL THE LIGHTS.
WHAT IS THIS?
OBSTETRICS, GYNECOLOGY AND MIDWIFERY.
MATERNITY IS THREE DOORS DOWN.
ARE YOU EXPECTING?
WATCH THAT MOUTH, HUMAN, OR I WILL TAKE IT FROM YOU.
THERE WERE TWO SKRULLS POSTED HERE. WHERE ARE THEY?
PRETTY SURE THEY WENT TO GET MORE SNACKS.
SNACKS?
THERE'S A MACHINE DOWN THE HALL.
THE, *UM*...CHUBBIER GUY REALLY LIKES CHEDDAR BUGLES, I GUESS.
AND THEY WERE ARGUING ABOUT SOMETHING CALLED KREE FIZZY RED. GOT SORT OF HEATED.
FIZZY.
RED.

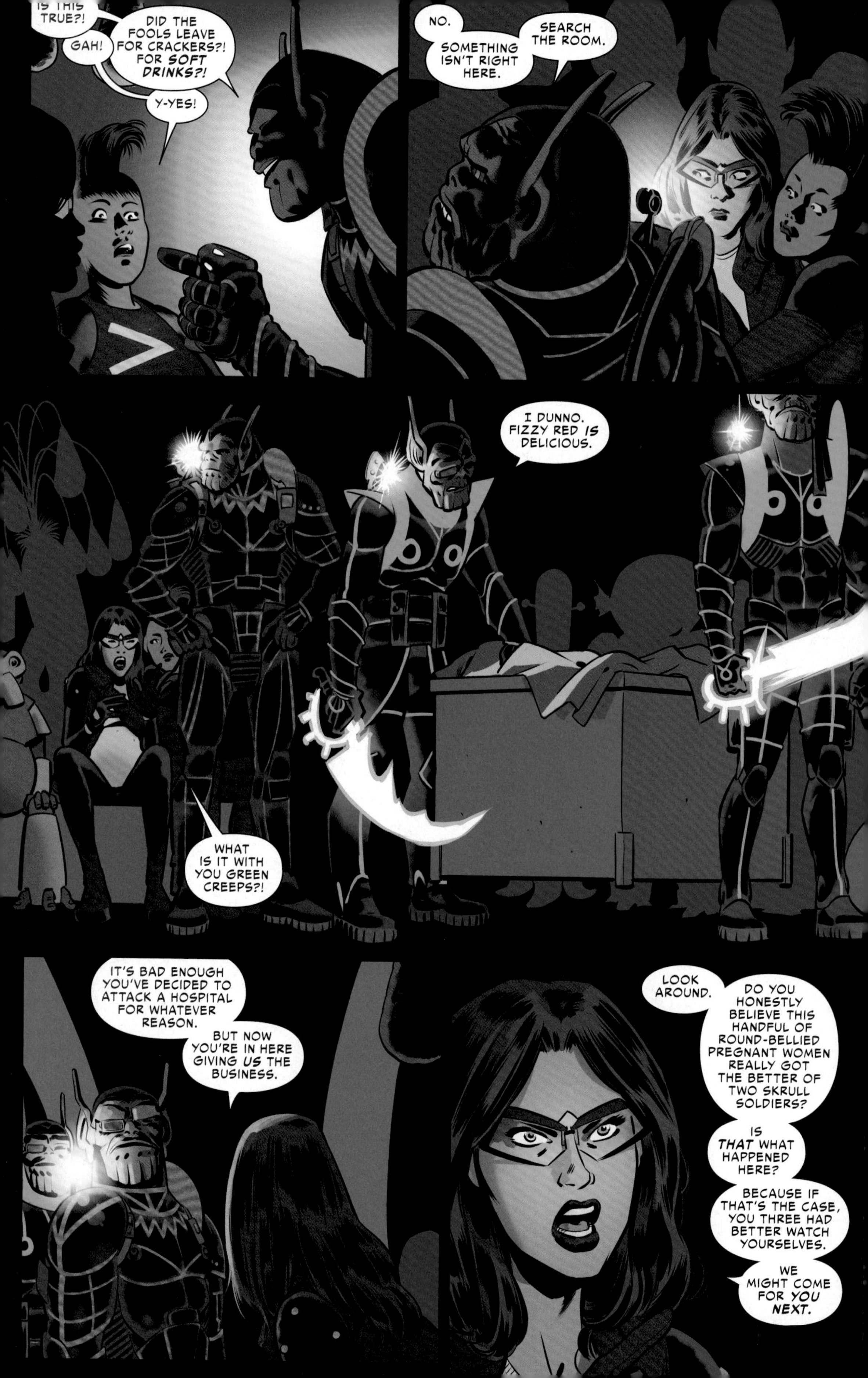
IS THIS TRUE?!
GAH!
DID THE FOOLS LEAVE FOR CRACKERS?! FOR SOFT DRINKS?!
Y-YES!
NO.
SOMETHING ISN'T RIGHT HERE.
SEARCH THE ROOM.
I DUNNO. FIZZY RED IS DELICIOUS.
WHAT IS IT WITH YOU GREEN CREEPS?!
IT'S BAD ENOUGH YOU'VE DECIDED TO ATTACK A HOSPITAL FOR WHATEVER REASON.
BUT NOW YOU'RE IN HERE GIVING US THE BUSINESS.
LOOK AROUND.
DO YOU HONESTLY BELIEVE THIS HANDFUL OF ROUND-BELLIED PREGNANT WOMEN REALLY GOT THE BETTER OF TWO SKRULL SOLDIERS?
IS THAT WHAT HAPPENED HERE?
BECAUSE IF THAT'S THE CASE, YOU THREE HAD BETTER WATCH YOURSELVES.
WE MIGHT COME FOR YOU NEXT.

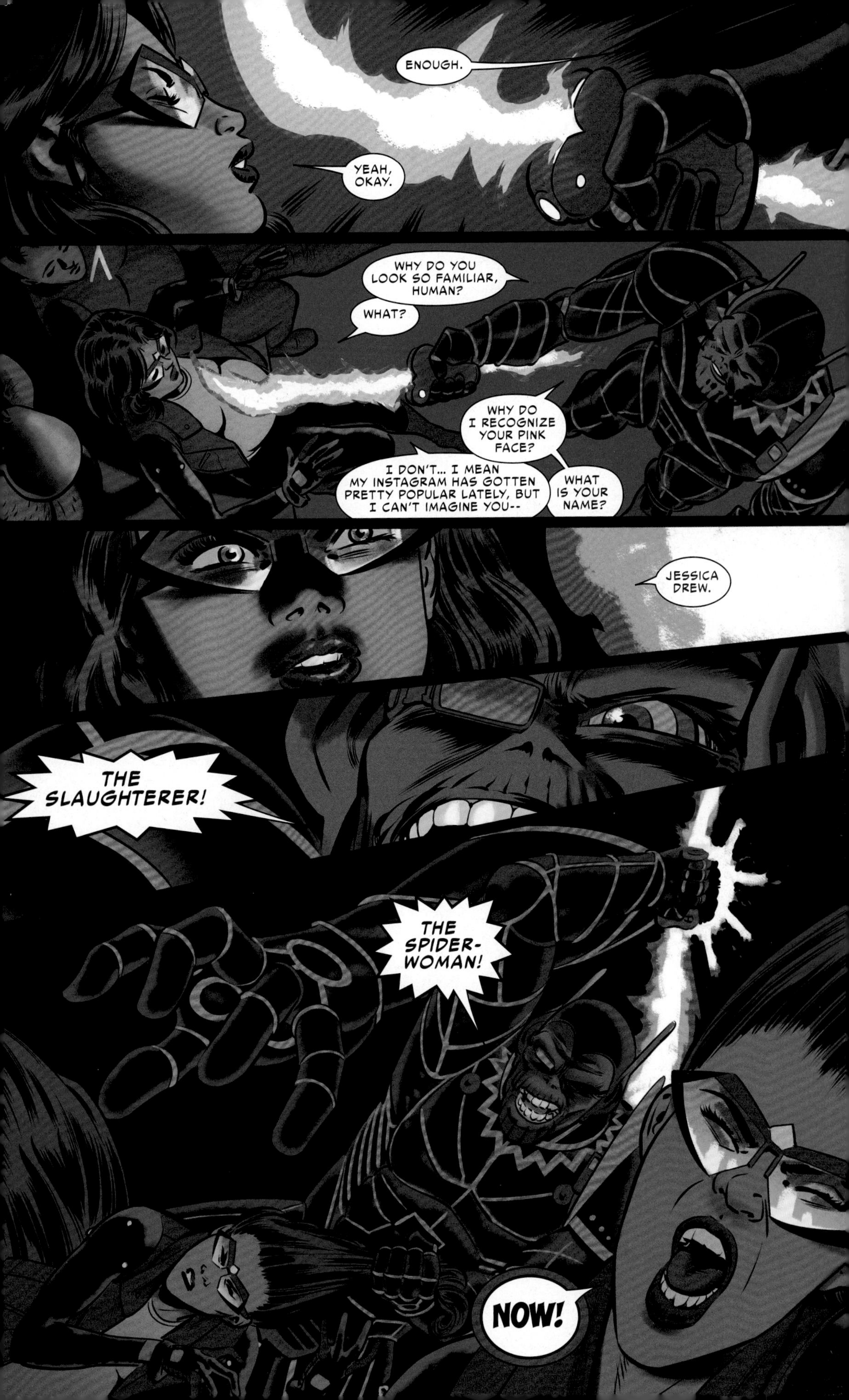
ENOUGH.
YEAH, OKAY.
WHY DO YOU LOOK SO FAMILIAR, HUMAN?
WHAT?
WHY DO I RECOGNIZE YOUR PINK FACE?
I DON'T... I MEAN MY INSTAGRAM HAS GOTTEN PRETTY POPULAR LATELY, BUT I CAN'T IMAGINE YOU--
WHAT IS YOUR NAME?
JESSICA DREW.
THE SLAUGHTERER!
THE SPIDER-WOMAN!
NOW!

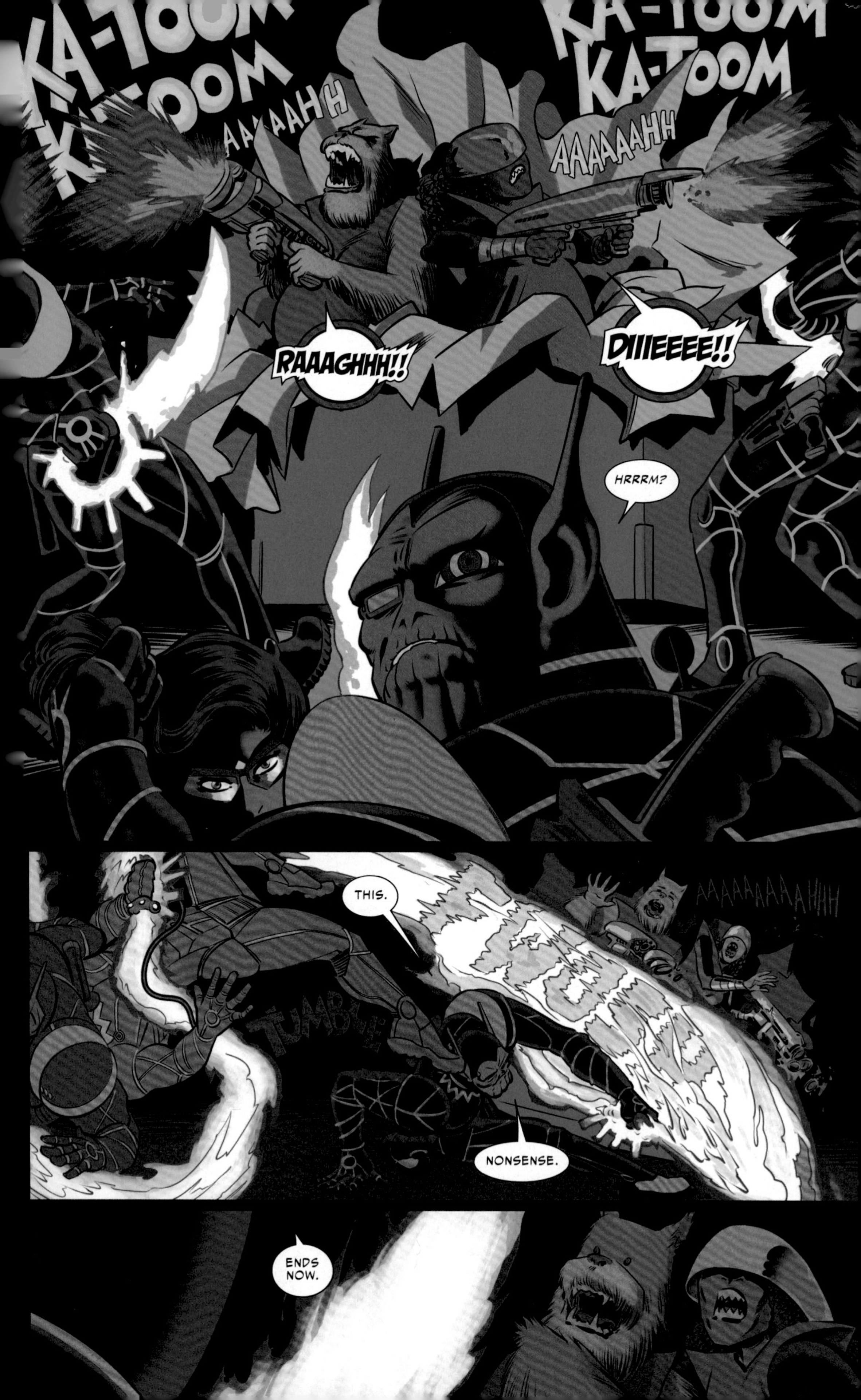
KA-TOOM
KA-TOOM
AAAAAHH
KA-TOOM
KA-TOOM
AAAAAAHH
RAAAGHHH!!
DIIIEEEE!!
HRRRM?
THIS.
AAAAAAAAAHHH
TUMBLE
NONSENSE.
ENDS NOW.

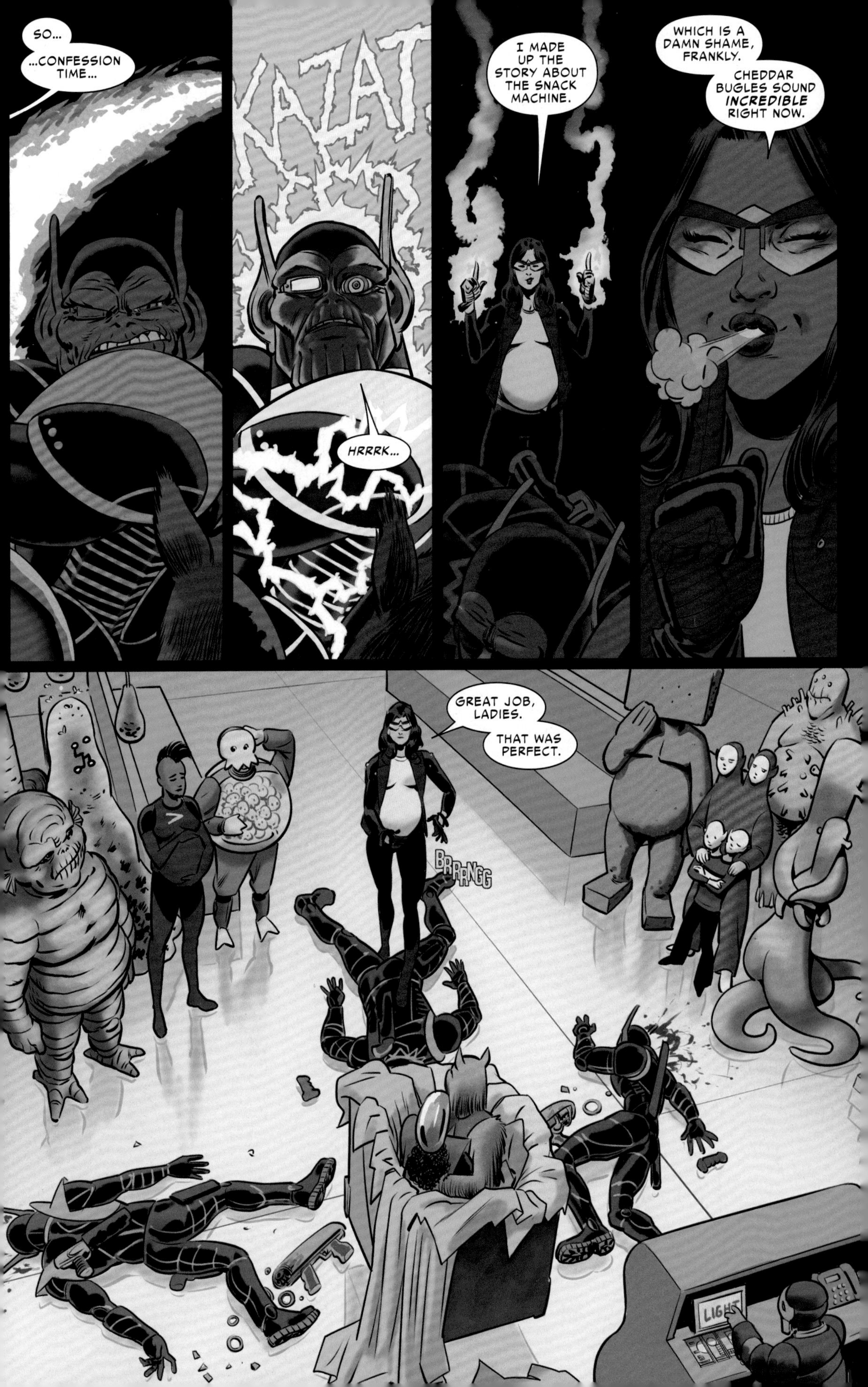
SO...
...CONFESSION TIME...
KAZAT
HRRRK...
I MADE UP THE STORY ABOUT THE SNACK MACHINE.
WHICH IS A DAMN SHAME, FRANKLY.
CHEDDAR BUGLES SOUND *INCREDIBLE* RIGHT NOW.
GREAT JOB, LADIES.
THAT WAS PERFECT.
BRRRRNGG
LIGHT

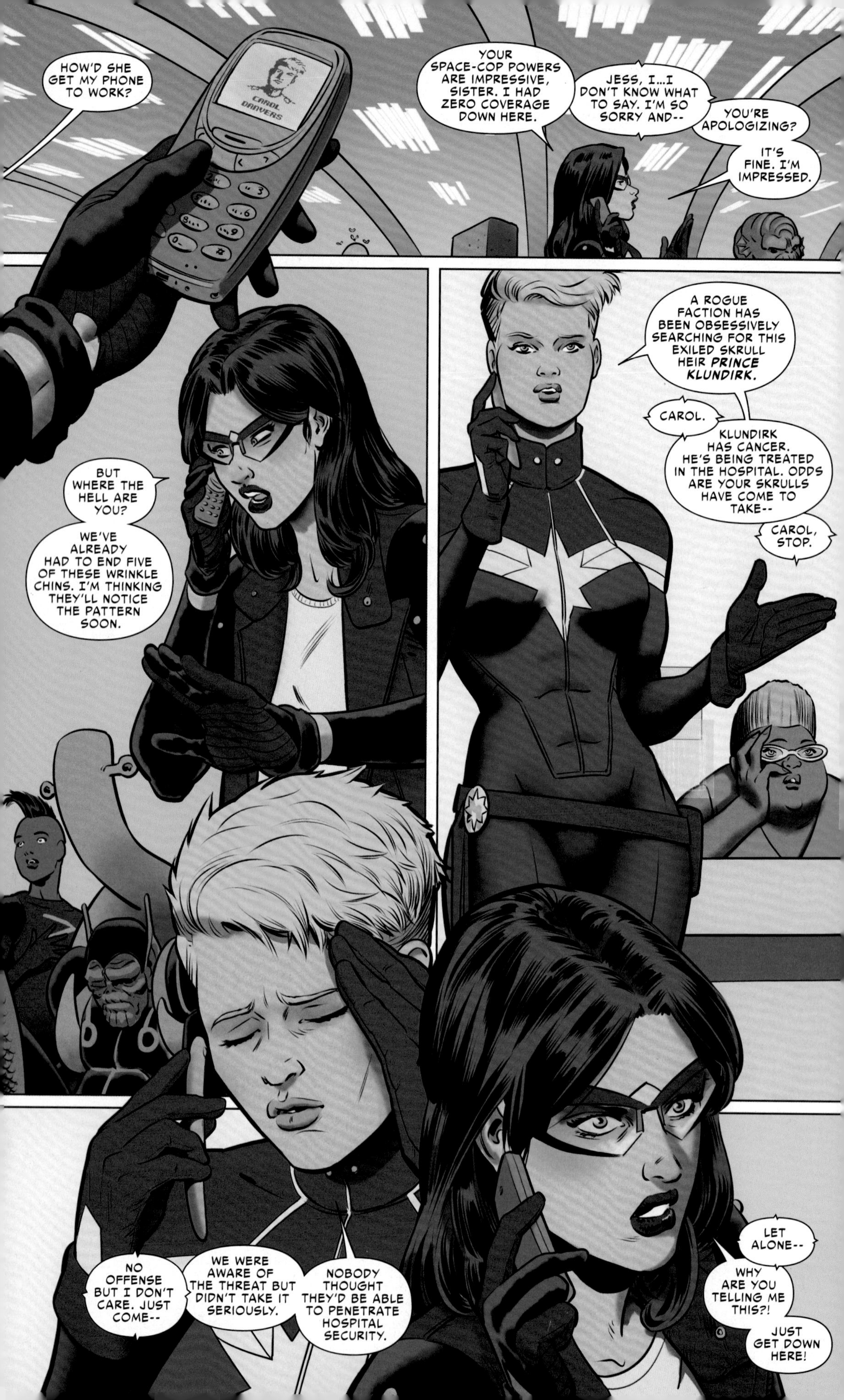
HOW'D SHE GET MY PHONE TO WORK?
CAROL DANVERS
YOUR SPACE-COP POWERS ARE IMPRESSIVE, SISTER. I HAD ZERO COVERAGE DOWN HERE.
JESS, I...I DON'T KNOW WHAT TO SAY. I'M SO SORRY AND--
YOU'RE APOLOGIZING?
IT'S FINE. I'M IMPRESSED.
BUT WHERE THE HELL ARE YOU?
WE'VE ALREADY HAD TO END FIVE OF THESE WRINKLE CHINS. I'M THINKING THEY'LL NOTICE THE PATTERN SOON.
A ROGUE FACTION HAS BEEN OBSESSIVELY SEARCHING FOR THIS EXILED SKRULL HEIR ***PRINCE KLUNDIRK.***
CAROL.
KLUNDIRK HAS CANCER. HE'S BEING TREATED IN THE HOSPITAL. ODDS ARE YOUR SKRULLS HAVE COME TO TAKE--
CAROL, STOP.
NO OFFENSE BUT I DON'T CARE. JUST COME--
WE WERE AWARE OF THE THREAT BUT DIDN'T TAKE IT SERIOUSLY.
NOBODY THOUGHT THEY'D BE ABLE TO PENETRATE HOSPITAL SECURITY.
LET ALONE--
WHY ARE YOU TELLING ME THIS?!
JUST GET DOWN HERE!

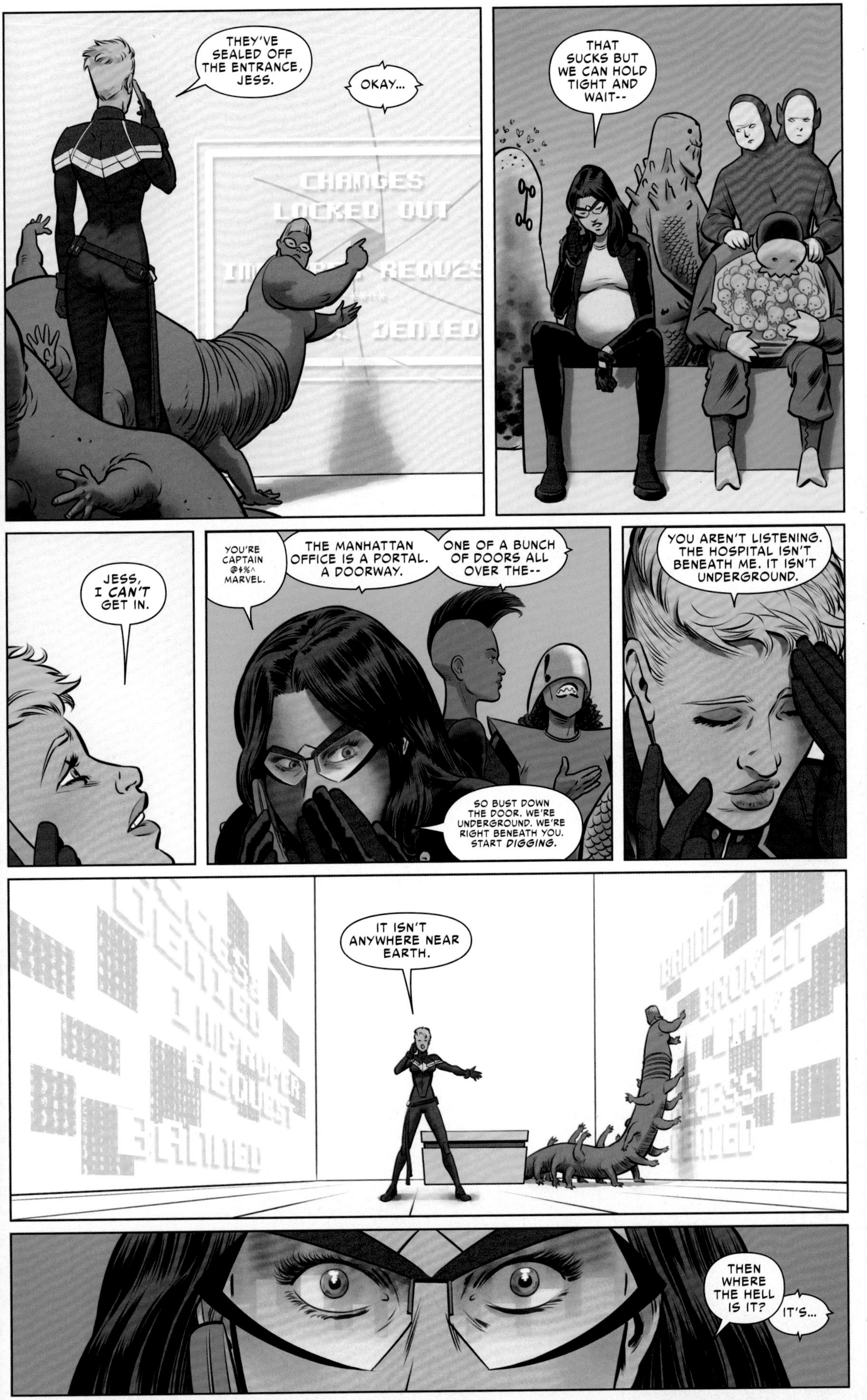
THEY'VE SEALED OFF THE ENTRANCE, JESS.
OKAY...
CHANGES LOCKED OUT
DENIED
THAT SUCKS BUT WE CAN HOLD TIGHT AND WAIT--
JESS, I *CAN'T* GET IN.
YOU'RE CAPTAIN @$%^ MARVEL.
THE MANHATTAN OFFICE IS A PORTAL. A DOORWAY.
ONE OF A BUNCH OF DOORS ALL OVER THE--
SO BUST DOWN THE DOOR. WE'RE UNDERGROUND. WE'RE RIGHT BENEATH YOU. START *DIGGING*.
YOU AREN'T LISTENING. THE HOSPITAL ISN'T BENEATH ME. IT ISN'T UNDERGROUND.
IT ISN'T ANYWHERE NEAR EARTH.
THEN WHERE THE HELL IS IT?
IT'S...

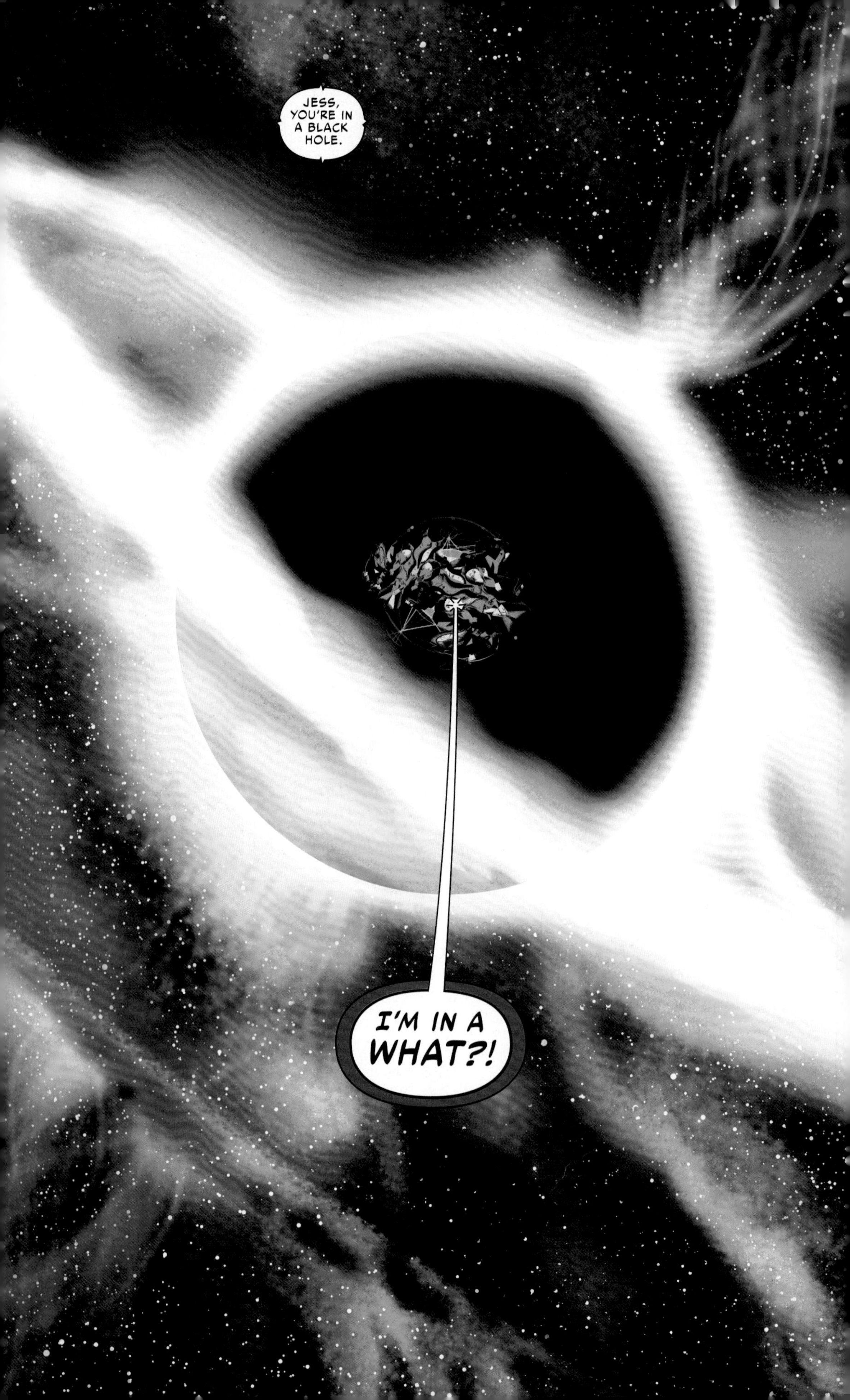
JESS, YOU'RE IN A BLACK HOLE.
I'M IN A WHAT?!

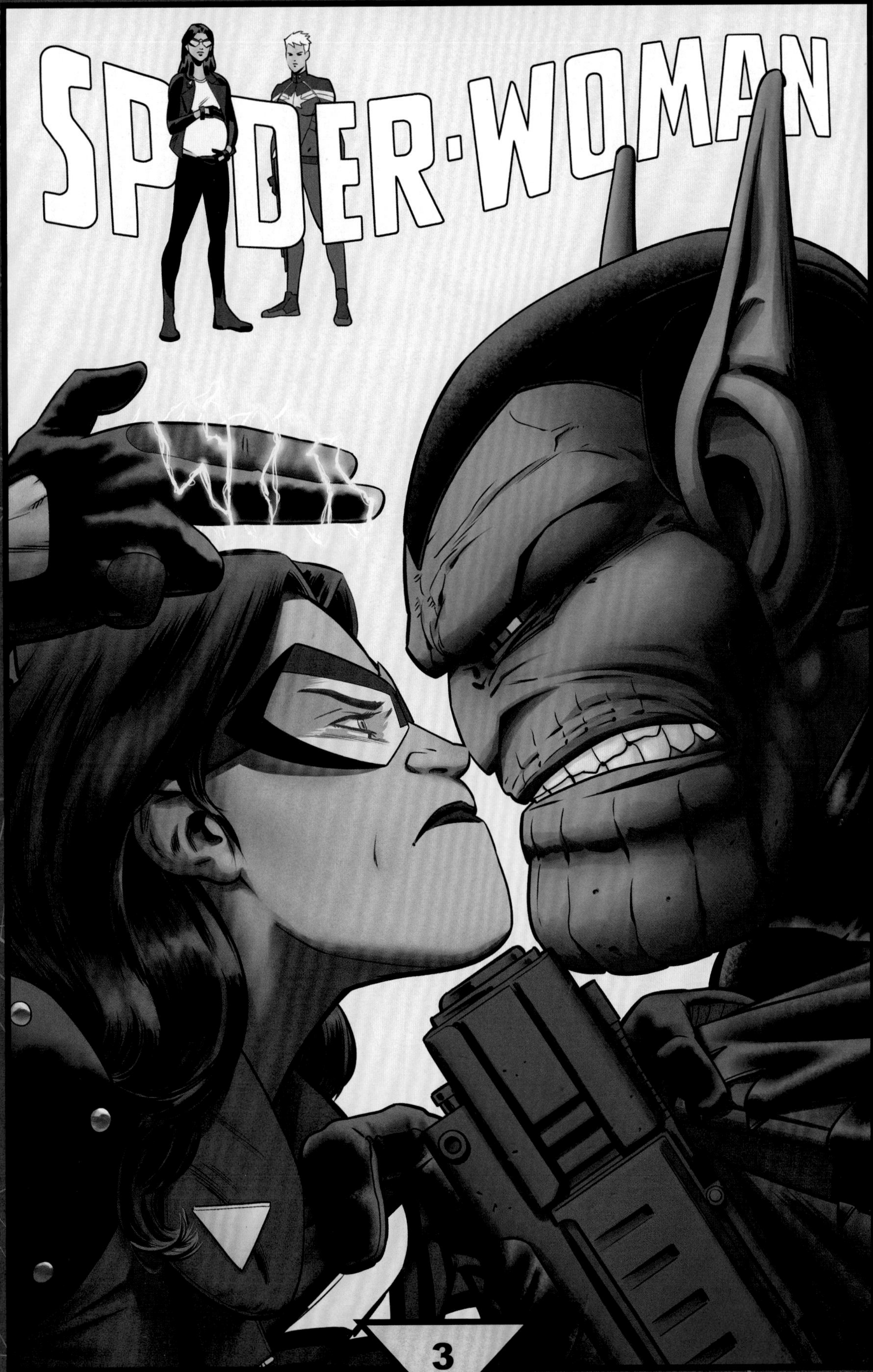
SPIDER-WOMAN
3

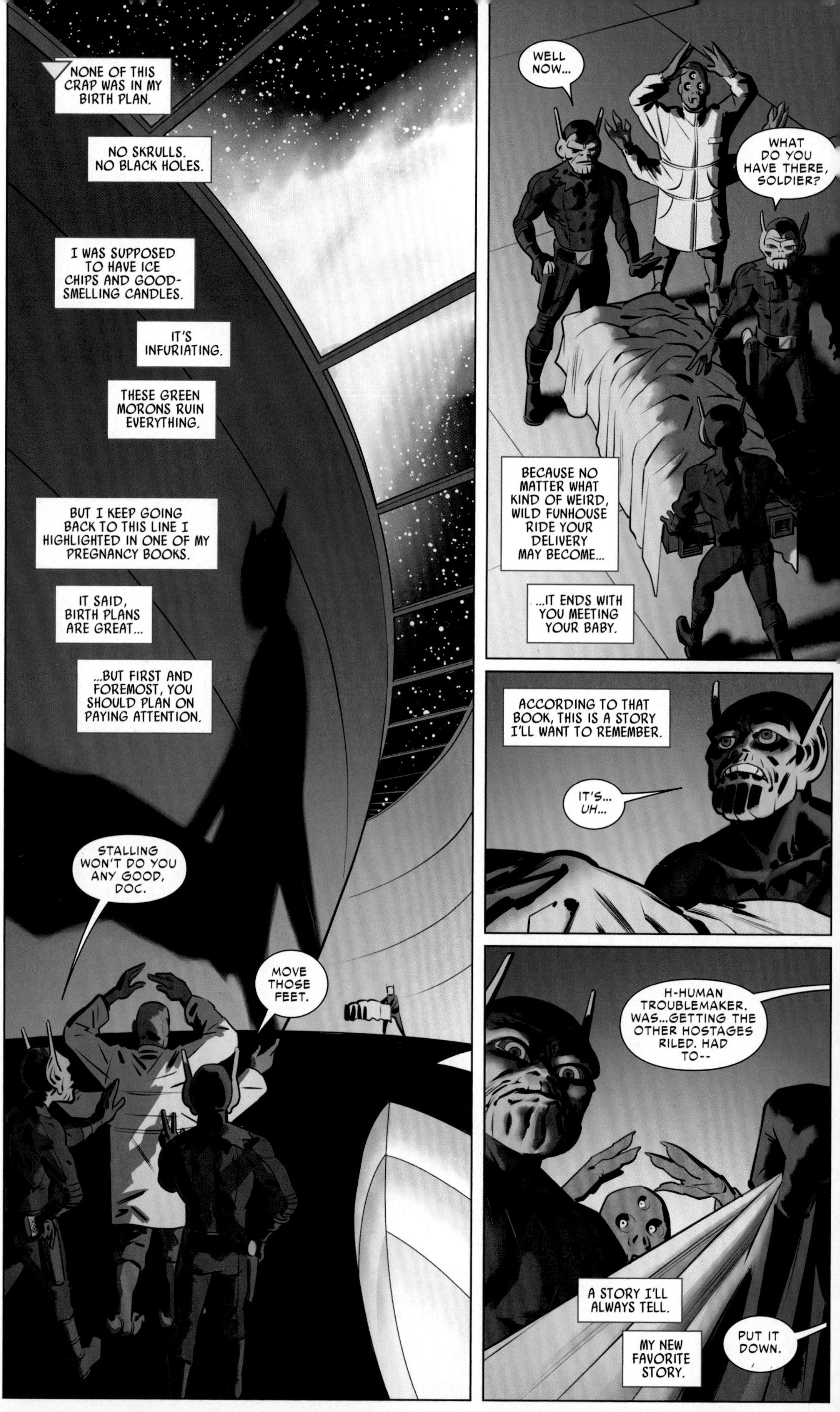

NONE OF THIS CRAP WAS IN MY BIRTH PLAN.
NO SKRULLS. NO BLACK HOLES.
I WAS SUPPOSED TO HAVE ICE CHIPS AND GOOD-SMELLING CANDLES.
IT'S INFURIATING.
THESE GREEN MORONS RUIN EVERYTHING.
BUT I KEEP GOING BACK TO THIS LINE I HIGHLIGHTED IN ONE OF MY PREGNANCY BOOKS.
IT SAID, BIRTH PLANS ARE GREAT...
...BUT FIRST AND FOREMOST, YOU SHOULD PLAN ON PAYING ATTENTION.
STALLING WON'T DO YOU ANY GOOD, DOC.
MOVE THOSE FEET.
WELL NOW...
WHAT DO YOU HAVE THERE, SOLDIER?
BECAUSE NO MATTER WHAT KIND OF WEIRD, WILD FUNHOUSE RIDE YOUR DELIVERY MAY BECOME...
...IT ENDS WITH YOU MEETING YOUR BABY.
ACCORDING TO THAT BOOK, THIS IS A STORY I'LL WANT TO REMEMBER.
IT'S... UH...
H-HUMAN TROUBLEMAKER. WAS...GETTING THE OTHER HOSTAGES RILED. HAD TO--
A STORY I'LL ALWAYS TELL.
MY NEW FAVORITE STORY.
PUT IT DOWN.

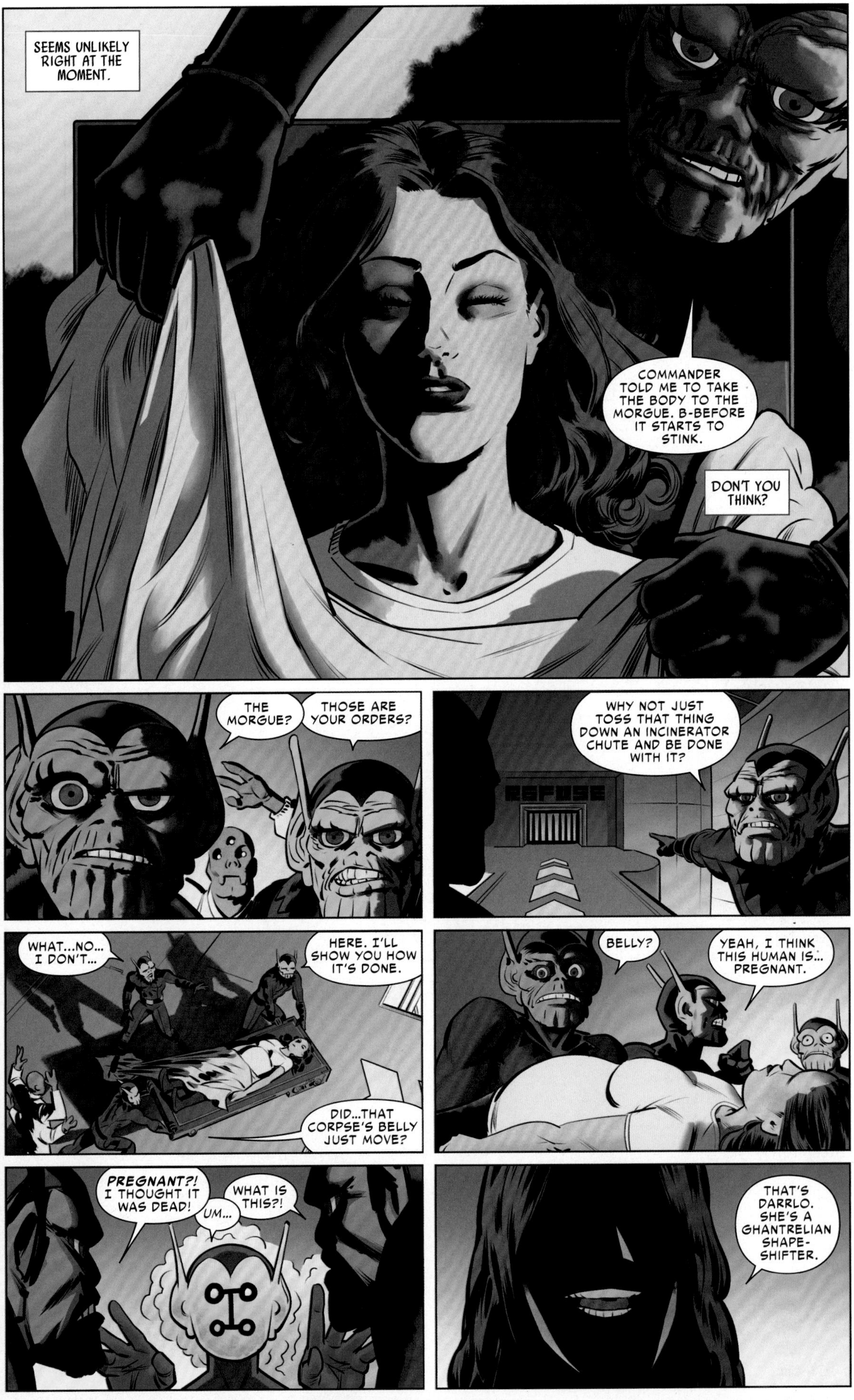
SEEMS UNLIKELY RIGHT AT THE MOMENT.
COMMANDER TOLD ME TO TAKE THE BODY TO THE MORGUE. B-BEFORE IT STARTS TO STINK.
DON'T YOU THINK?
THE MORGUE?
THOSE ARE YOUR ORDERS?
WHY NOT JUST TOSS THAT THING DOWN AN INCINERATOR CHUTE AND BE DONE WITH IT?
REFUSE
WHAT...NO... I DON'T...
HERE. I'LL SHOW YOU HOW IT'S DONE.
DID...THAT CORPSE'S BELLY JUST MOVE?
BELLY?
YEAH, I THINK THIS HUMAN IS... PREGNANT.
PREGNANT?! I THOUGHT IT WAS DEAD!
UM...
WHAT IS THIS?!
THAT'S DARRLO. SHE'S A GHANTRELIAN SHAPE-SHIFTER.

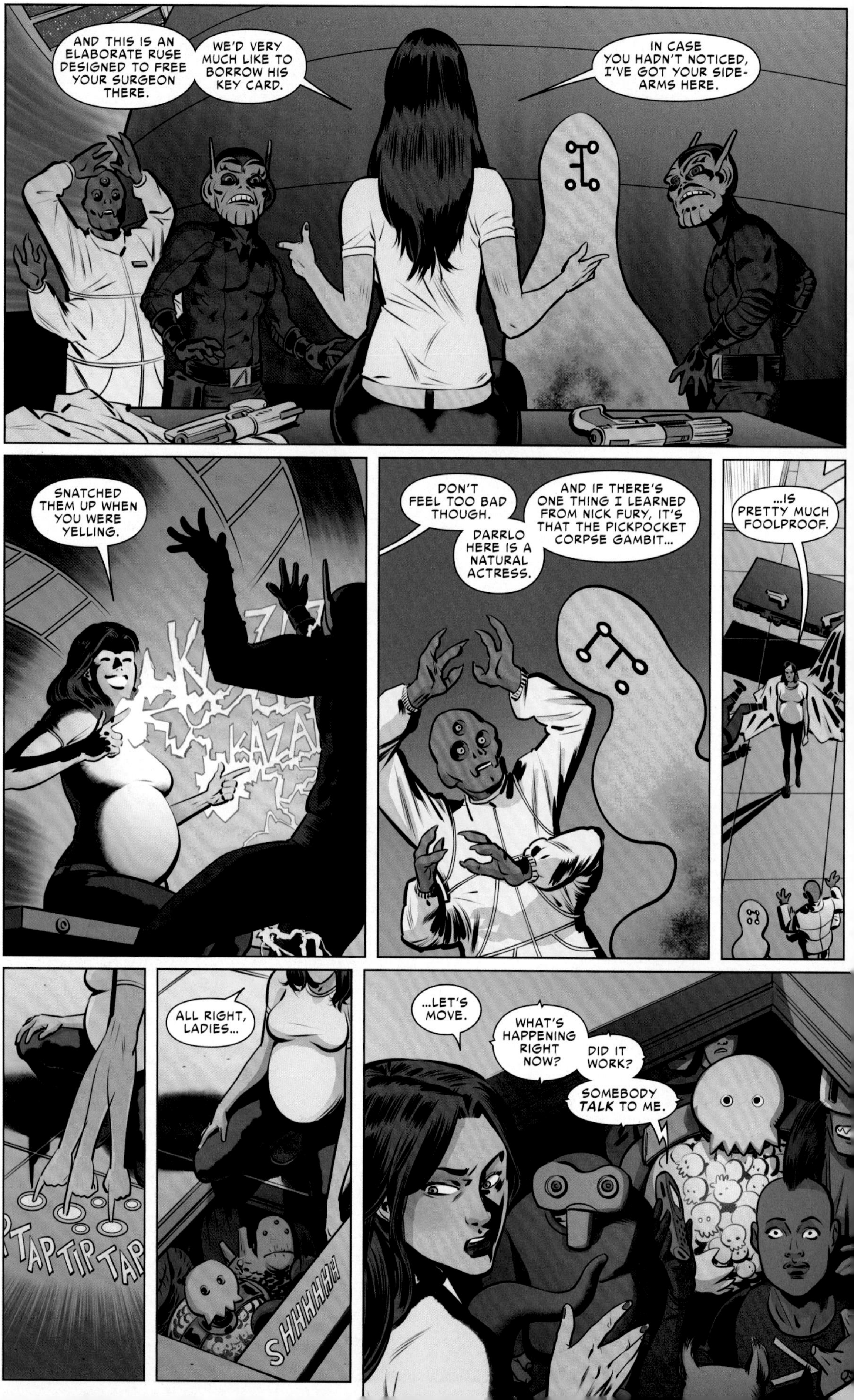
AND THIS IS AN ELABORATE RUSE DESIGNED TO FREE YOUR SURGEON THERE.
WE'D VERY MUCH LIKE TO BORROW HIS KEY CARD.
IN CASE YOU HADN'T NOTICED, I'VE GOT YOUR SIDE-ARMS HERE.
SNATCHED THEM UP WHEN YOU WERE YELLING.
KAZAK
DON'T FEEL TOO BAD THOUGH.
DARRLO HERE IS A NATURAL ACTRESS.
AND IF THERE'S ONE THING I LEARNED FROM NICK FURY, IT'S THAT THE PICKPOCKET CORPSE GAMBIT...
...IS PRETTY MUCH FOOLPROOF.
TAP TIP TAP
ALL RIGHT, LADIES...
SHHHHHH
...LET'S MOVE.
WHAT'S HAPPENING RIGHT NOW?
DID IT WORK?
SOMEBODY *TALK* TO ME.

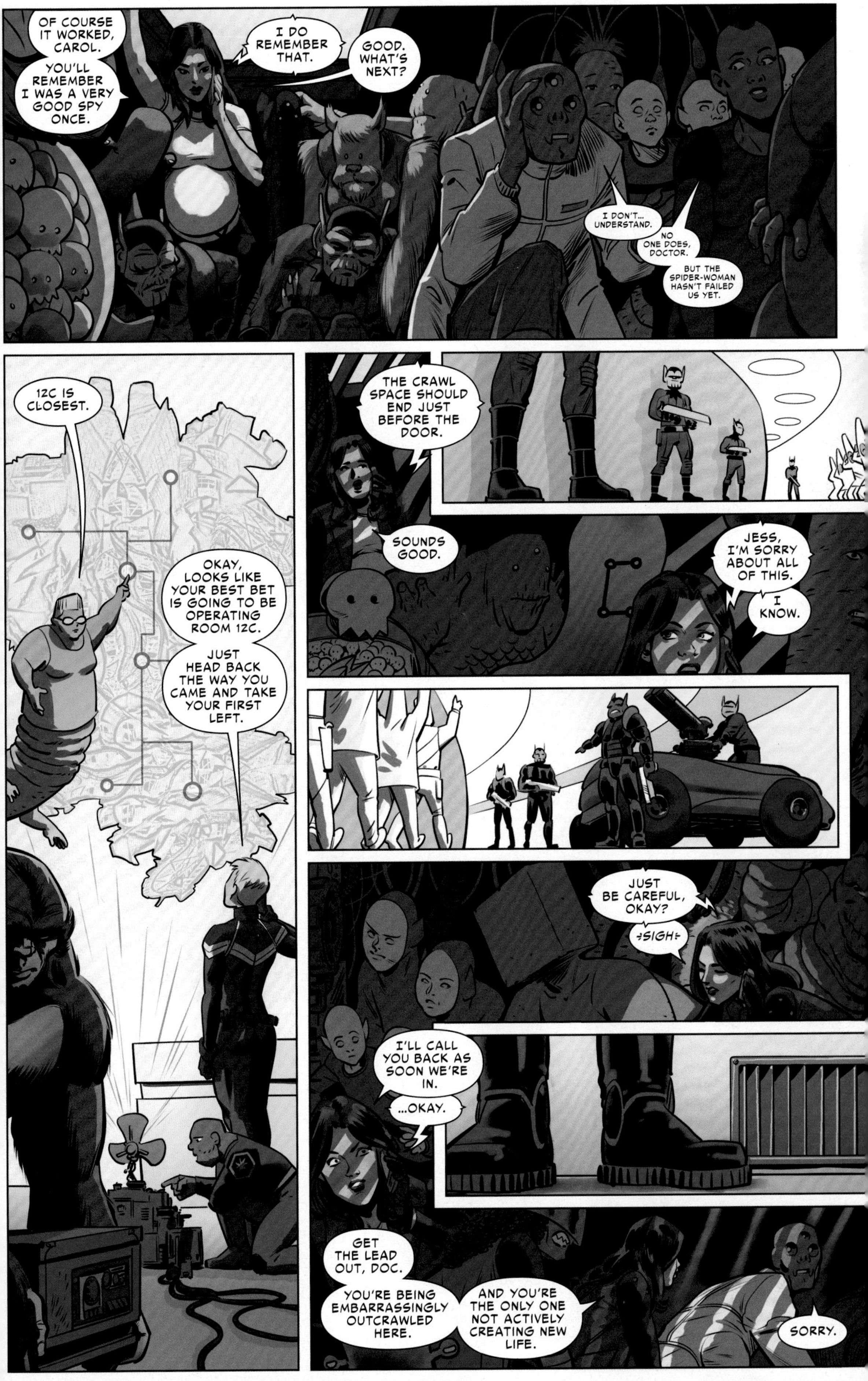
OF COURSE IT WORKED, CAROL.
YOU'LL REMEMBER I WAS A VERY GOOD SPY ONCE.
I DO REMEMBER THAT.
GOOD. WHAT'S NEXT?
I DON'T... UNDERSTAND.
NO ONE DOES, DOCTOR.
BUT THE SPIDER-WOMAN HASN'T FAILED US YET.
12C IS CLOSEST.
OKAY, LOOKS LIKE YOUR BEST BET IS GOING TO BE OPERATING ROOM 12C.
JUST HEAD BACK THE WAY YOU CAME AND TAKE YOUR FIRST LEFT.
THE CRAWL SPACE SHOULD END JUST BEFORE THE DOOR.
SOUNDS GOOD.
JESS, I'M SORRY ABOUT ALL OF THIS.
I KNOW.
JUST BE CAREFUL, OKAY?
SIGH
I'LL CALL YOU BACK AS SOON WE'RE IN.
...OKAY.
GET THE LEAD OUT, DOC.
YOU'RE BEING EMBARRASSINGLY OUTCRAWLED HERE.
AND YOU'RE THE ONLY ONE NOT ACTIVELY CREATING NEW LIFE.
SORRY.

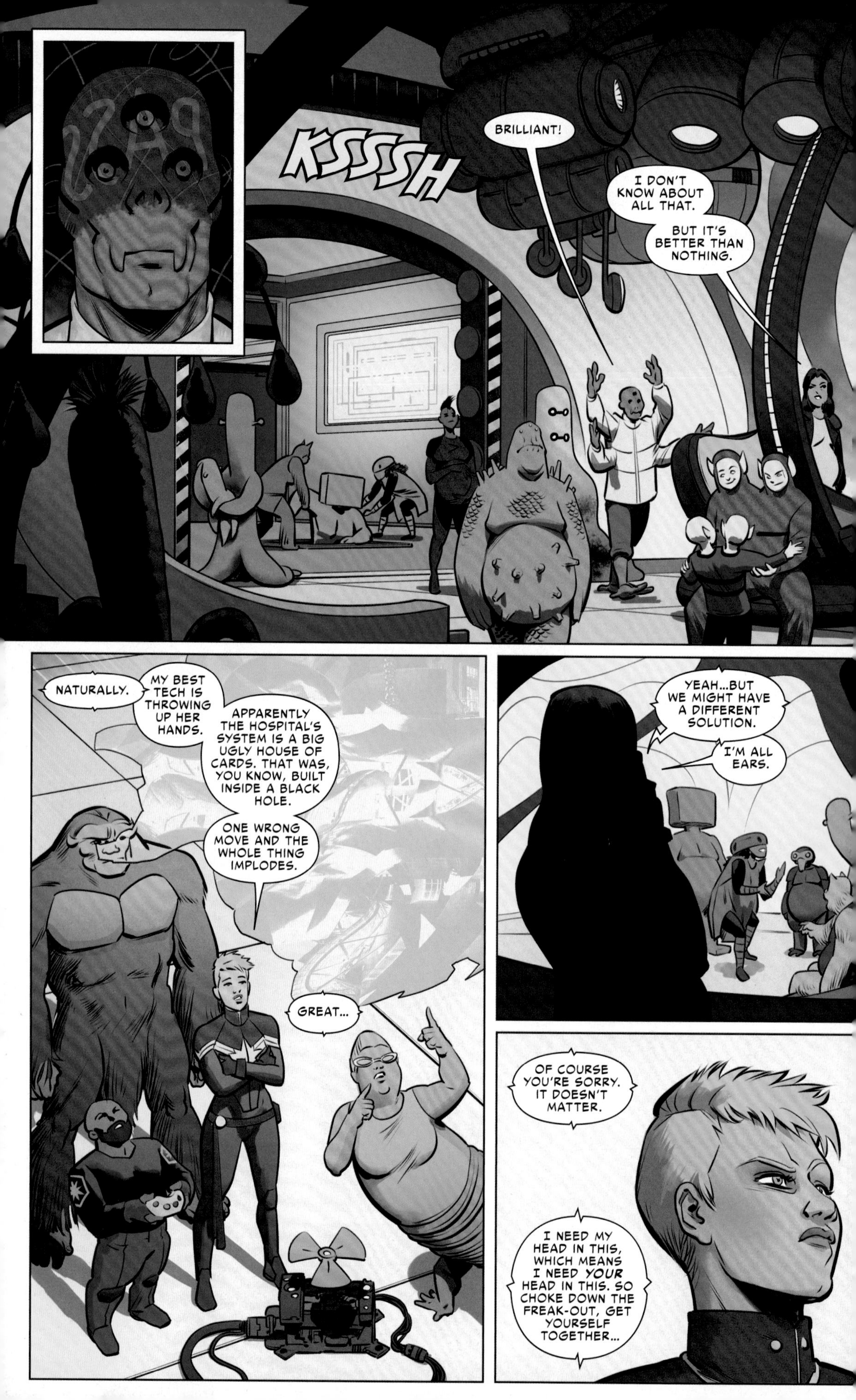
KSSSH
BRILLIANT!
I DON'T KNOW ABOUT ALL THAT.
BUT IT'S BETTER THAN NOTHING.
NATURALLY.
MY BEST TECH IS THROWING UP HER HANDS.
APPARENTLY THE HOSPITAL'S SYSTEM IS A BIG UGLY HOUSE OF CARDS. THAT WAS, YOU KNOW, BUILT INSIDE A BLACK HOLE.
ONE WRONG MOVE AND THE WHOLE THING IMPLODES.
GREAT...
YEAH...BUT WE MIGHT HAVE A DIFFERENT SOLUTION.
I'M ALL EARS.
OF COURSE YOU'RE SORRY. IT DOESN'T MATTER.
I NEED MY HEAD IN THIS, WHICH MEANS I NEED *YOUR* HEAD IN THIS. SO CHOKE DOWN THE FREAK-OUT, GET YOURSELF TOGETHER...

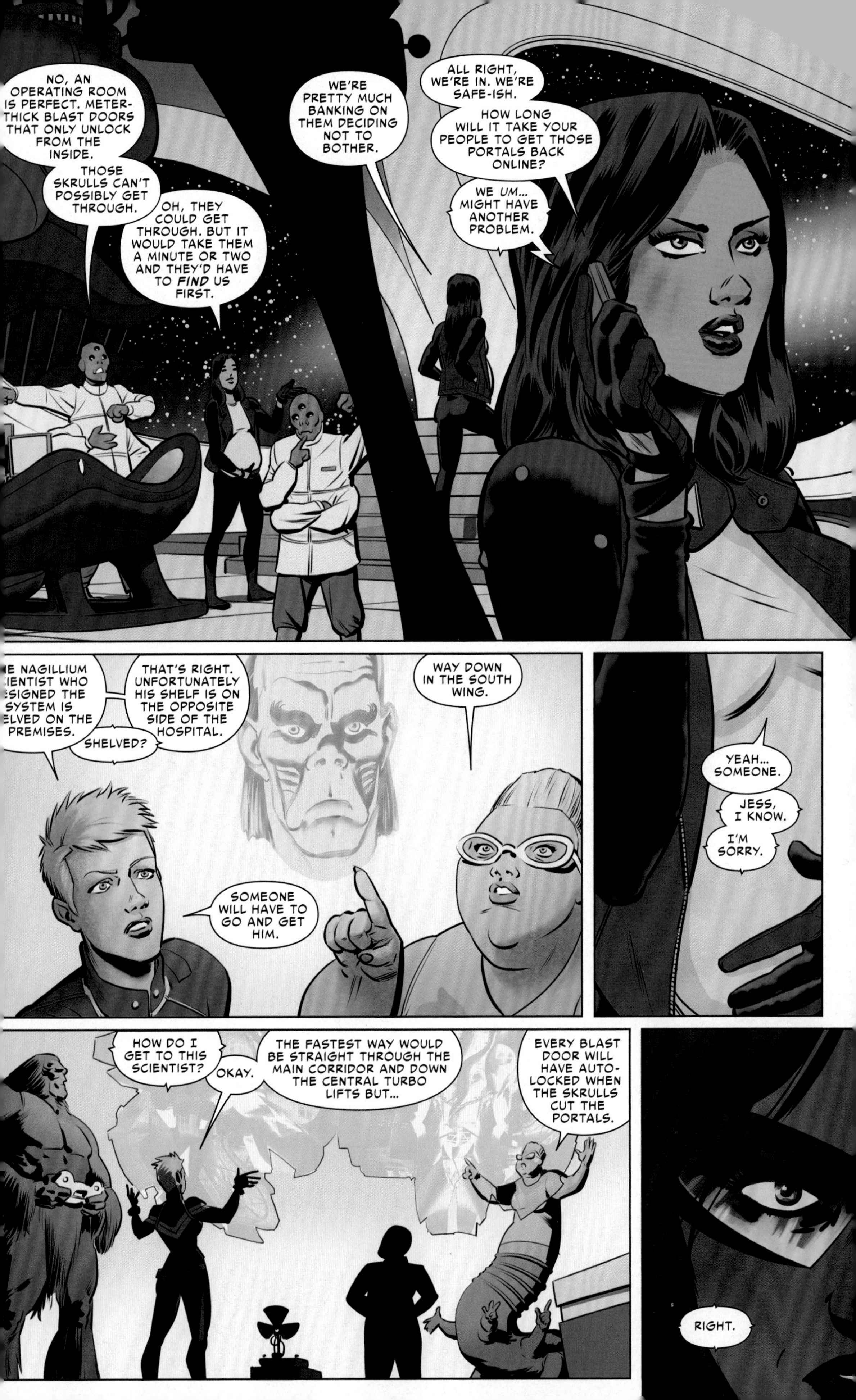
NO, AN OPERATING ROOM IS PERFECT. METER-THICK BLAST DOORS THAT ONLY UNLOCK FROM THE INSIDE.
THOSE SKRULLS CAN'T POSSIBLY GET THROUGH.
OH, THEY COULD GET THROUGH. BUT IT WOULD TAKE THEM A MINUTE OR TWO AND THEY'D HAVE TO *FIND* US FIRST.
WE'RE PRETTY MUCH BANKING ON THEM DECIDING NOT TO BOTHER.
ALL RIGHT, WE'RE IN. WE'RE SAFE-ISH.
HOW LONG WILL IT TAKE YOUR PEOPLE TO GET THOSE PORTALS BACK ONLINE?
WE *UM*... MIGHT HAVE ANOTHER PROBLEM.
E NAGILLIUM CIENTIST WHO ESIGNED THE SYSTEM IS ELVED ON THE PREMISES.
SHELVED?
THAT'S RIGHT. UNFORTUNATELY HIS SHELF IS ON THE OPPOSITE SIDE OF THE HOSPITAL.
WAY DOWN IN THE SOUTH WING.
SOMEONE WILL HAVE TO GO AND GET HIM.
YEAH... SOMEONE.
JESS, I KNOW.
I'M SORRY.
HOW DO I GET TO THIS SCIENTIST?
OKAY.
THE FASTEST WAY WOULD BE STRAIGHT THROUGH THE MAIN CORRIDOR AND DOWN THE CENTRAL TURBO LIFTS BUT...
EVERY BLAST DOOR WILL HAVE AUTO-LOCKED WHEN THE SKRULLS CUT THE PORTALS.
RIGHT.

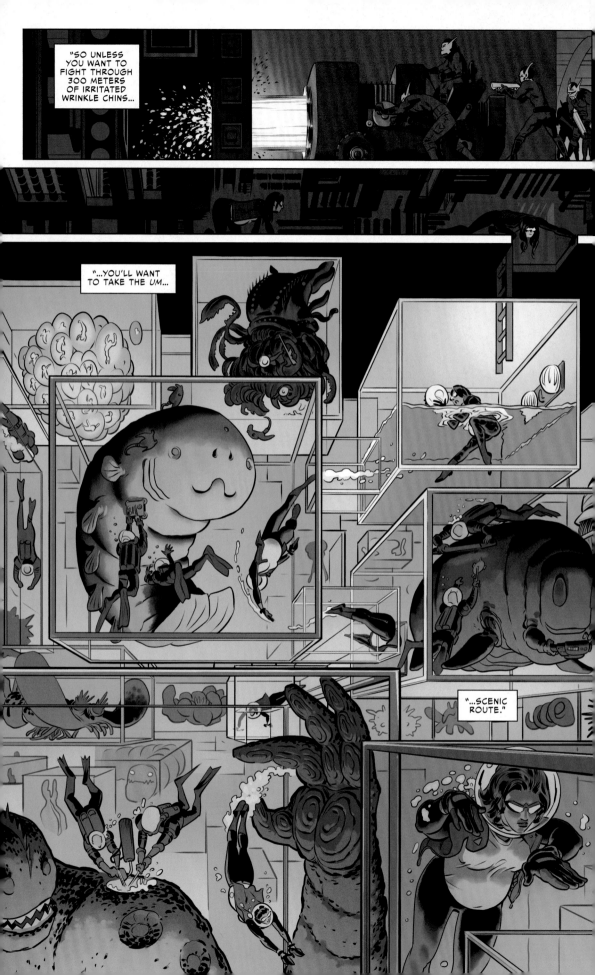

"SO UNLESS YOU WANT TO FIGHT THROUGH 300 METERS OF IRRITATED WRINKLE CHINS...

"...YOU'LL WANT TO TAKE THE *UM*...

"...SCENIC ROUTE."

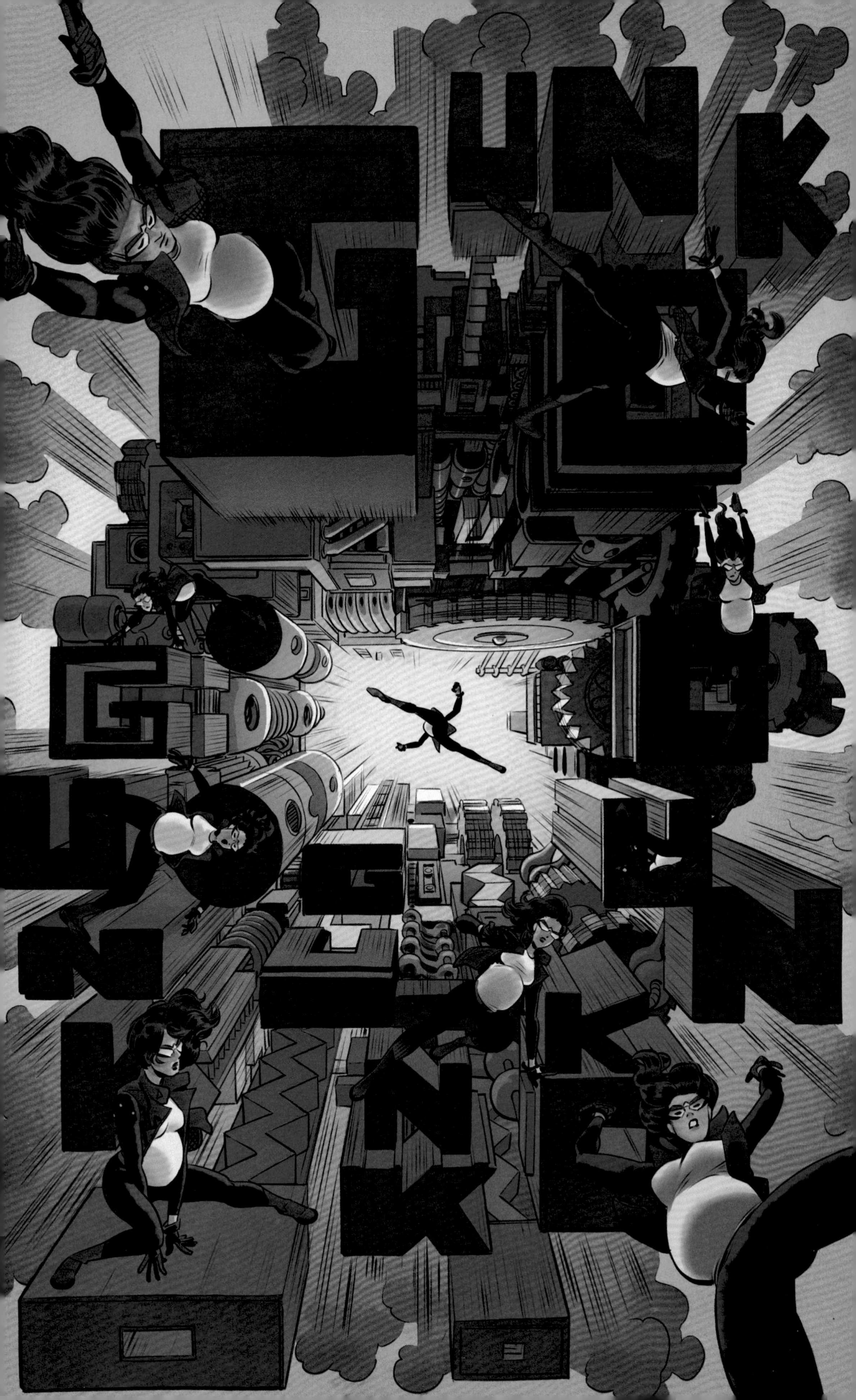

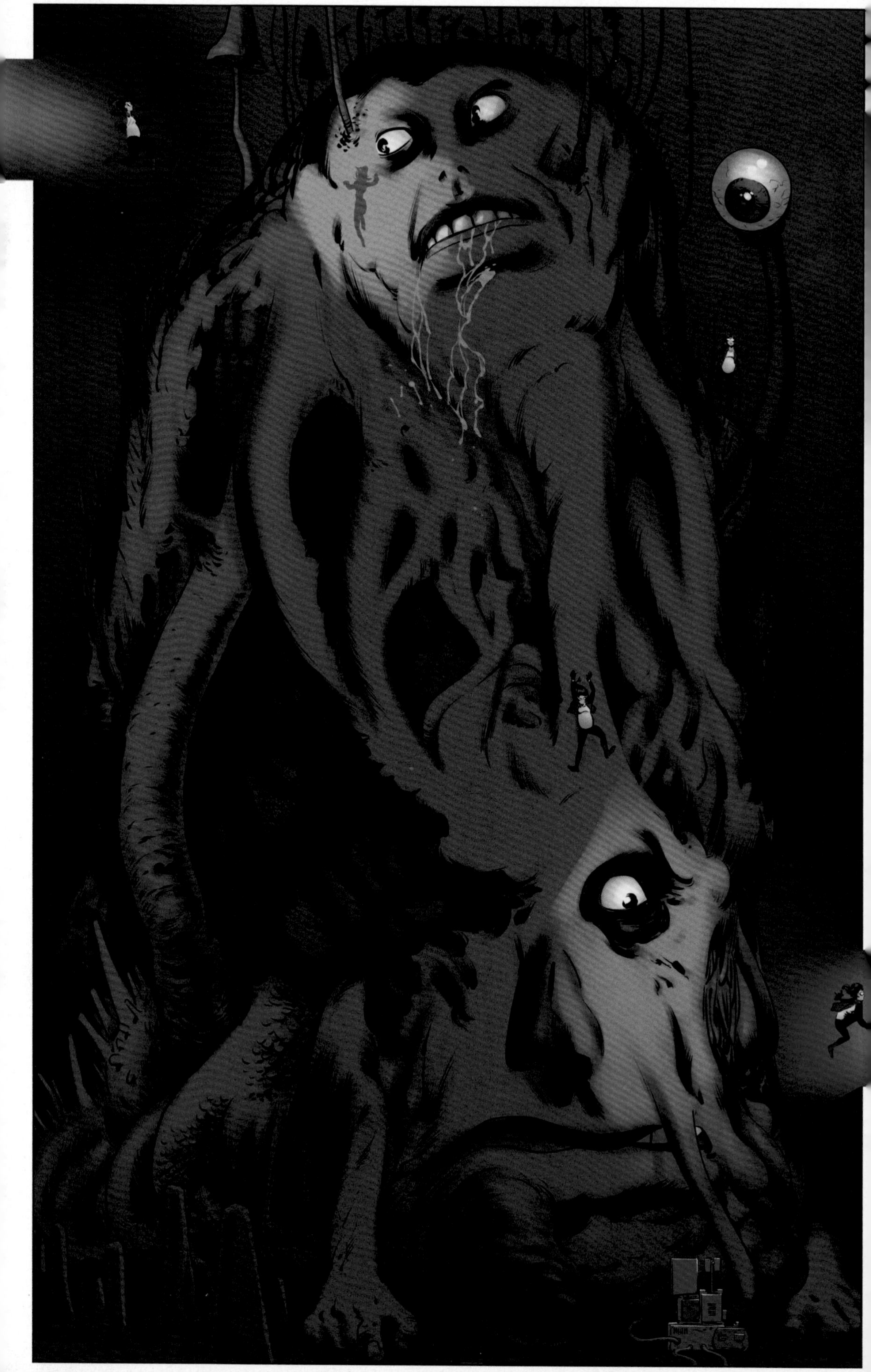

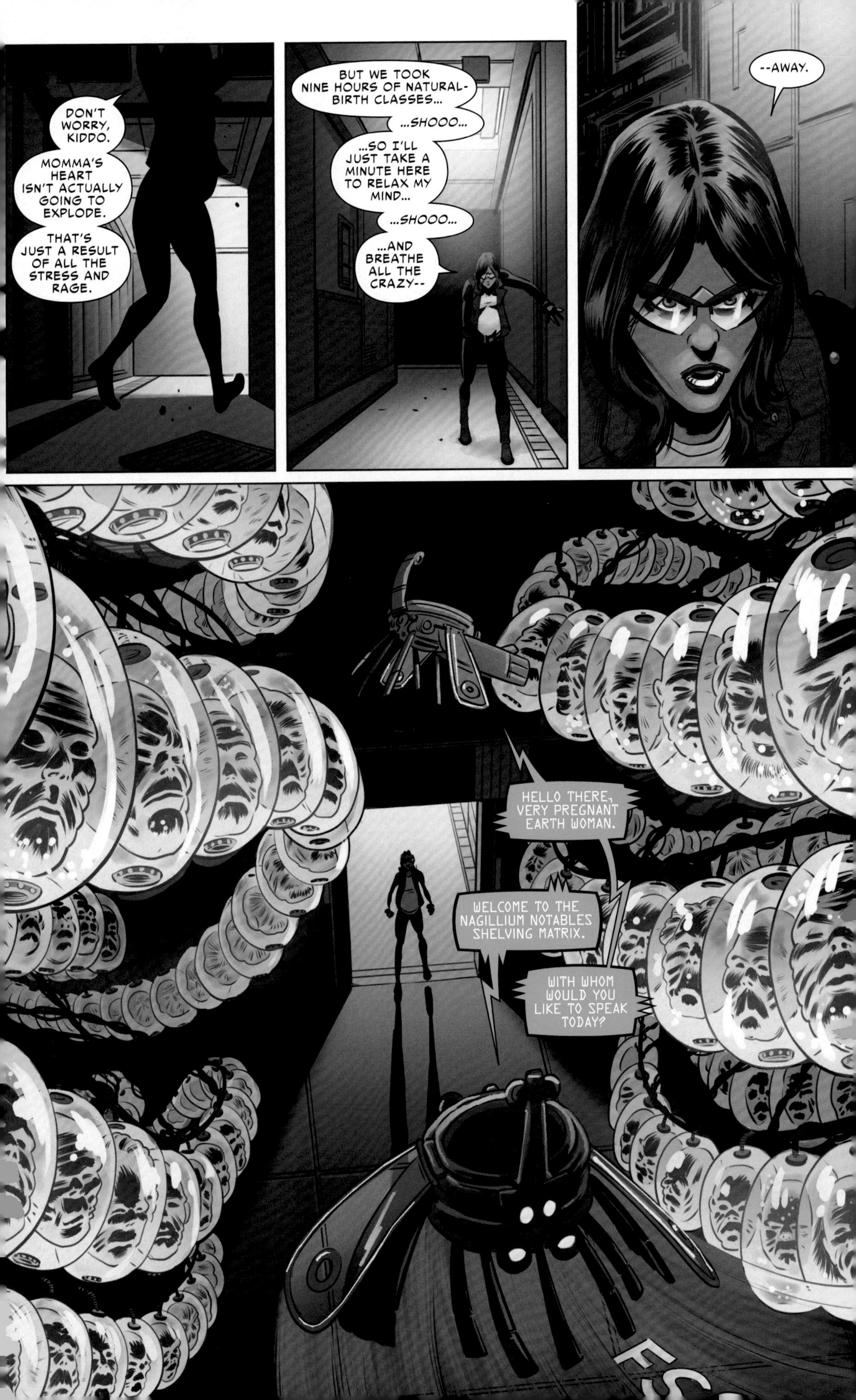
DON'T WORRY, KIDDO.
MOMMA'S HEART ISN'T ACTUALLY GOING TO EXPLODE.
THAT'S JUST A RESULT OF ALL THE STRESS AND RAGE.
BUT WE TOOK NINE HOURS OF NATURAL-BIRTH CLASSES...
...SHOOO...
...SO I'LL JUST TAKE A MINUTE HERE TO RELAX MY MIND...
...SHOOO...
...AND BREATHE ALL THE CRAZY--
--AWAY.
HELLO THERE, VERY PREGNANT EARTH WOMAN.
WELCOME TO THE NAGILLIUM NOTABLES SHELVING MATRIX.
WITH WHOM WOULD YOU LIKE TO SPEAK TODAY?

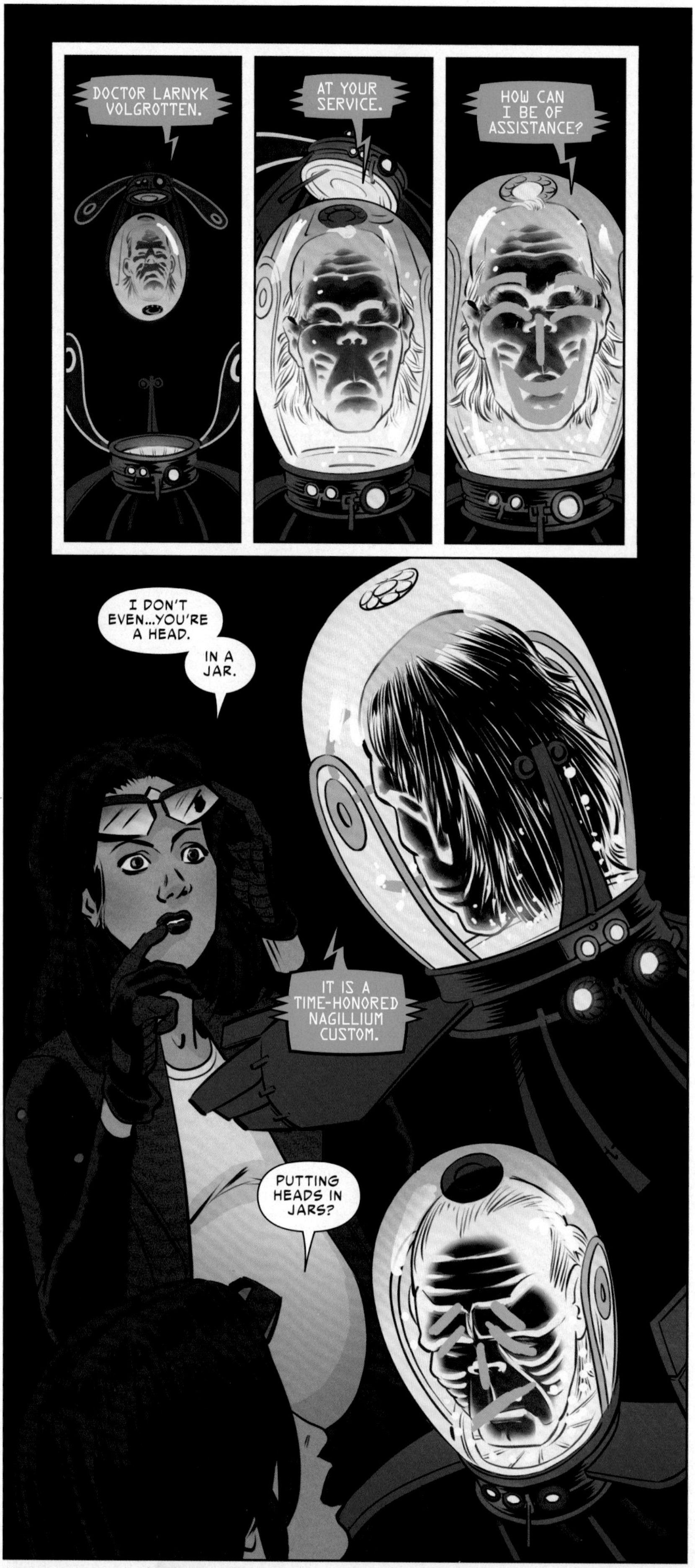
DOCTOR LARNYK VOLGROTTEN.
AT YOUR SERVICE.
HOW CAN I BE OF ASSISTANCE?
I DON'T EVEN...YOU'RE A HEAD.
IN A JAR.
IT IS A TIME-HONORED NAGILLIUM CUSTOM.
PUTTING HEADS IN JARS?

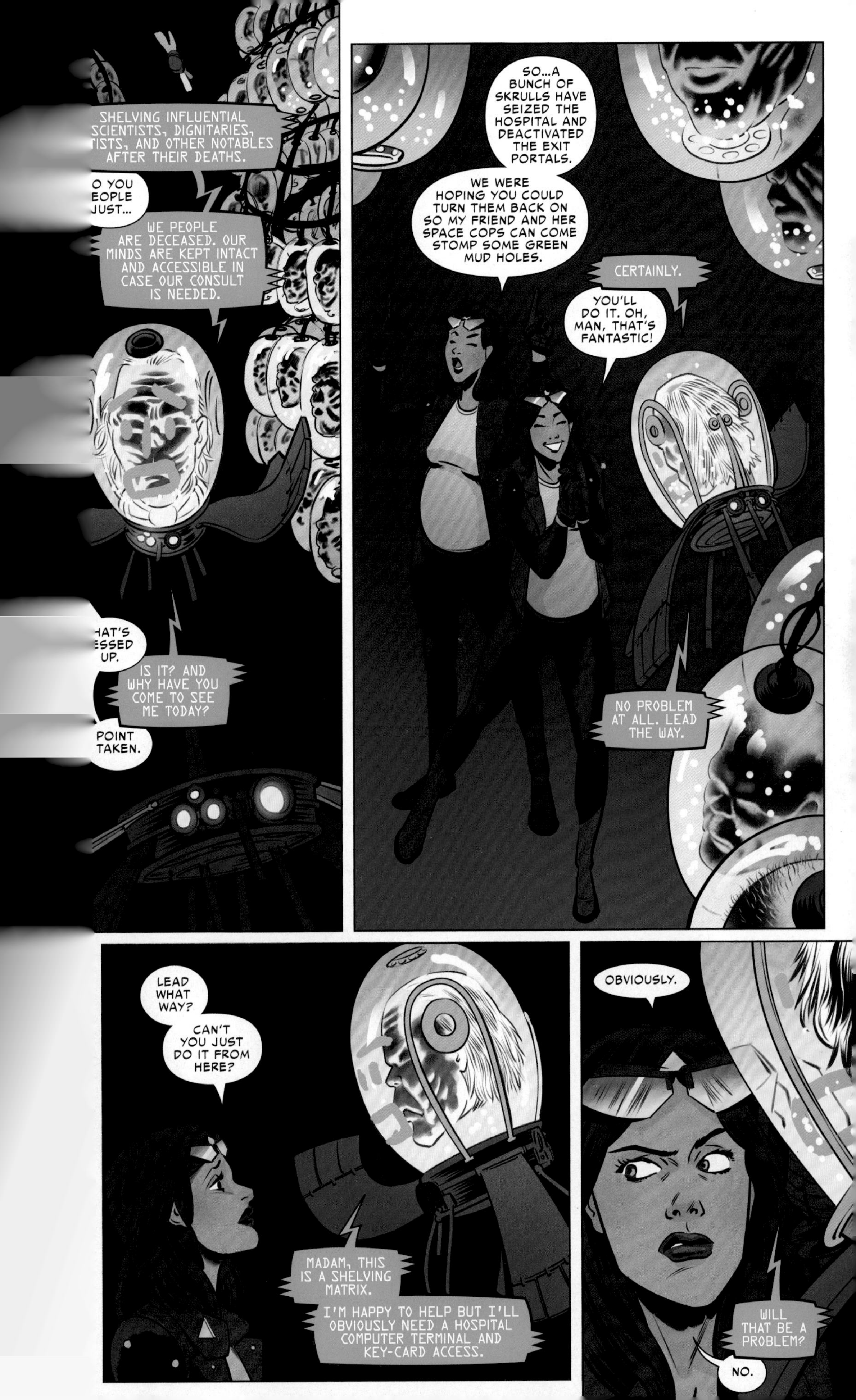
SHELVING INFLUENTIAL SCIENTISTS, DIGNITARIES, TISTS, AND OTHER NOTABLES AFTER THEIR DEATHS.
O YOU EOPLE JUST...
WE PEOPLE ARE DECEASED. OUR MINDS ARE KEPT INTACT AND ACCESSIBLE IN CASE OUR CONSULT IS NEEDED.
HAT'S ESSED UP.
IS IT? AND WHY HAVE YOU COME TO SEE ME TODAY?
POINT TAKEN.
SO...A BUNCH OF SKRULLS HAVE SEIZED THE HOSPITAL AND DEACTIVATED THE EXIT PORTALS.
WE WERE HOPING YOU COULD TURN THEM BACK ON SO MY FRIEND AND HER SPACE COPS CAN COME STOMP SOME GREEN MUD HOLES.
CERTAINLY.
YOU'LL DO IT. OH, MAN, THAT'S FANTASTIC!
NO PROBLEM AT ALL. LEAD THE WAY.
LEAD WHAT WAY?
CAN'T YOU JUST DO IT FROM HERE?
MADAM, THIS IS A SHELVING MATRIX.
I'M HAPPY TO HELP BUT I'LL OBVIOUSLY NEED A HOSPITAL COMPUTER TERMINAL AND KEY-CARD ACCESS.
OBVIOUSLY.
WILL THAT BE A PROBLEM?
NO.

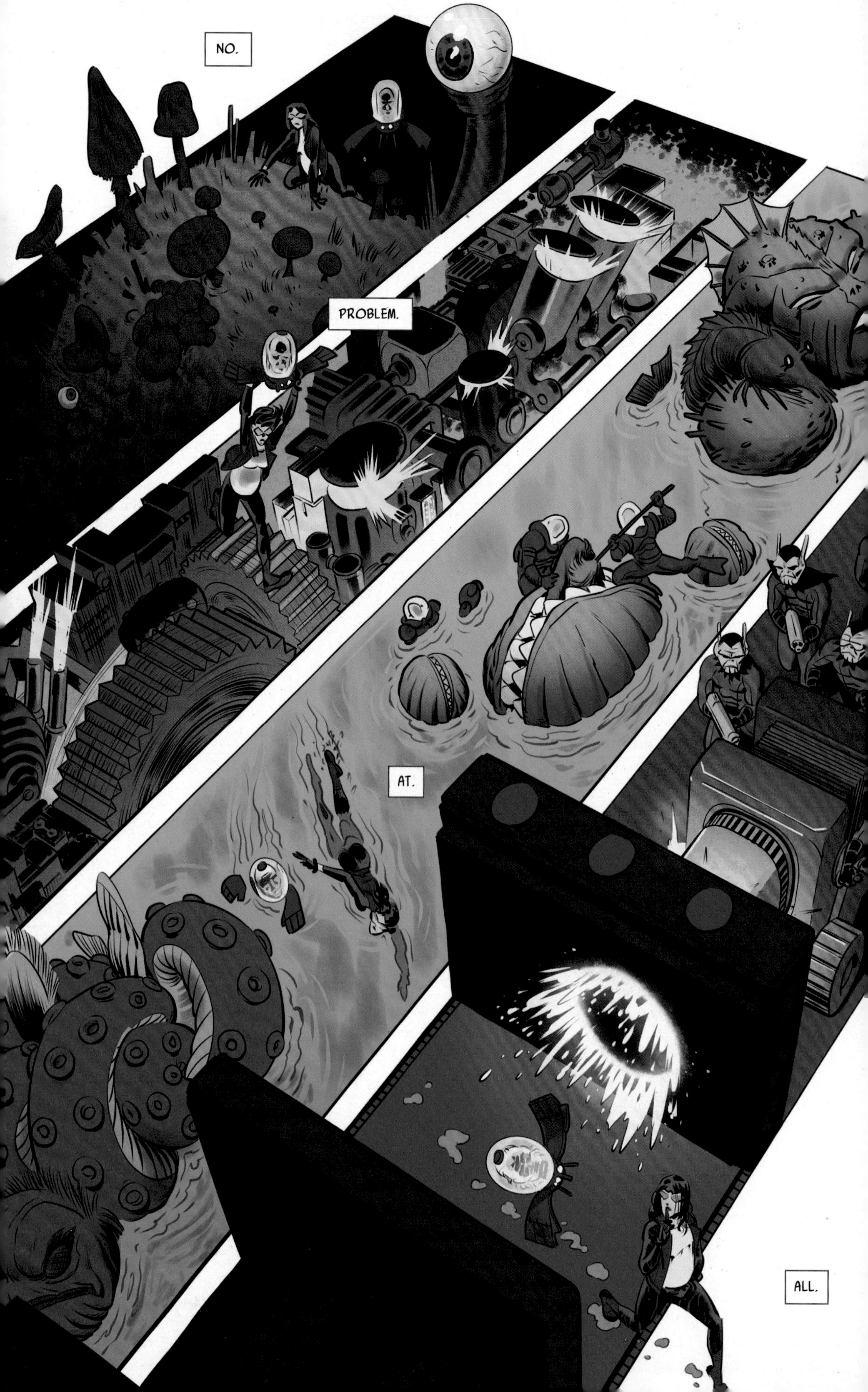
NO.
PROBLEM.
AT.
ALL.

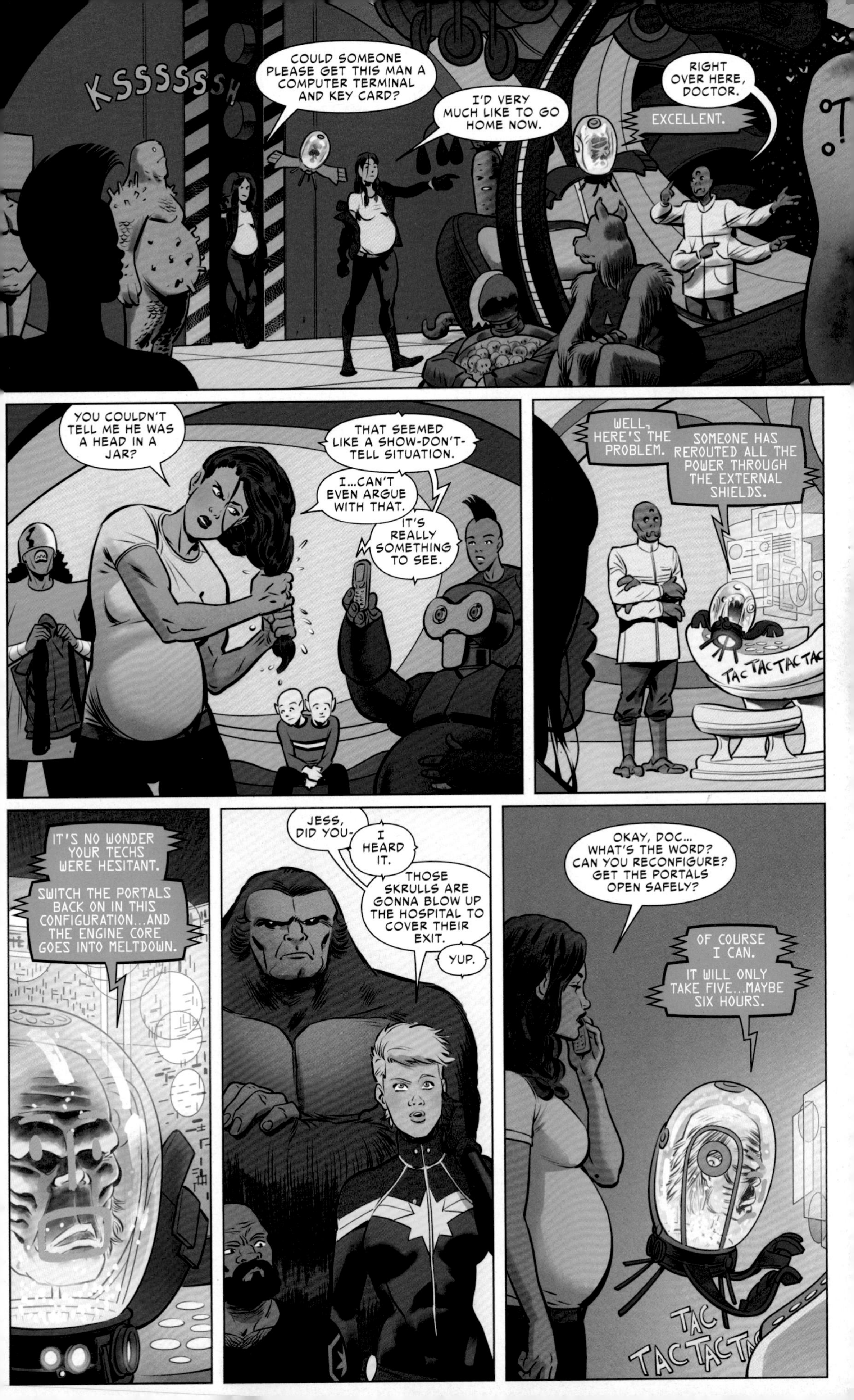
KSSSSSSSH
COULD SOMEONE PLEASE GET THIS MAN A COMPUTER TERMINAL AND KEY CARD?
I'D VERY MUCH LIKE TO GO HOME NOW.
RIGHT OVER HERE, DOCTOR.
EXCELLENT.
YOU COULDN'T TELL ME HE WAS A HEAD IN A JAR?
THAT SEEMED LIKE A SHOW-DON'T-TELL SITUATION.
I...CAN'T EVEN ARGUE WITH THAT.
IT'S REALLY SOMETHING TO SEE.
WELL, HERE'S THE PROBLEM.
SOMEONE HAS REROUTED ALL THE POWER THROUGH THE EXTERNAL SHIELDS.
TAC TAC TAC TAC TAC
IT'S NO WONDER YOUR TECHS WERE HESITANT.
SWITCH THE PORTALS BACK ON IN THIS CONFIGURATION...AND THE ENGINE CORE GOES INTO MELTDOWN.
JESS, DID YOU-
I HEARD IT.
THOSE SKRULLS ARE GONNA BLOW UP THE HOSPITAL TO COVER THEIR EXIT.
YUP.
OKAY, DOC... WHAT'S THE WORD? CAN YOU RECONFIGURE? GET THE PORTALS OPEN SAFELY?
OF COURSE I CAN.
IT WILL ONLY TAKE FIVE...MAYBE SIX HOURS.
TAC TAC TAC TAC

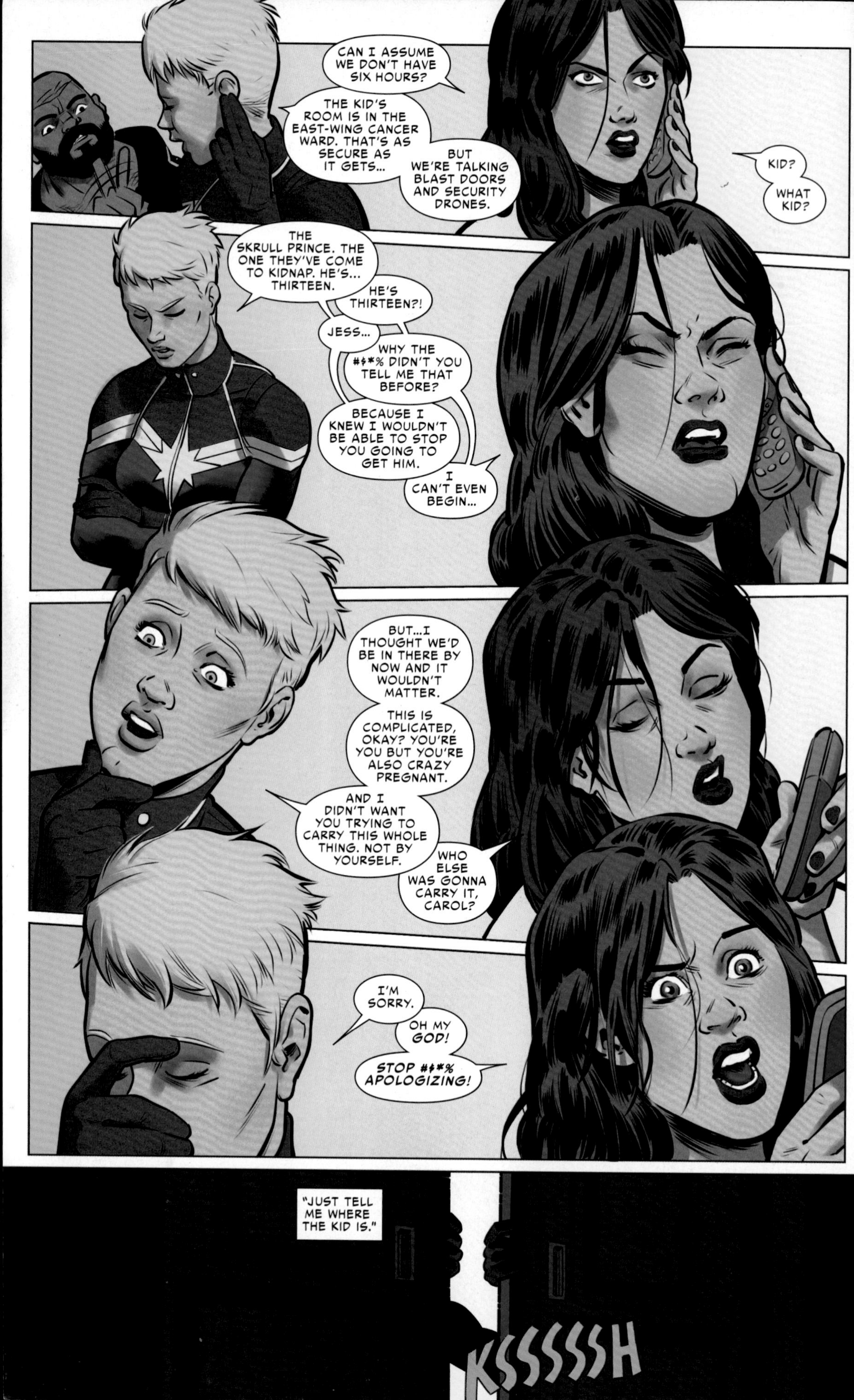
CAN I ASSUME WE DON'T HAVE SIX HOURS?
THE KID'S ROOM IS IN THE EAST-WING CANCER WARD. THAT'S AS SECURE AS IT GETS...
BUT WE'RE TALKING BLAST DOORS AND SECURITY DRONES.
KID?
WHAT KID?
THE SKRULL PRINCE. THE ONE THEY'VE COME TO KIDNAP. HE'S... THIRTEEN.
HE'S THIRTEEN?!
JESS...
WHY THE #$*% DIDN'T YOU TELL ME THAT BEFORE?
BECAUSE I KNEW I WOULDN'T BE ABLE TO STOP YOU GOING TO GET HIM.
I CAN'T EVEN BEGIN...
BUT...I THOUGHT WE'D BE IN THERE BY NOW AND IT WOULDN'T MATTER.
THIS IS COMPLICATED, OKAY? YOU'RE YOU BUT YOU'RE ALSO CRAZY PREGNANT.
AND I DIDN'T WANT YOU TRYING TO CARRY THIS WHOLE THING. NOT BY YOURSELF.
WHO ELSE WAS GONNA CARRY IT, CAROL?
I'M SORRY.
OH MY GOD!
STOP #$*% APOLOGIZING!
"JUST TELL ME WHERE THE KID IS."
KSSSSSH

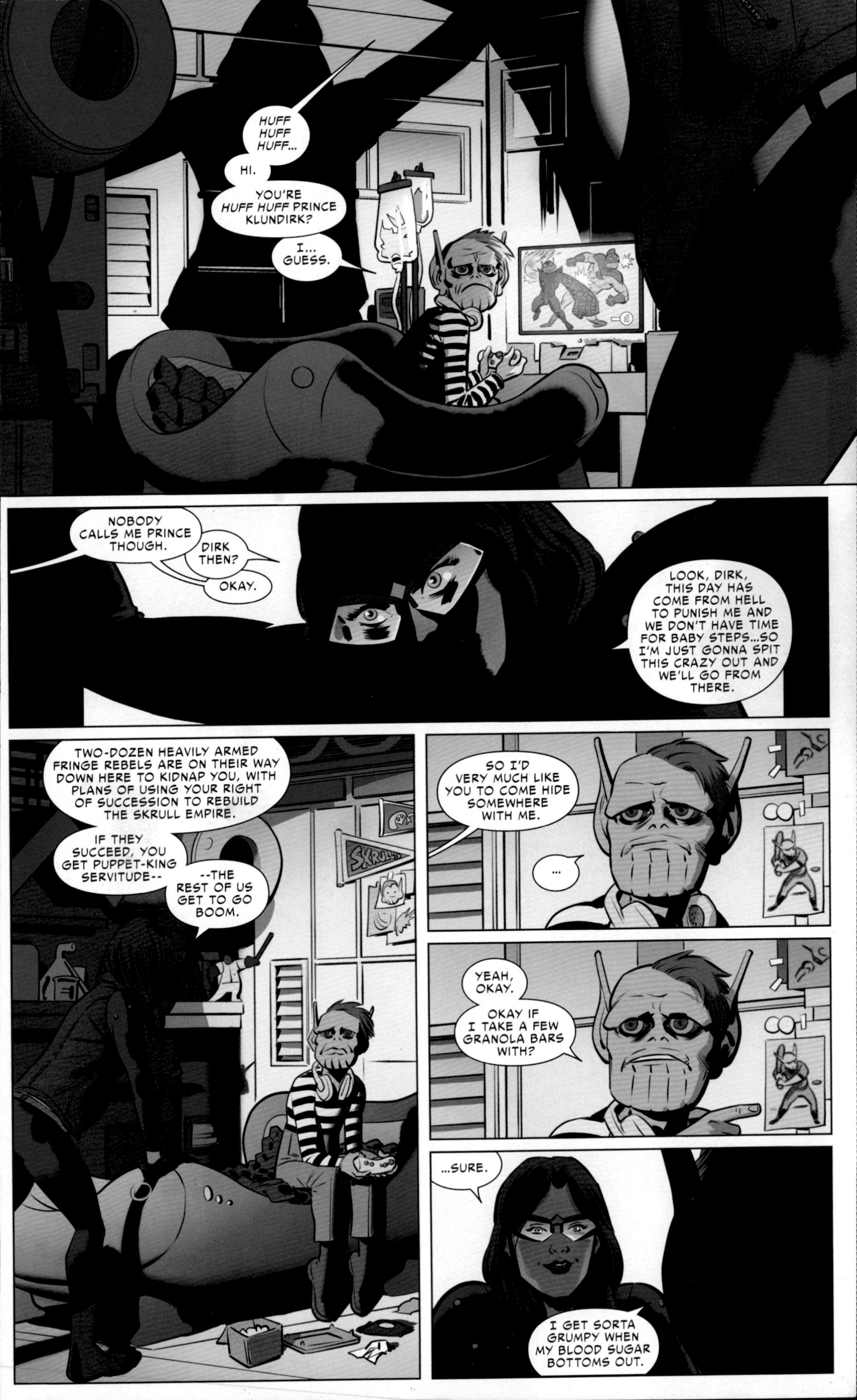
HUFF HUFF HUFF...
HI.
YOU'RE HUFF HUFF PRINCE KLUNDIRK?
I... GUESS.
NOBODY CALLS ME PRINCE THOUGH.
DIRK THEN?
OKAY.
LOOK, DIRK, THIS DAY HAS COME FROM HELL TO PUNISH ME AND WE DON'T HAVE TIME FOR BABY STEPS...SO I'M JUST GONNA SPIT THIS CRAZY OUT AND WE'LL GO FROM THERE.
TWO-DOZEN HEAVILY ARMED FRINGE REBELS ARE ON THEIR WAY DOWN HERE TO KIDNAP YOU, WITH PLANS OF USING YOUR RIGHT OF SUCCESSION TO REBUILD THE SKRULL EMPIRE.
IF THEY SUCCEED, YOU GET PUPPET-KING SERVITUDE--
--THE REST OF US GET TO GO BOOM.
SKRULLS
SO I'D VERY MUCH LIKE YOU TO COME HIDE SOMEWHERE WITH ME.
...
YEAH, OKAY.
OKAY IF I TAKE A FEW GRANOLA BARS WITH?
...SURE.
I GET SORTA GRUMPY WHEN MY BLOOD SUGAR BOTTOMS OUT.

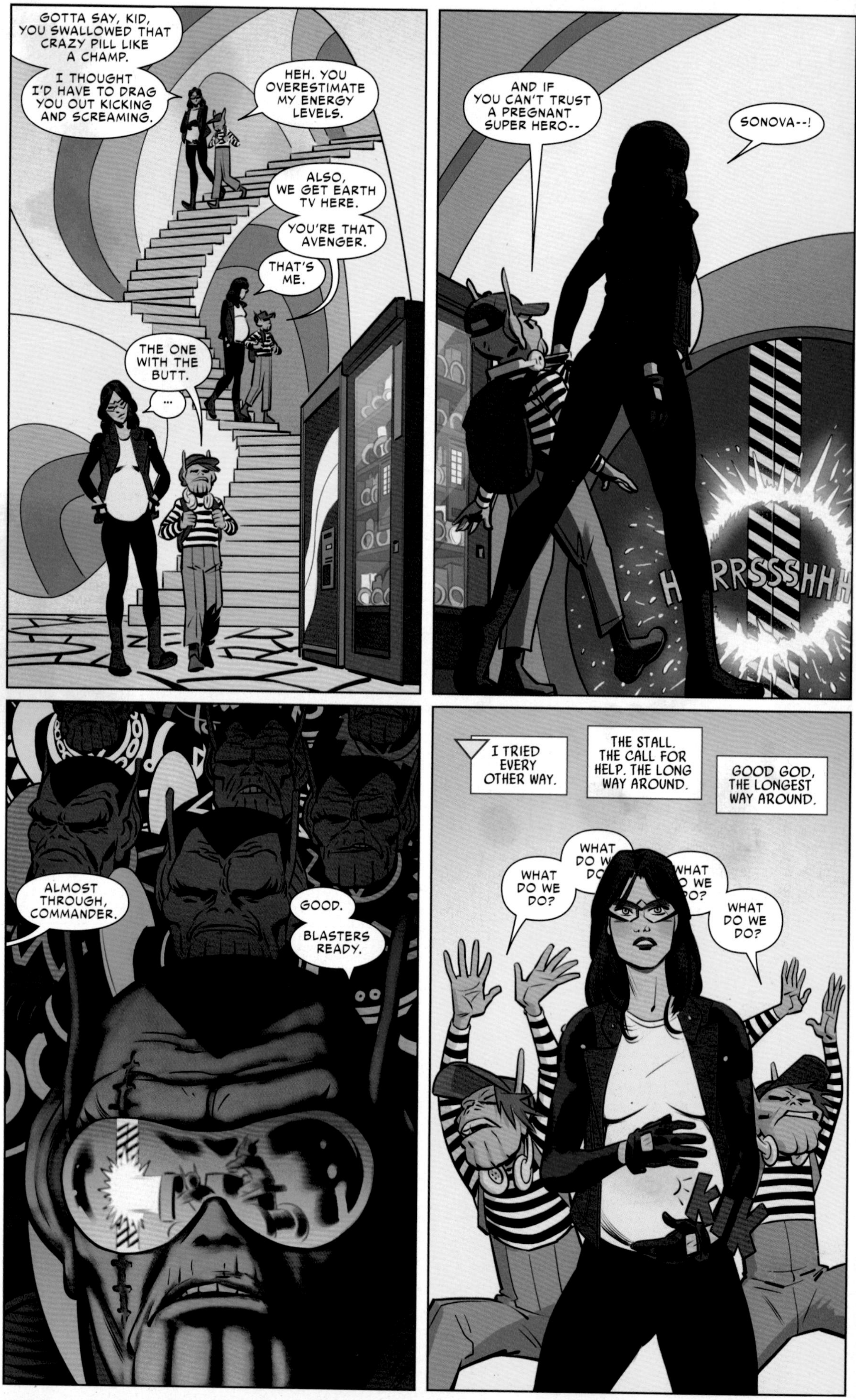

GOTTA SAY, KID, YOU SWALLOWED THAT CRAZY PILL LIKE A CHAMP.
I THOUGHT I'D HAVE TO DRAG YOU OUT KICKING AND SCREAMING.
HEH. YOU OVERESTIMATE MY ENERGY LEVELS.
ALSO, WE GET EARTH TV HERE.
YOU'RE THAT AVENGER.
THAT'S ME.
THE ONE WITH THE BUTT.
...
AND IF YOU CAN'T TRUST A PREGNANT SUPER HERO--
SONOVA--!
HRRSSSHHH
ALMOST THROUGH, COMMANDER.
GOOD.
BLASTERS READY.
I TRIED EVERY OTHER WAY.
THE STALL. THE CALL FOR HELP. THE LONG WAY AROUND.
GOOD GOD, THE LONGEST WAY AROUND.
WHAT DO WE DO?
WHAT DO WE DO?
WHAT DO WE DO?
WHAT DO WE DO?
KIK

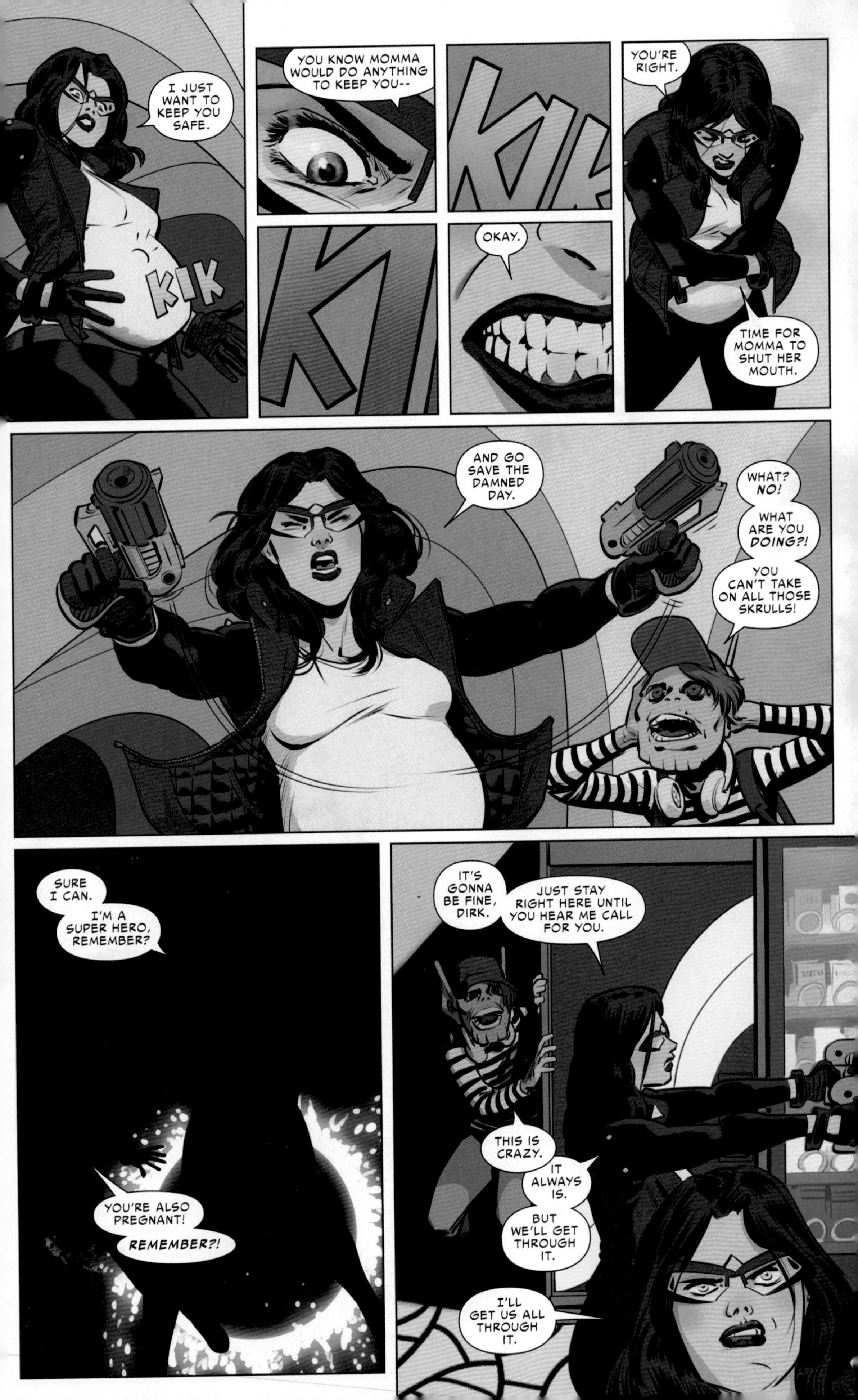
I JUST WANT TO KEEP YOU SAFE.
KIK
YOU KNOW MOMMA WOULD DO ANYTHING TO KEEP YOU--
KIK
YOU'RE RIGHT.
KIK
OKAY.
TIME FOR MOMMA TO SHUT HER MOUTH.
AND GO SAVE THE DAMNED DAY.
WHAT? NO!
WHAT ARE YOU DOING?!
YOU CAN'T TAKE ON ALL THOSE SKRULLS!
SURE I CAN.
I'M A SUPER HERO, REMEMBER?
YOU'RE ALSO PREGNANT!
REMEMBER?!
IT'S GONNA BE FINE, DIRK.
JUST STAY RIGHT HERE UNTIL YOU HEAR ME CALL FOR YOU.
THIS IS CRAZY.
IT ALWAYS IS.
BUT WE'LL GET THROUGH IT.
I'LL GET US ALL THROUGH IT.

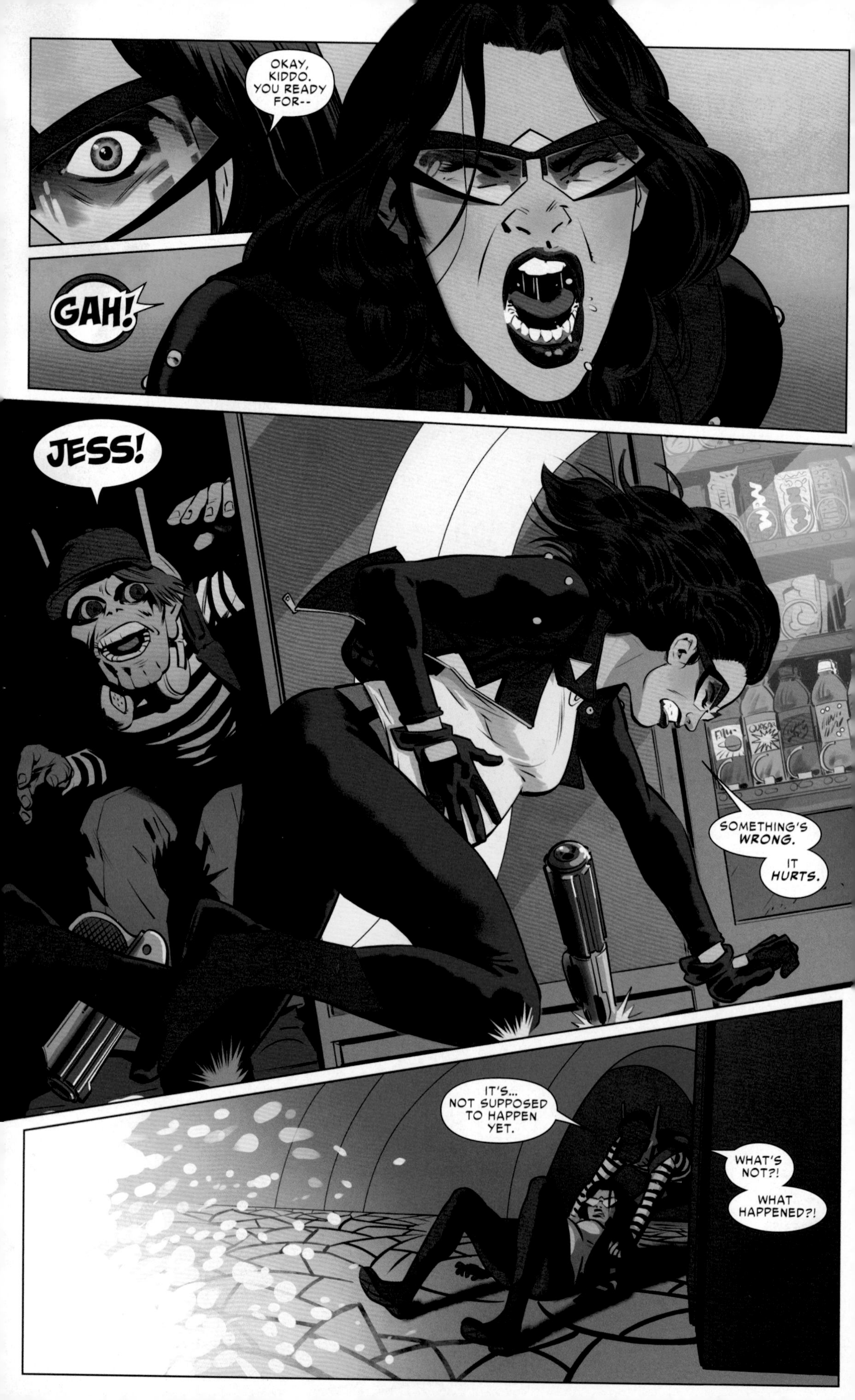
OKAY, KIDDO. YOU READY FOR--
GAH!
JESS!
SOMETHING'S WRONG.
IT HURTS.
IT'S... NOT SUPPOSED TO HAPPEN YET.
WHAT'S NOT?!
WHAT HAPPENED?!

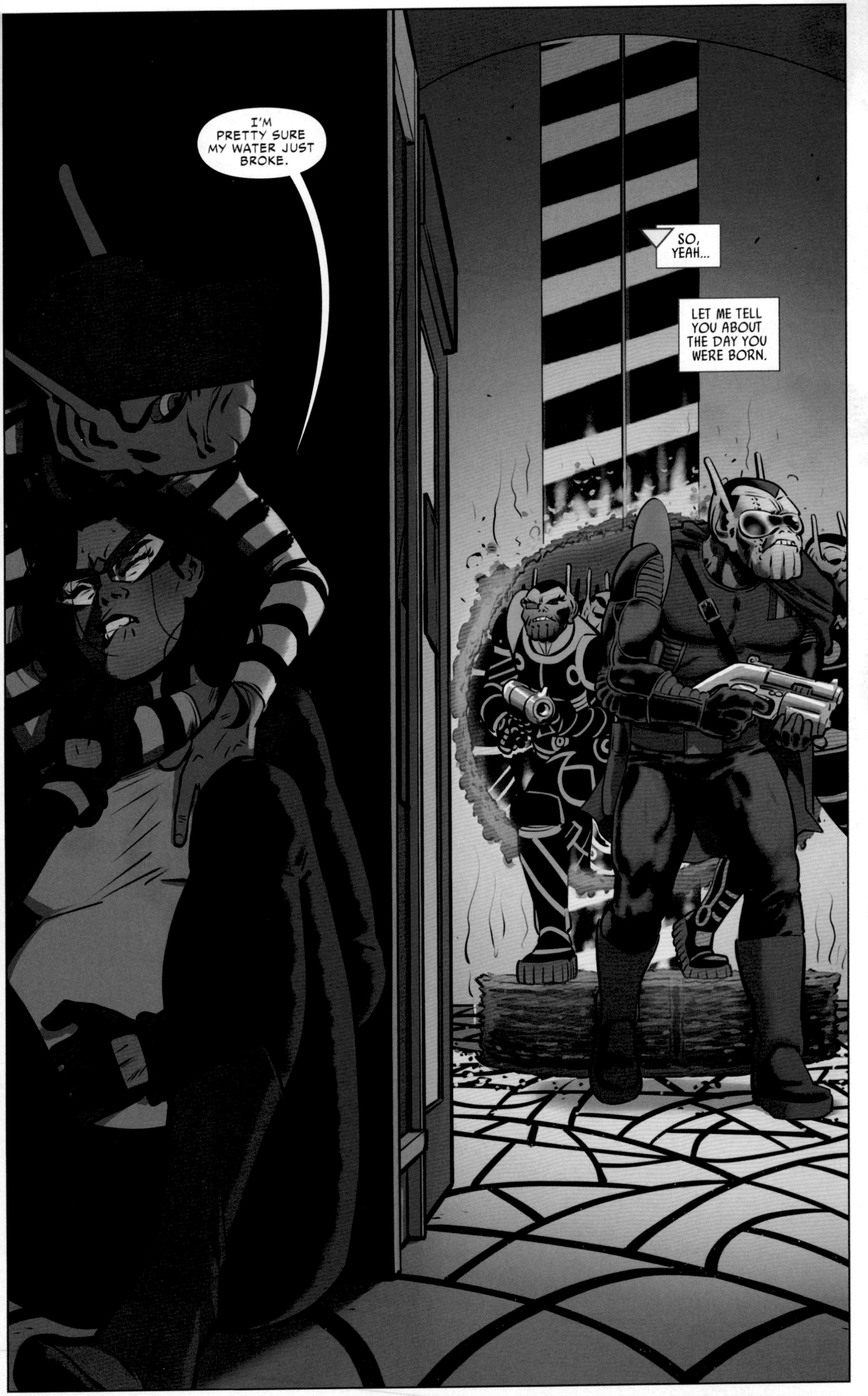
I'M PRETTY SURE MY WATER JUST BROKE.
SO, YEAH...
LET ME TELL YOU ABOUT THE DAY YOU WERE BORN.

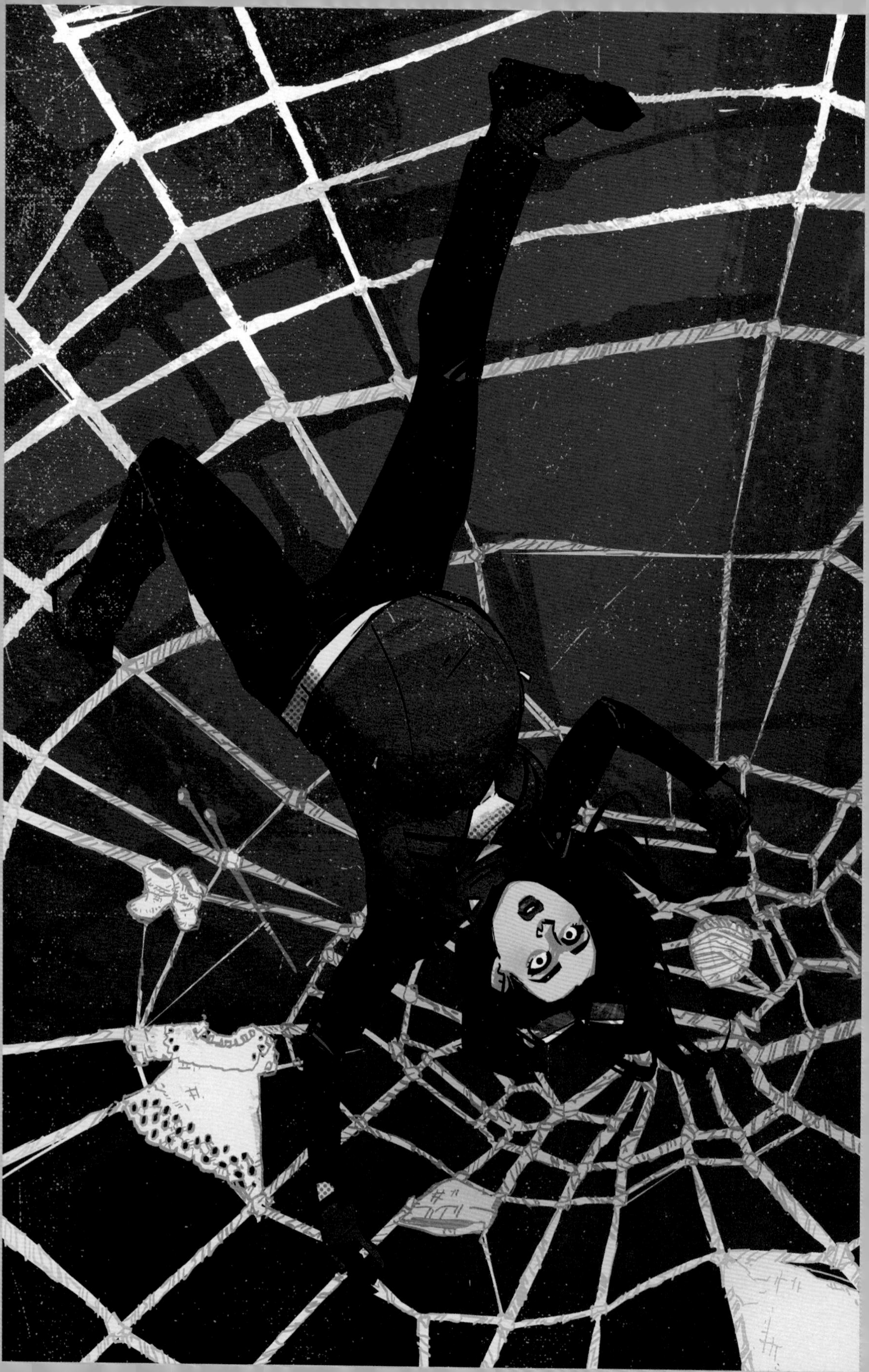

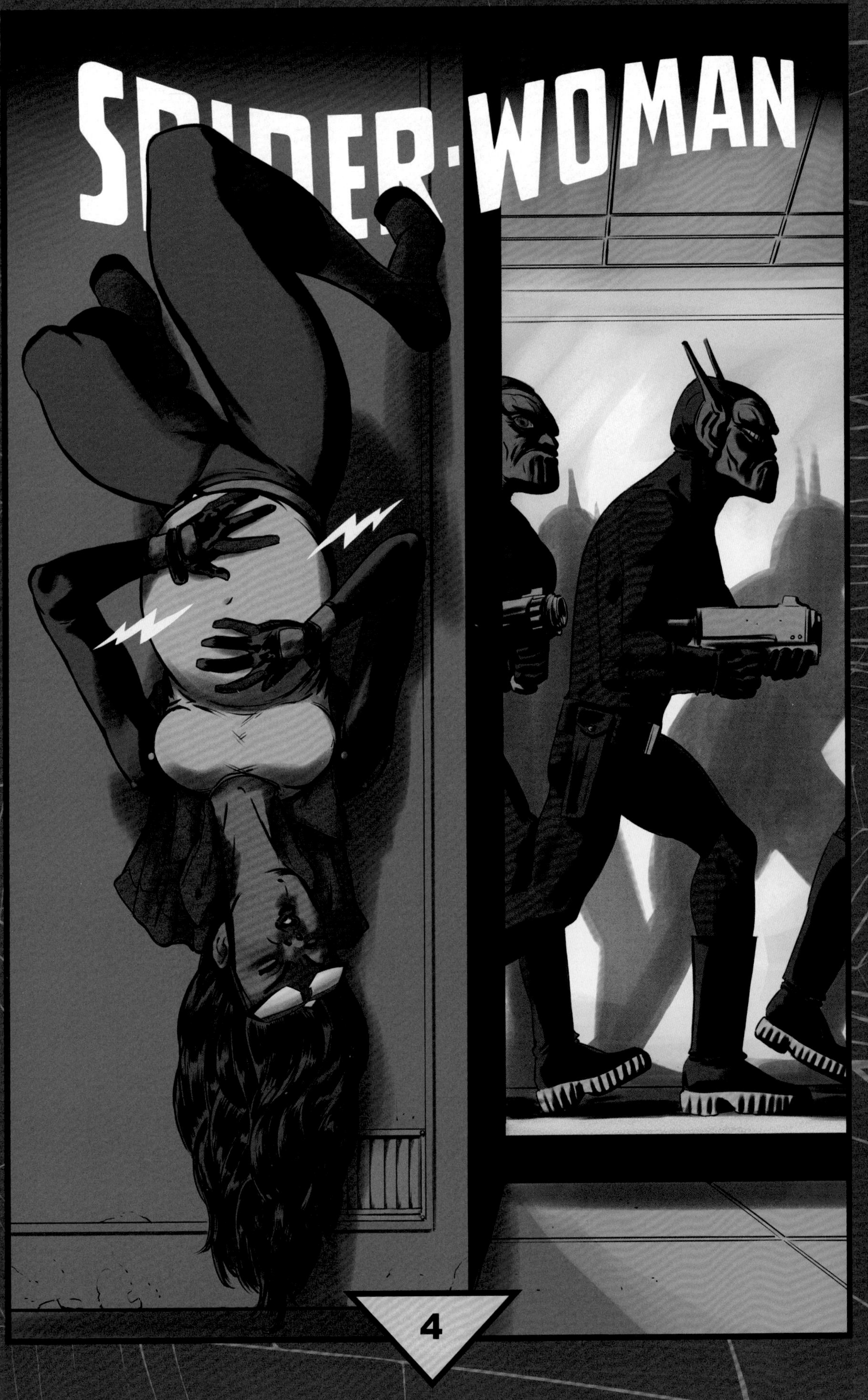
SPIDER-WOMAN
4

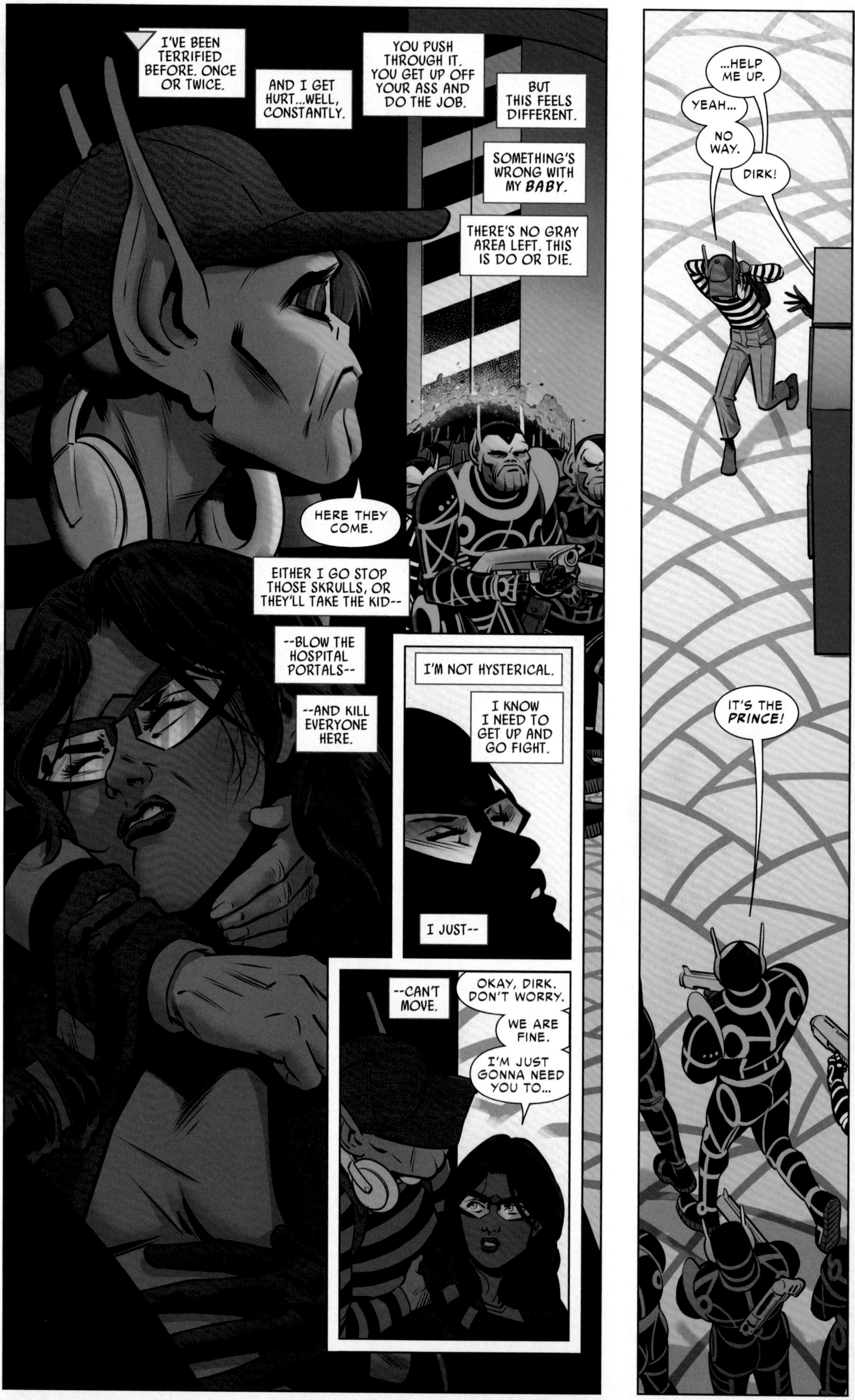
I'VE BEEN TERRIFIED BEFORE. ONCE OR TWICE.
AND I GET HURT...WELL, CONSTANTLY.
YOU PUSH THROUGH IT. YOU GET UP OFF YOUR ASS AND DO THE JOB.
BUT THIS FEELS DIFFERENT.
SOMETHING'S WRONG WITH MY BABY.
THERE'S NO GRAY AREA LEFT. THIS IS DO OR DIE.
HERE THEY COME.
EITHER I GO STOP THOSE SKRULLS, OR THEY'LL TAKE THE KID--
--BLOW THE HOSPITAL PORTALS--
--AND KILL EVERYONE HERE.
I'M NOT HYSTERICAL.
I KNOW I NEED TO GET UP AND GO FIGHT.
I JUST--
--CAN'T MOVE.
OKAY, DIRK. DON'T WORRY.
WE ARE FINE.
I'M JUST GONNA NEED YOU TO...
...HELP ME UP.
YEAH...
NO WAY.
DIRK!
IT'S THE PRINCE!

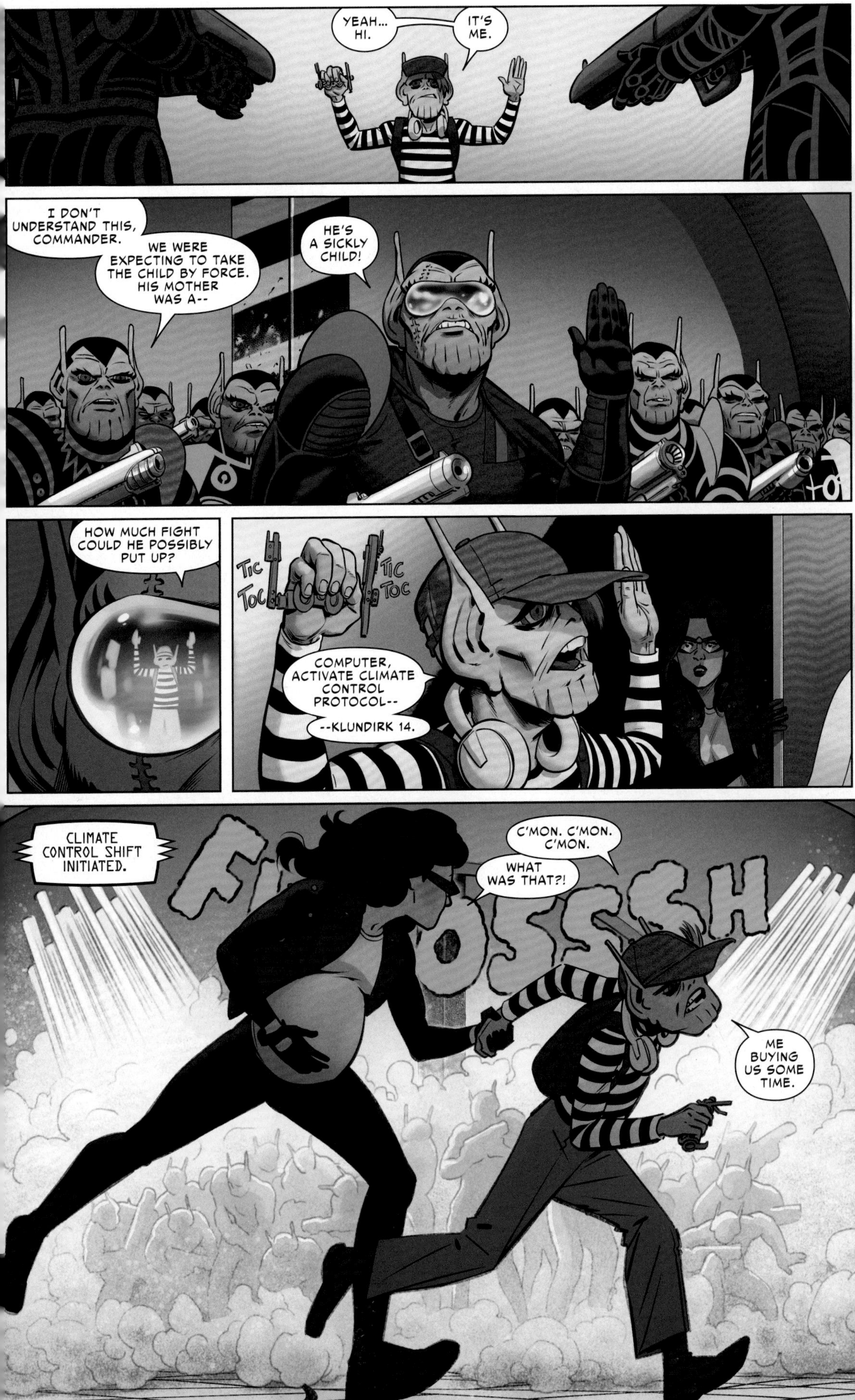
YEAH... HI.
IT'S ME.
I DON'T UNDERSTAND THIS, COMMANDER.
WE WERE EXPECTING TO TAKE THE CHILD BY FORCE. HIS MOTHER WAS A--
HE'S A SICKLY CHILD!
HOW MUCH FIGHT COULD HE POSSIBLY PUT UP?
TIC TOC
TIC TOC
COMPUTER, ACTIVATE CLIMATE CONTROL PROTOCOL--
--KLUNDIRK 14.
CLIMATE CONTROL SHIFT INITIATED.
FOOSSSH
C'MON. C'MON. C'MON.
WHAT WAS THAT?!
ME BUYING US SOME TIME.

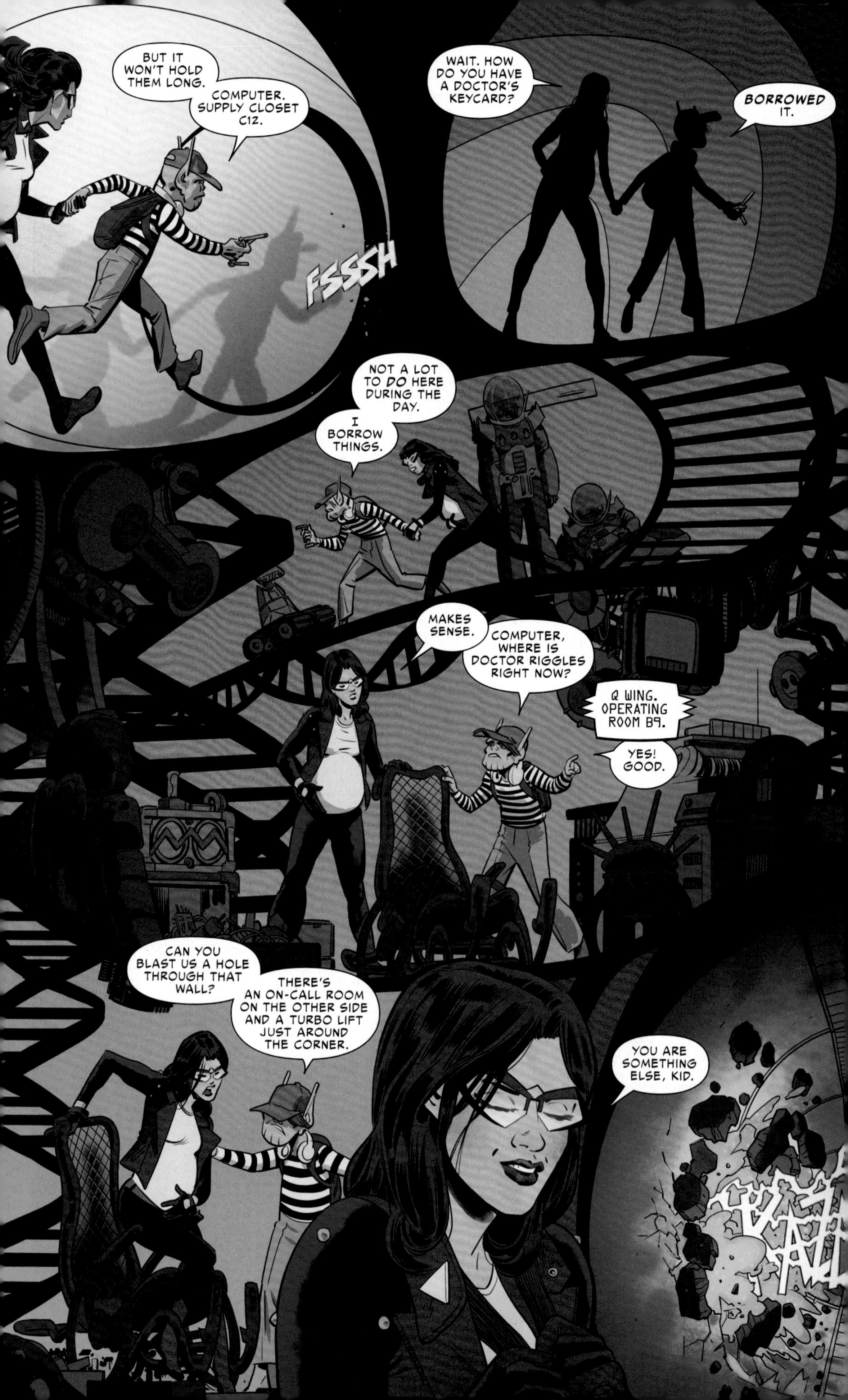
BUT IT WON'T HOLD THEM LONG.
COMPUTER. SUPPLY CLOSET C12.
FSSSH
WAIT. HOW DO YOU HAVE A DOCTOR'S KEYCARD?
BORROWED IT.
NOT A LOT TO DO HERE DURING THE DAY.
I BORROW THINGS.
MAKES SENSE.
COMPUTER, WHERE IS DOCTOR RIGGLES RIGHT NOW?
Q WING. OPERATING ROOM B9.
YES! GOOD.
CAN YOU BLAST US A HOLE THROUGH THAT WALL?
THERE'S AN ON-CALL ROOM ON THE OTHER SIDE AND A TURBO LIFT JUST AROUND THE CORNER.
YOU ARE SOMETHING ELSE, KID.

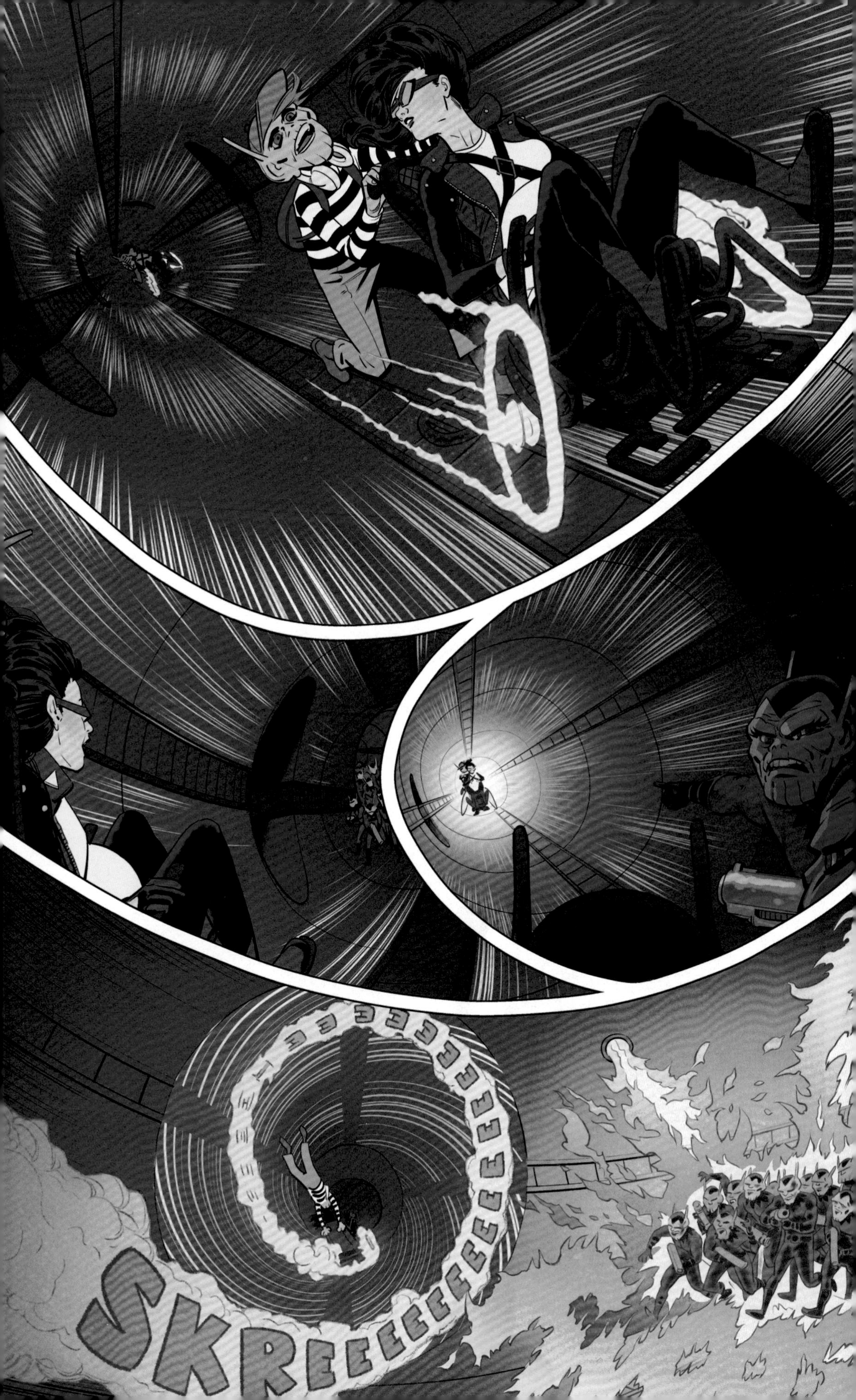
SKREEEEEEEEEEEEEEEEEEEEEEEEEEE

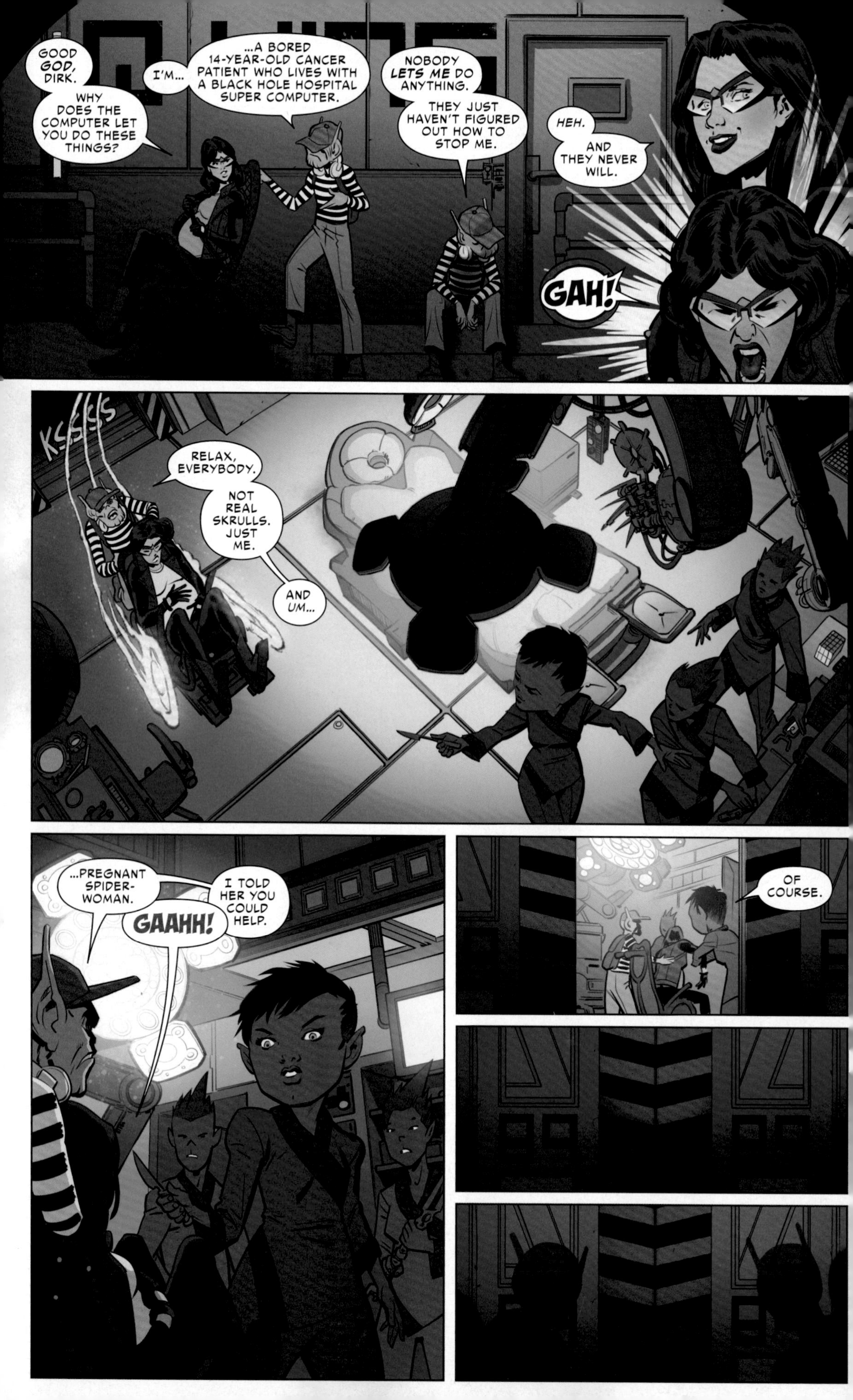

GOOD GOD, DIRK.
WHY DOES THE COMPUTER LET YOU DO THESE THINGS?
I'M...
...A BORED 14-YEAR-OLD CANCER PATIENT WHO LIVES WITH A BLACK HOLE HOSPITAL SUPER COMPUTER.
NOBODY LETS ME DO ANYTHING.
THEY JUST HAVEN'T FIGURED OUT HOW TO STOP ME.
HEH.
AND THEY NEVER WILL.
GAH!
KSSSS
RELAX, EVERYBODY.
NOT REAL SKRULLS. JUST ME.
AND UM...
...PREGNANT SPIDER-WOMAN.
GAAHH!
I TOLD HER YOU COULD HELP.
OF COURSE.

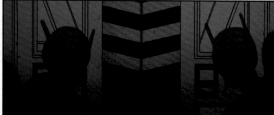

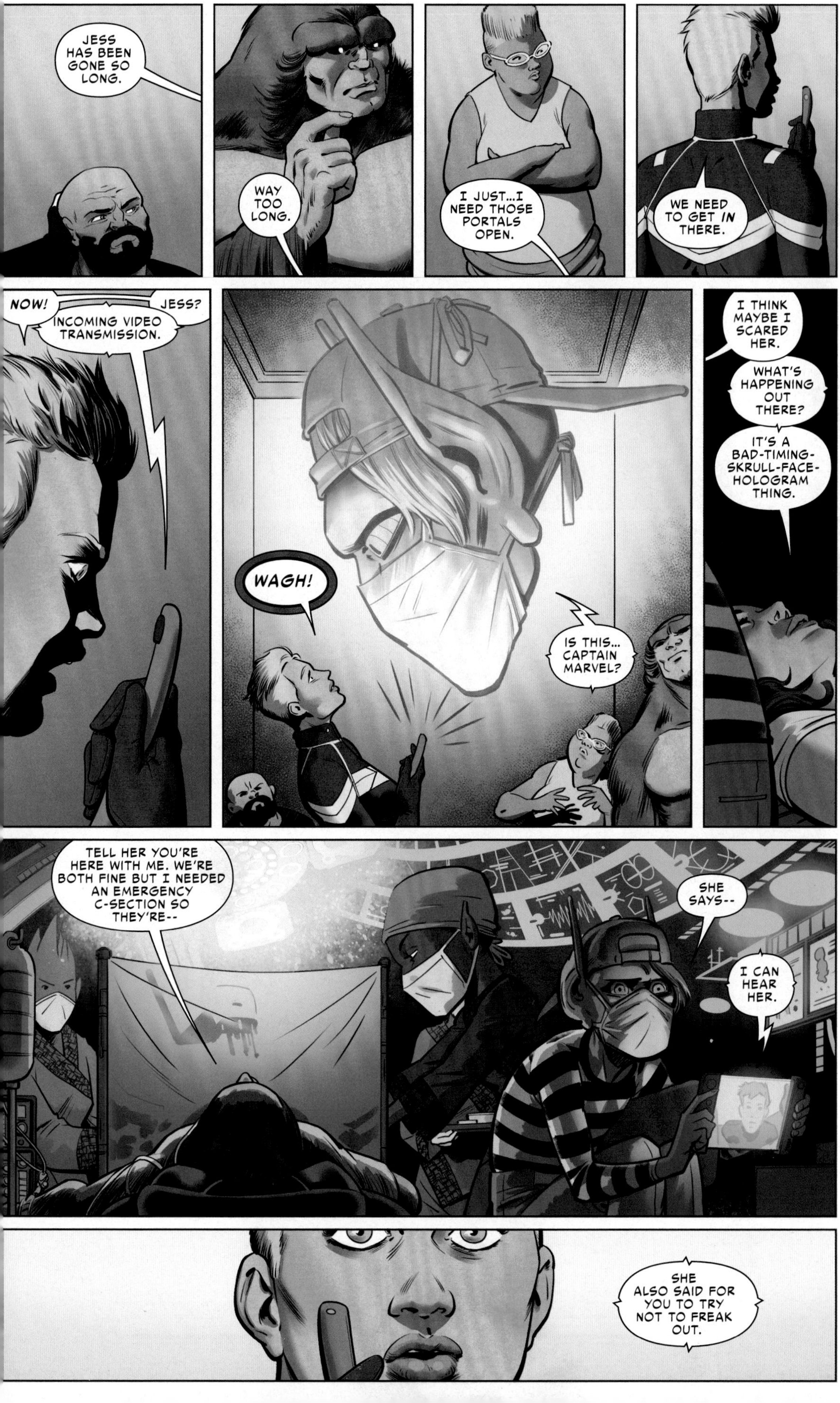
JESS HAS BEEN GONE SO LONG.
WAY TOO LONG.
I JUST...I NEED THOSE PORTALS OPEN.
WE NEED TO GET *IN* THERE.
NOW!
JESS?
INCOMING VIDEO TRANSMISSION.
WAGH!
IS THIS... CAPTAIN MARVEL?
I THINK MAYBE I SCARED HER.
WHAT'S HAPPENING OUT THERE?
IT'S A BAD-TIMING-SKRULL-FACE-HOLOGRAM THING.
TELL HER YOU'RE HERE WITH ME. WE'RE BOTH FINE BUT I NEEDED AN EMERGENCY C-SECTION SO THEY'RE--
SHE SAYS--
I CAN HEAR HER.
SHE ALSO SAID FOR YOU TO TRY NOT TO FREAK OUT.

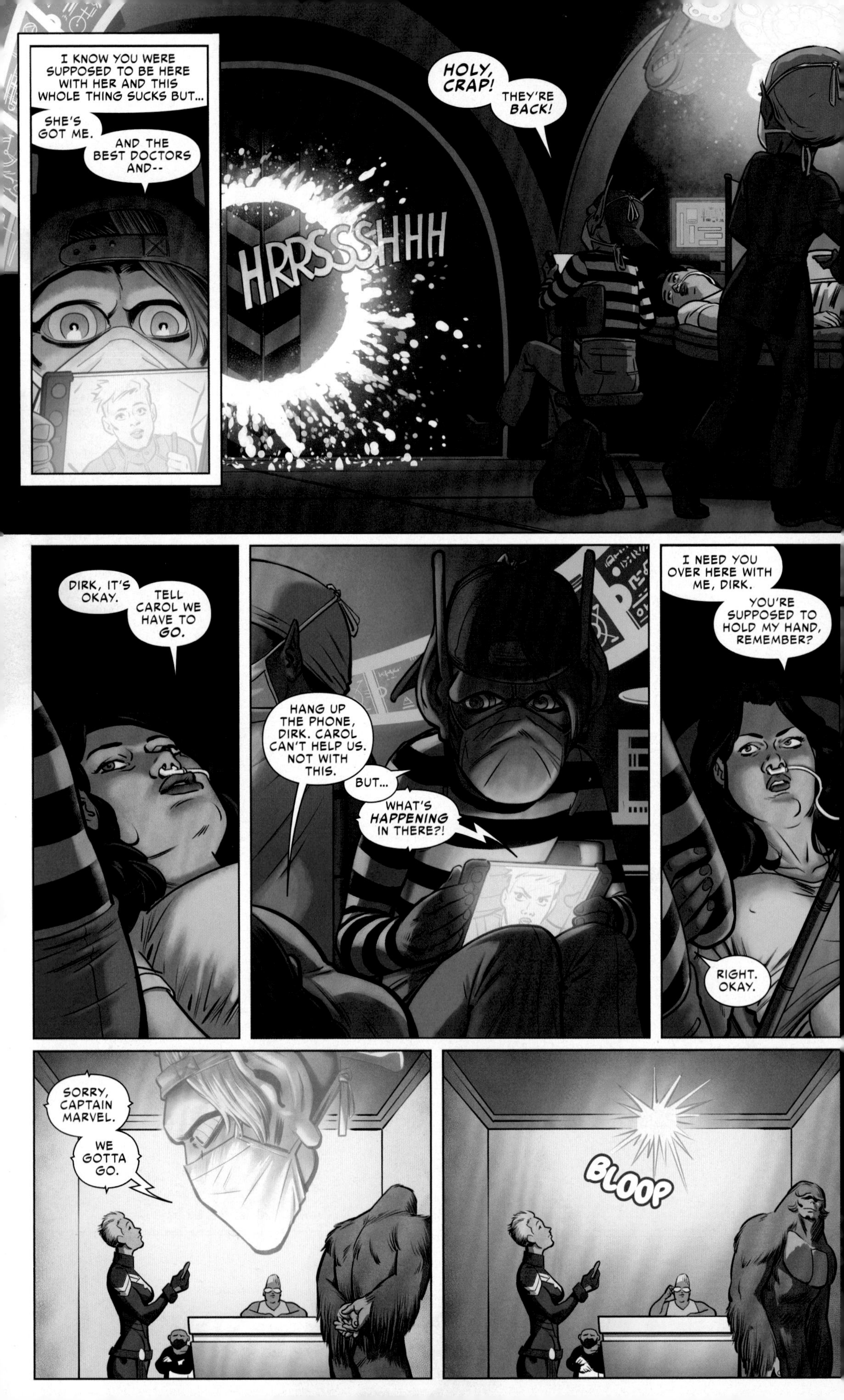
I KNOW YOU WERE SUPPOSED TO BE HERE WITH HER AND THIS WHOLE THING SUCKS BUT...
SHE'S GOT ME.
AND THE BEST DOCTORS AND--
HRRSSSHHH
HOLY, CRAP!
THEY'RE BACK!
DIRK, IT'S OKAY.
TELL CAROL WE HAVE TO GO.
HANG UP THE PHONE, DIRK. CAROL CAN'T HELP US. NOT WITH THIS.
BUT...
WHAT'S HAPPENING IN THERE?!
I NEED YOU OVER HERE WITH ME, DIRK.
YOU'RE SUPPOSED TO HOLD MY HAND, REMEMBER?
RIGHT. OKAY.
SORRY, CAPTAIN MARVEL.
WE GOTTA GO.
BLOOP

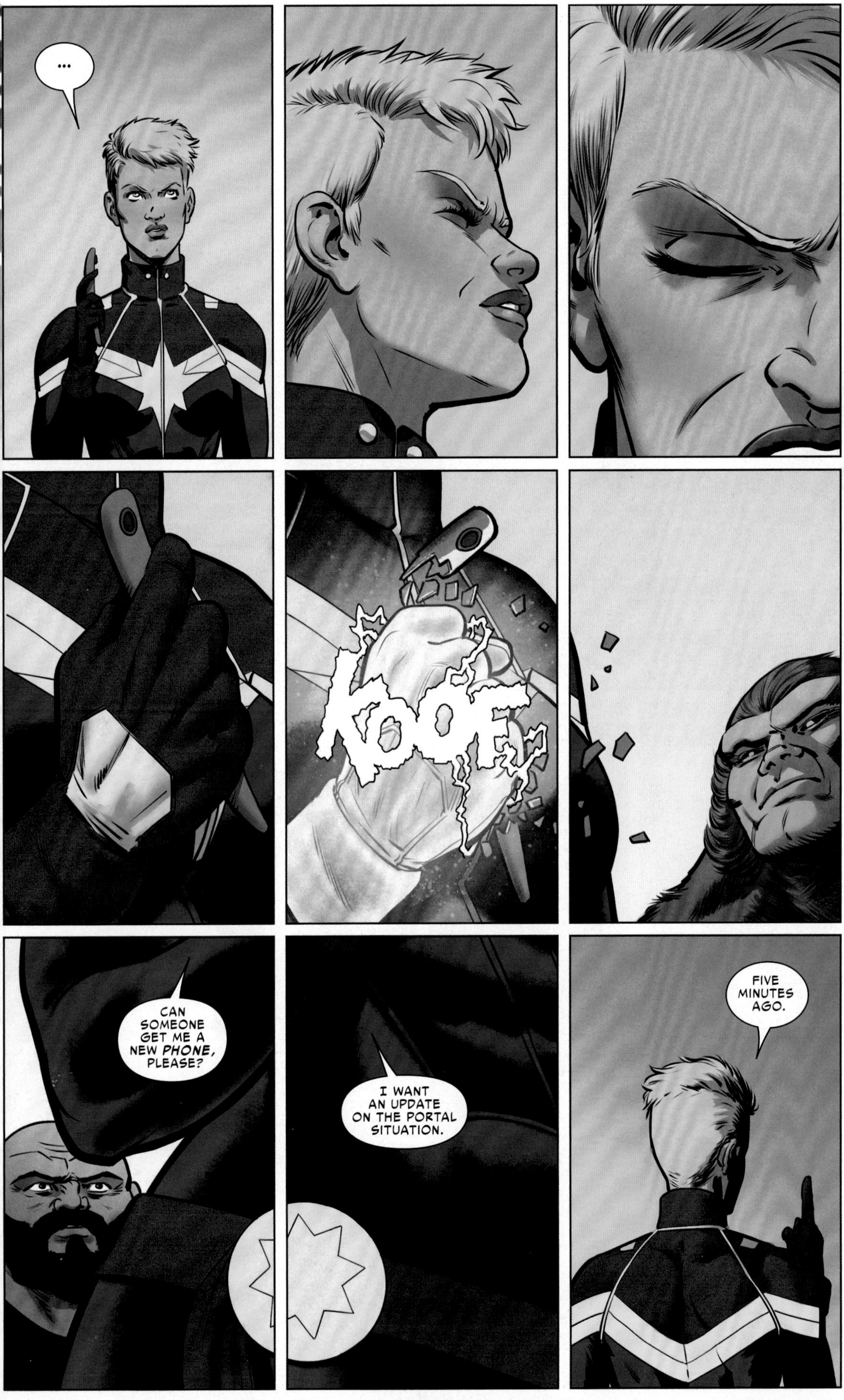
...
KOOF
CAN SOMEONE GET ME A NEW PHONE, PLEASE?
I WANT AN UPDATE ON THE PORTAL SITUATION.
FIVE MINUTES AGO.

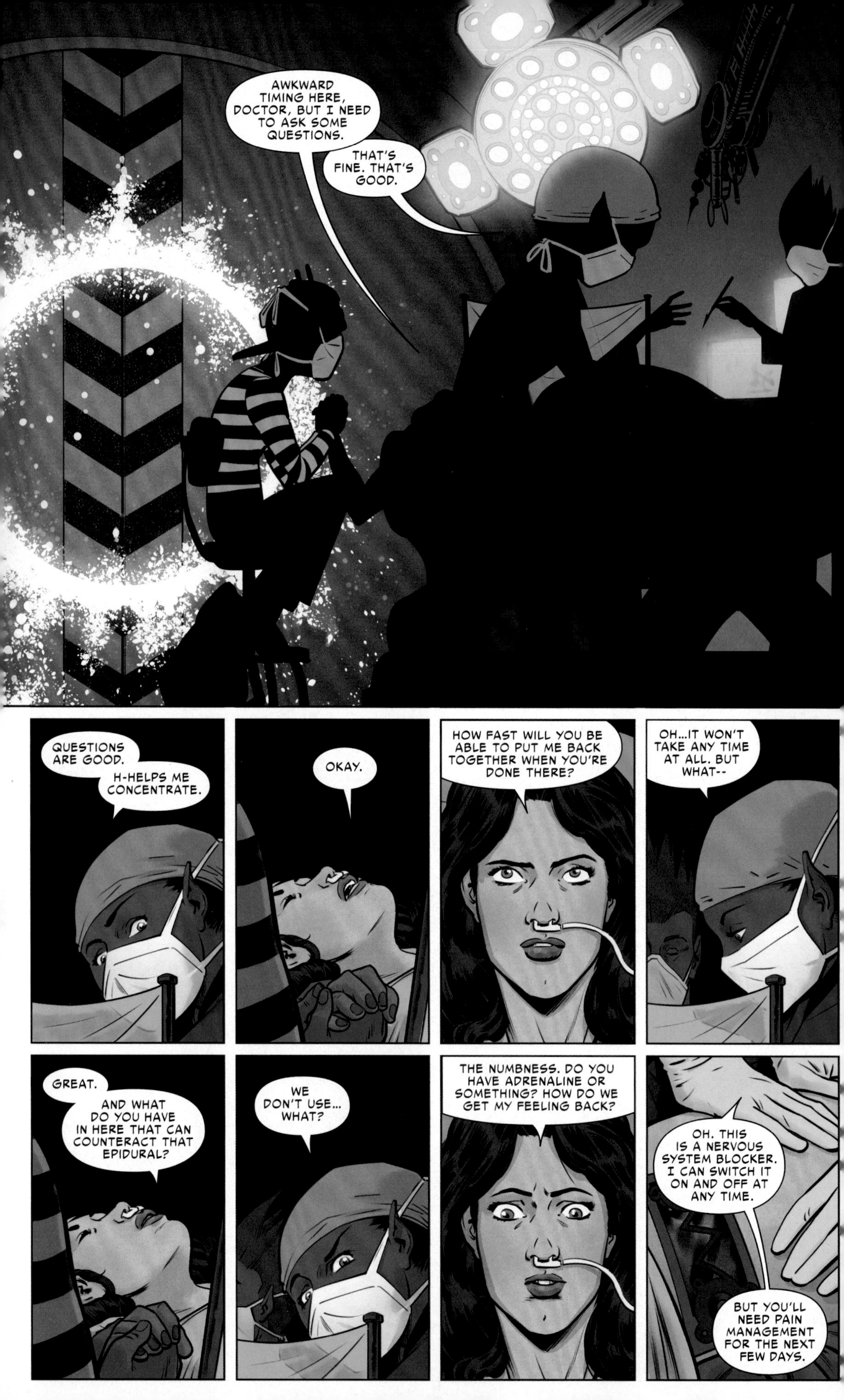
AWKWARD TIMING HERE, DOCTOR, BUT I NEED TO ASK SOME QUESTIONS.
THAT'S FINE. THAT'S GOOD.
QUESTIONS ARE GOOD.
H-HELPS ME CONCENTRATE.
OKAY.
HOW FAST WILL YOU BE ABLE TO PUT ME BACK TOGETHER WHEN YOU'RE DONE THERE?
OH...IT WON'T TAKE ANY TIME AT ALL. BUT WHAT--
GREAT.
AND WHAT DO YOU HAVE IN HERE THAT CAN COUNTERACT THAT EPIDURAL?
WE DON'T USE... WHAT?
THE NUMBNESS. DO YOU HAVE ADRENALINE OR SOMETHING? HOW DO WE GET MY FEELING BACK?
OH. THIS IS A NERVOUS SYSTEM BLOCKER. I CAN SWITCH IT ON AND OFF AT ANY TIME.
BUT YOU'LL NEED PAIN MANAGEMENT FOR THE NEXT FEW DAYS.

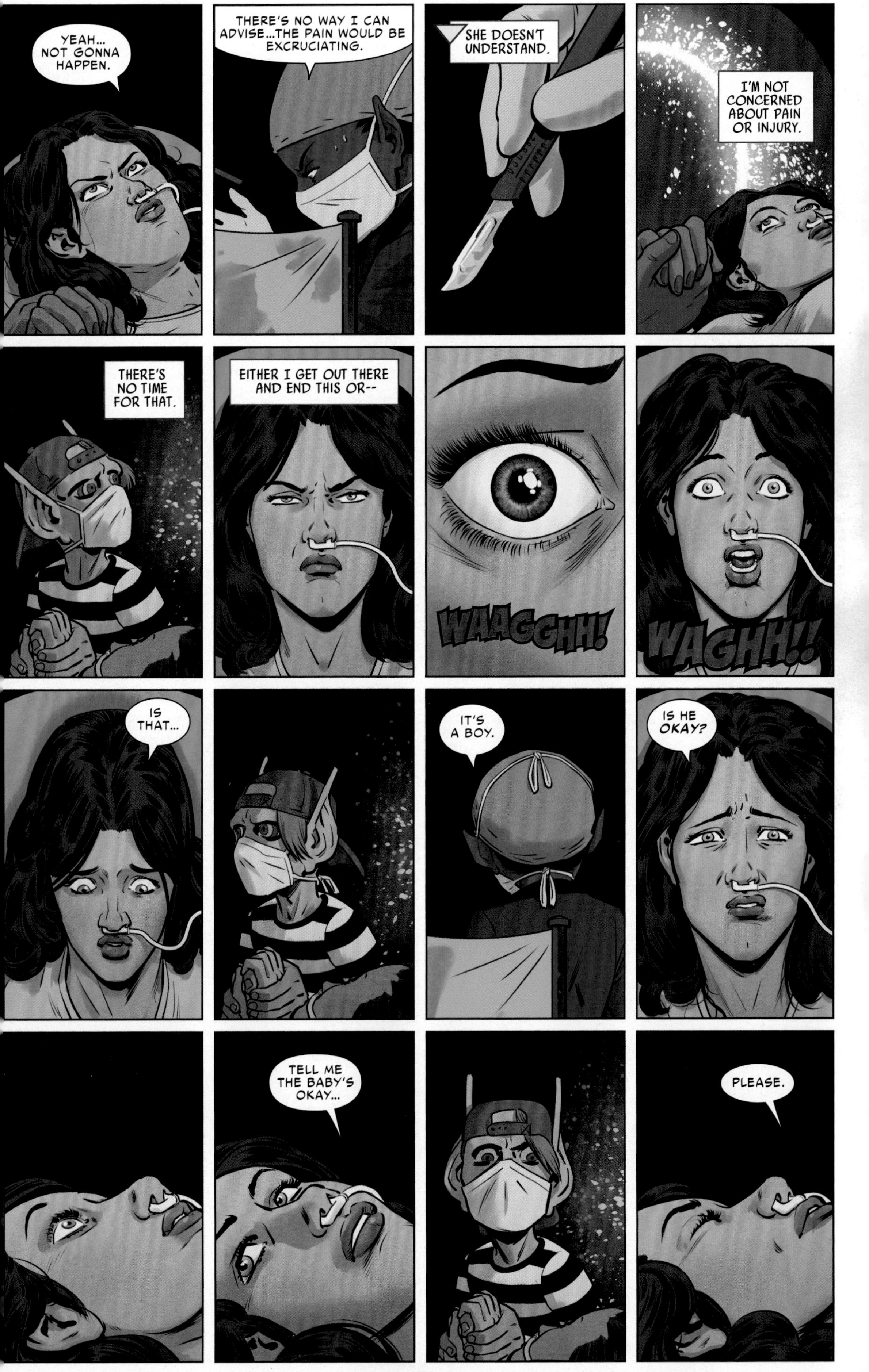
YEAH... NOT GONNA HAPPEN.
THERE'S NO WAY I CAN ADVISE...THE PAIN WOULD BE EXCRUCIATING.
SHE DOESN'T UNDERSTAND.
I'M NOT CONCERNED ABOUT PAIN OR INJURY.
THERE'S NO TIME FOR THAT.
EITHER I GET OUT THERE AND END THIS OR--
WAAGGHH!
WAGHH!!
IS THAT...
IT'S A BOY.
IS HE OKAY?
TELL ME THE BABY'S OKAY...
PLEASE.

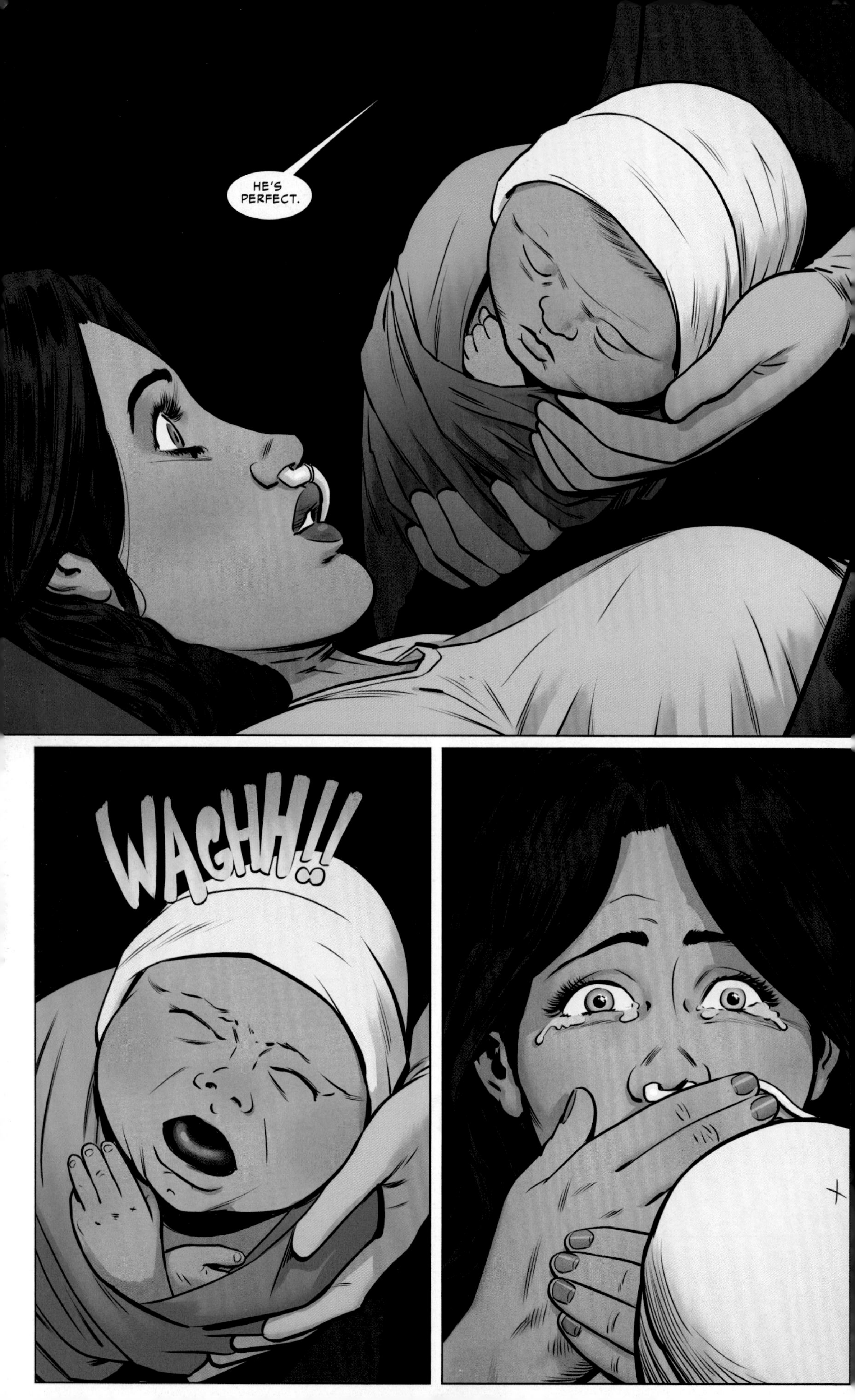
HE'S PERFECT.
WAGHH!!!

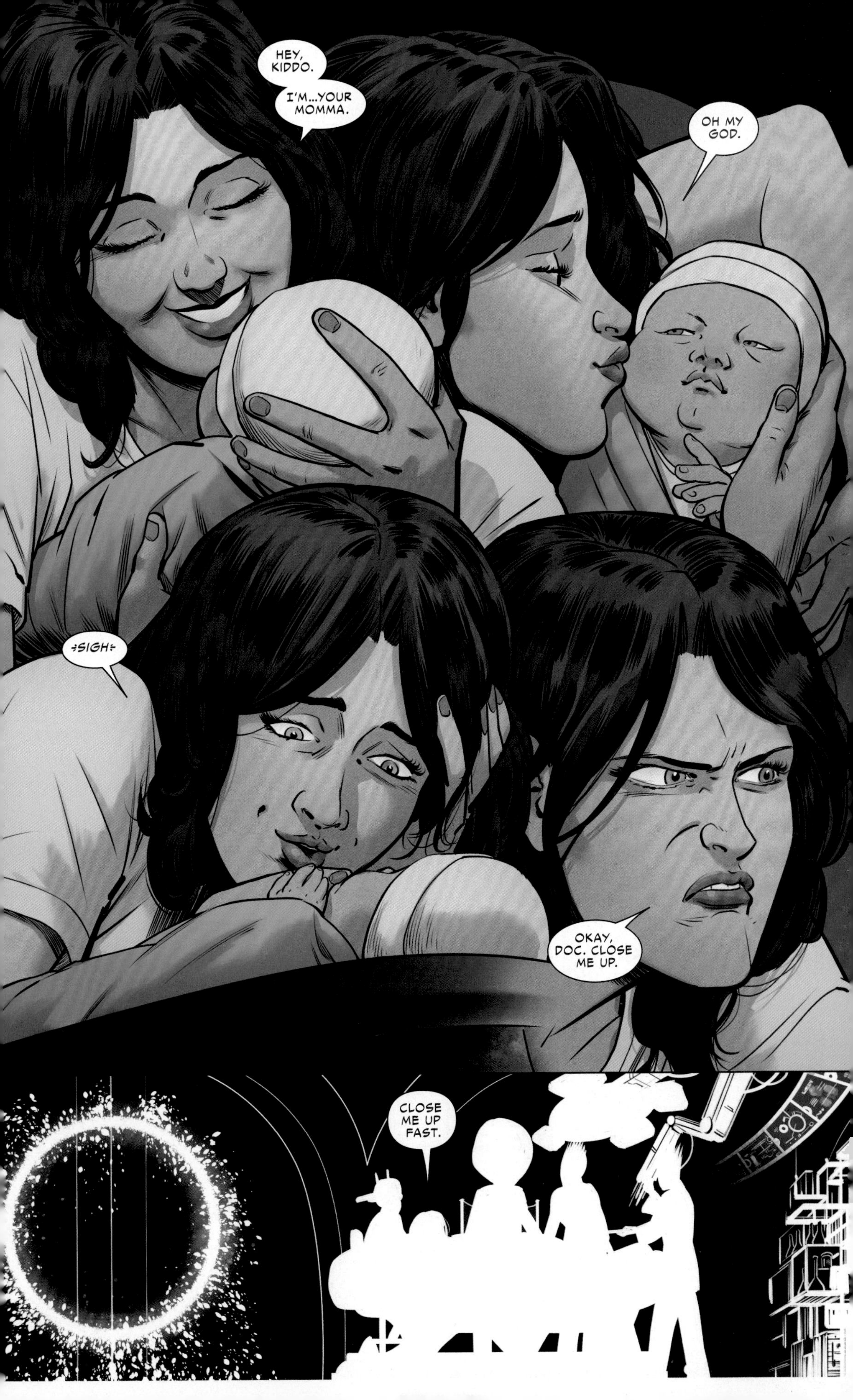
HEY, KIDDO.
I'M...YOUR MOMMA.
OH MY GOD.
=SIGH=
OKAY, DOC. CLOSE ME UP.
CLOSE ME UP FAST.

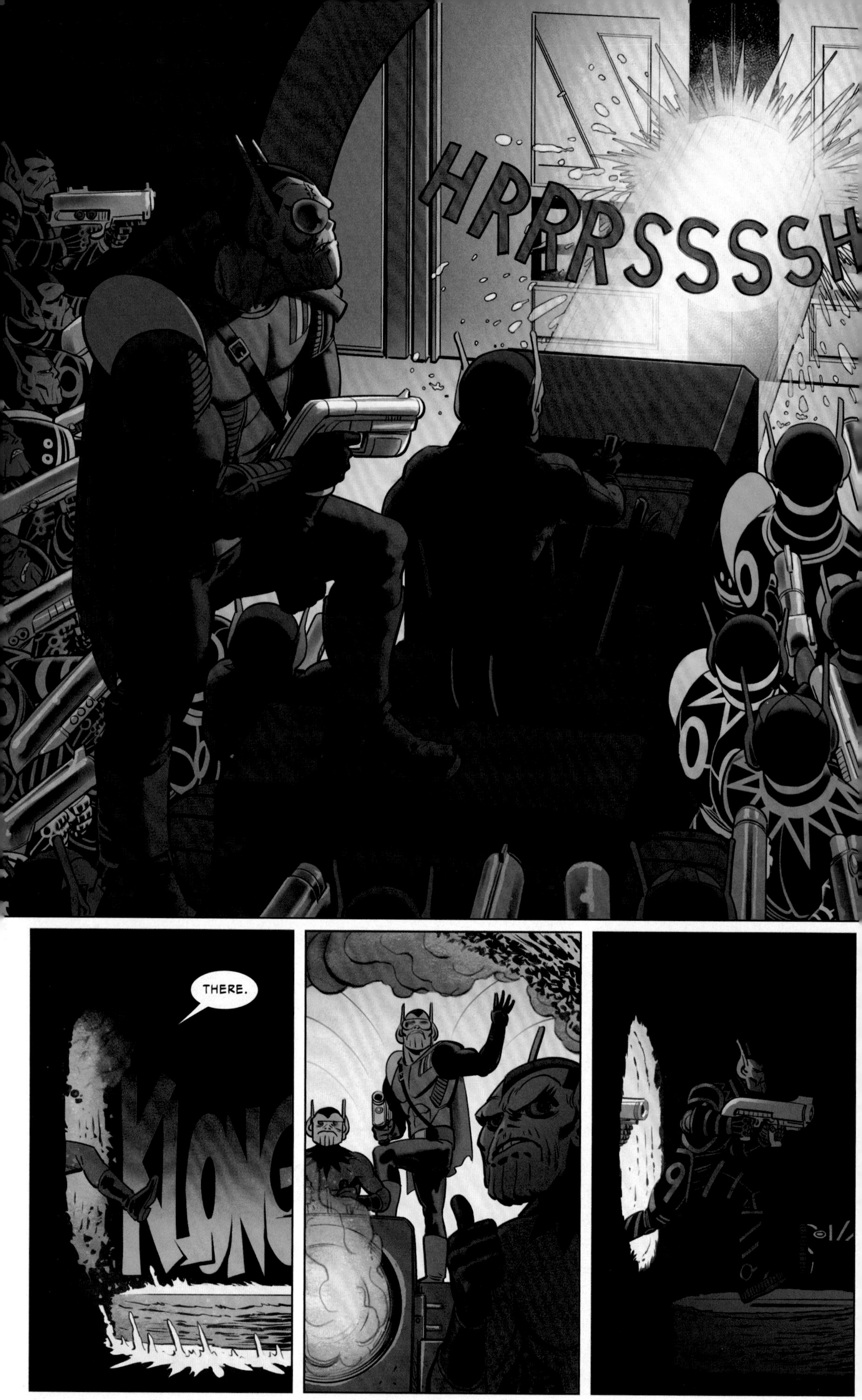
HRRRSSSSH
THERE.

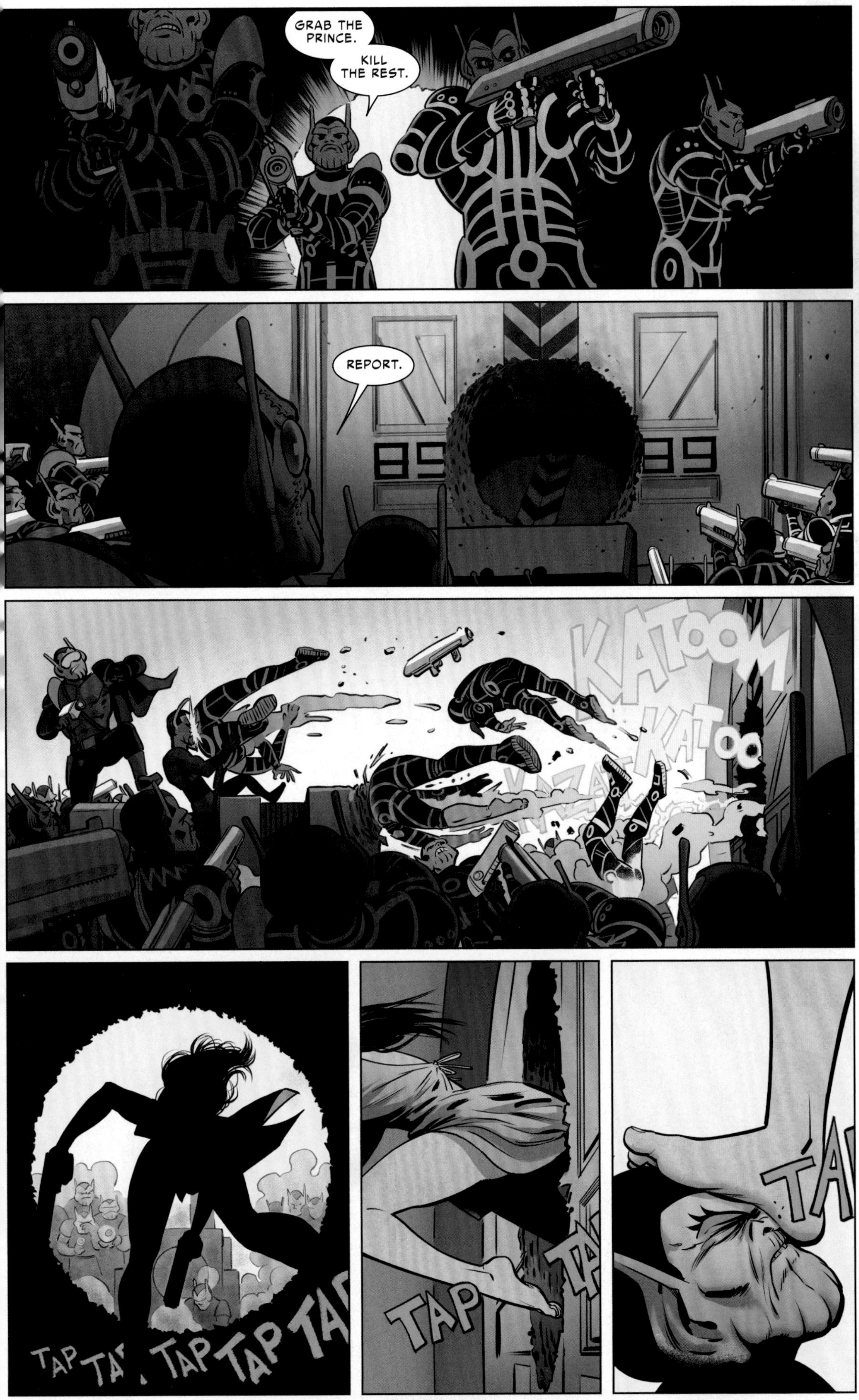
GRAB THE PRINCE.
KILL THE REST.
REPORT.
KATOOM
TAP
TAP
TAP
TAP

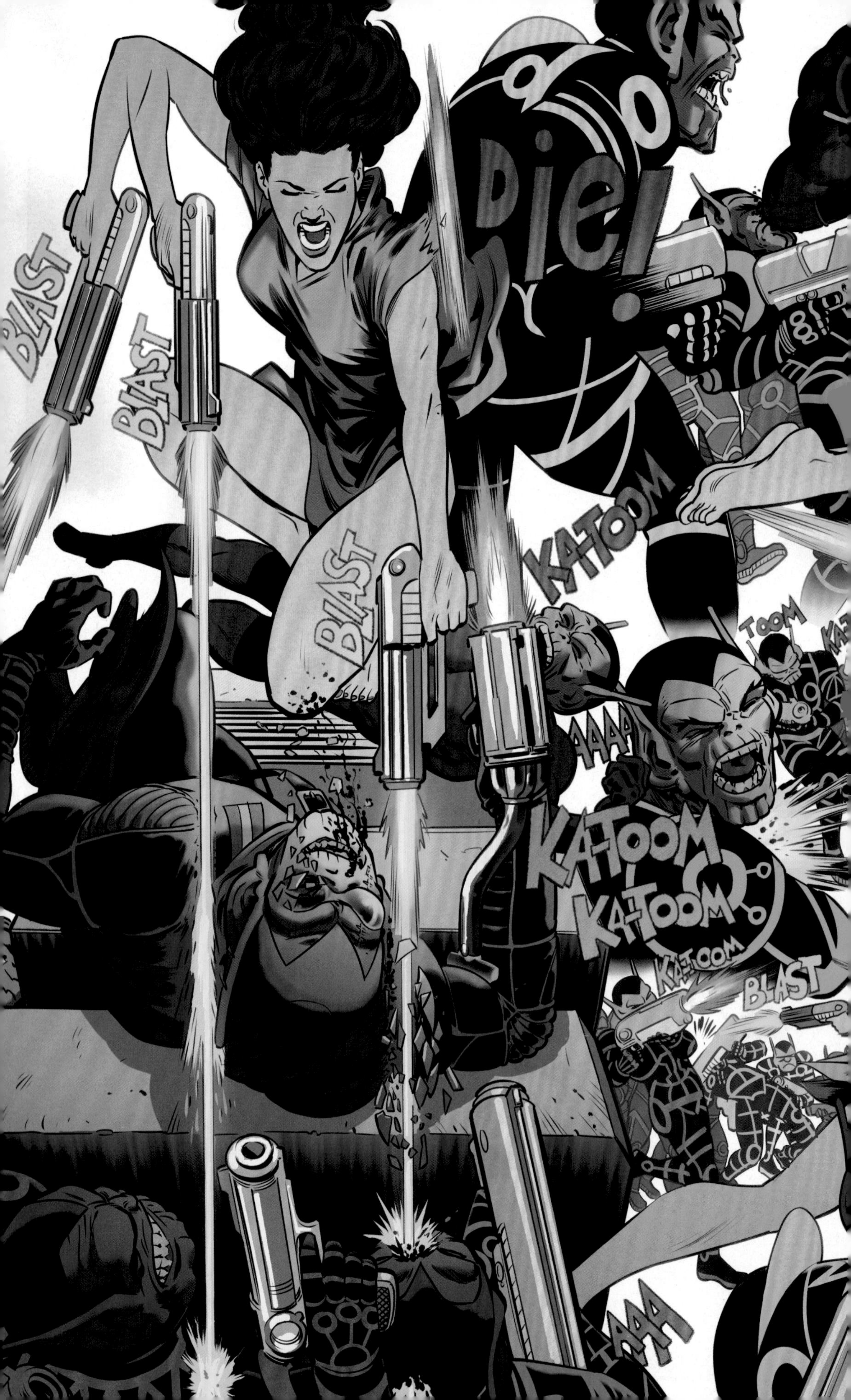
DIE!
BLAST
BLAST
BLAST
BLAST
KA-TOOM
TOOM
AAAA
KA-TOOM
KA-TOOM
KA-TOOM
BLAST
AAAA

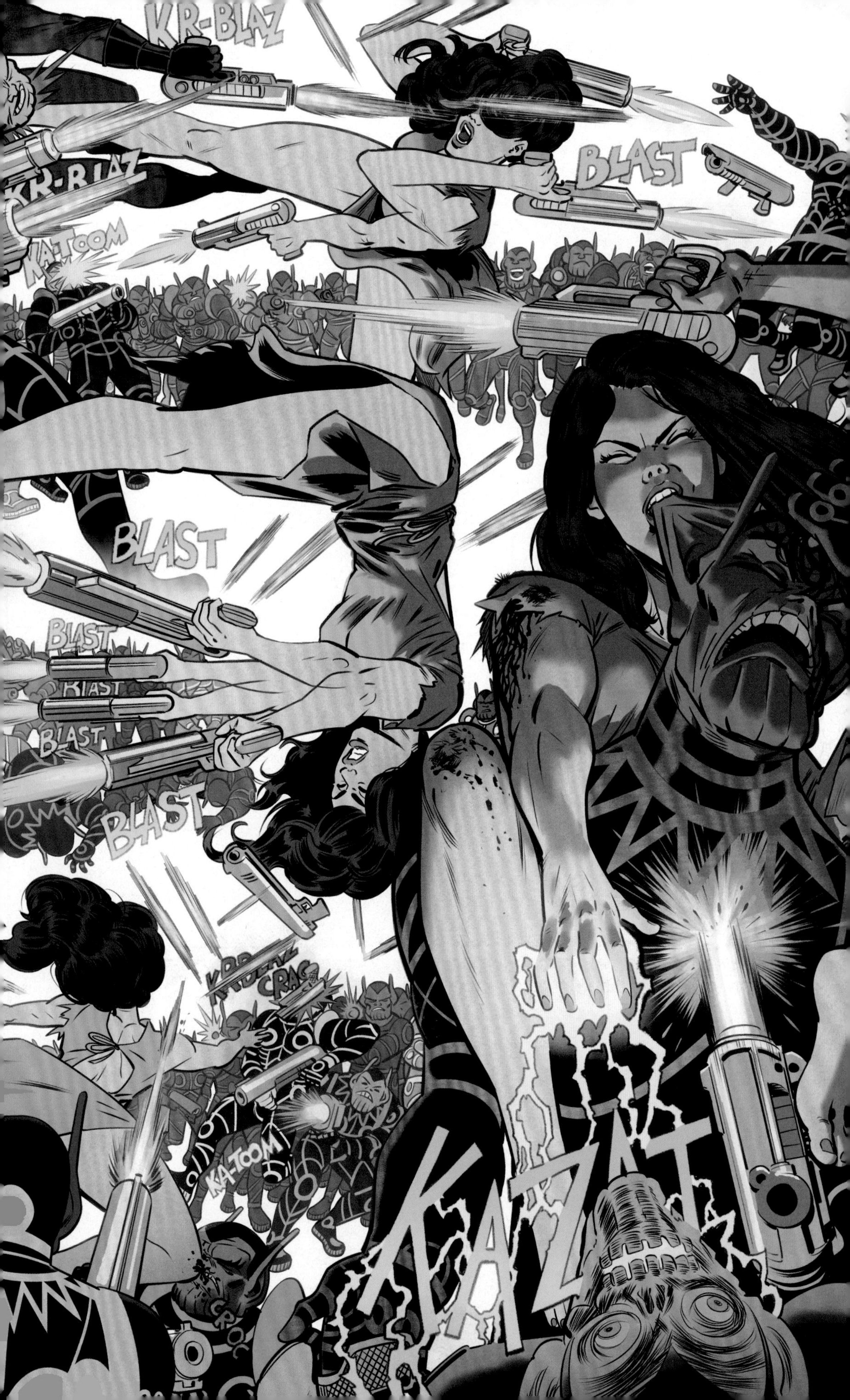
KR-BLAZ
KR-BLAZ
BLAST
KA-TOOM
BLAST
BLAST
BLAST
BLAST
BLAST
CRAC
KA-TOOM
KAZAT

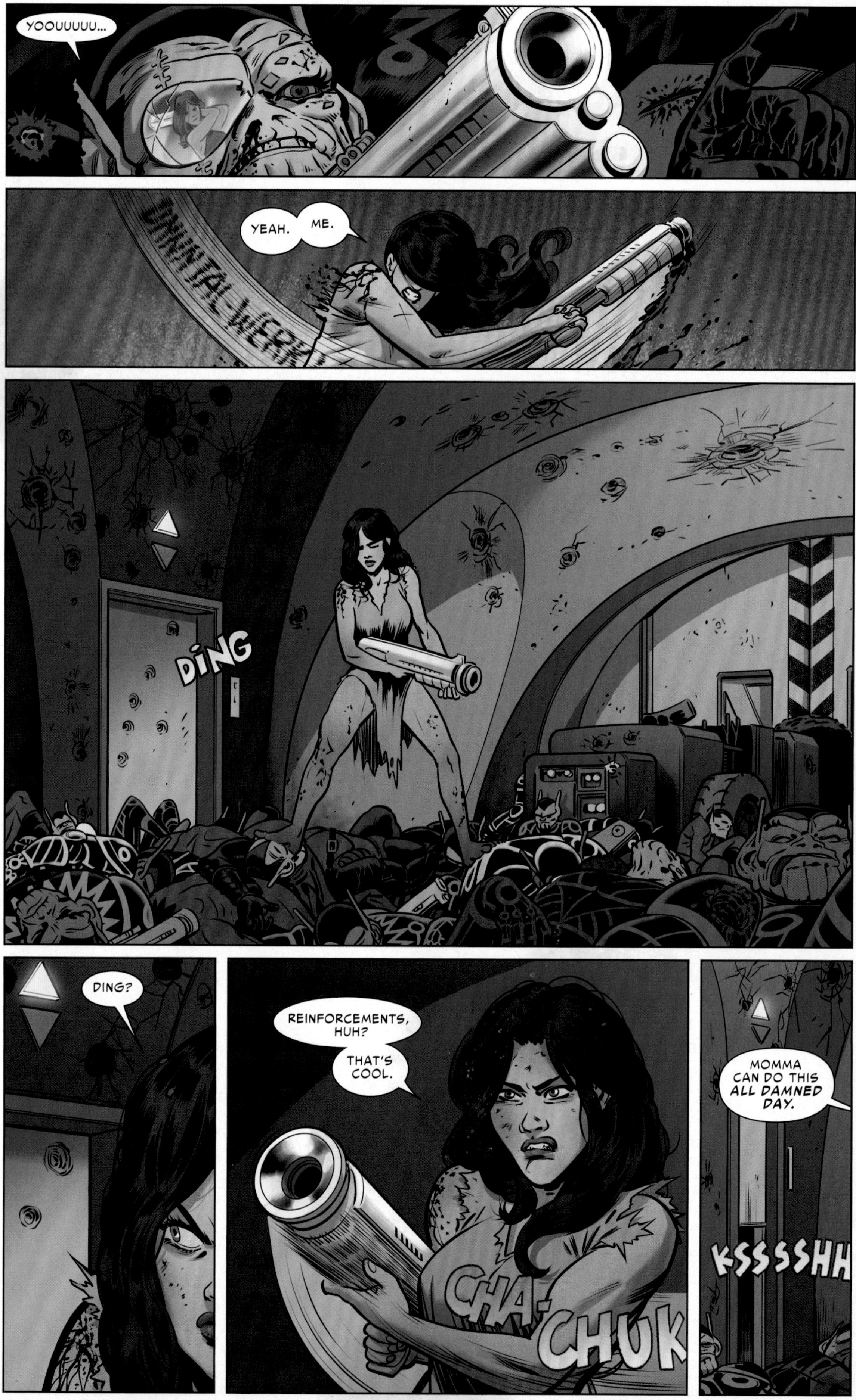
YOOUUUUU...
YEAH.
ME.
DING
DING?
REINFORCEMENTS, HUH?
THAT'S COOL.
CHA-CHUK
MOMMA CAN DO THIS ALL DAMNED DAY.
KSSSSHH

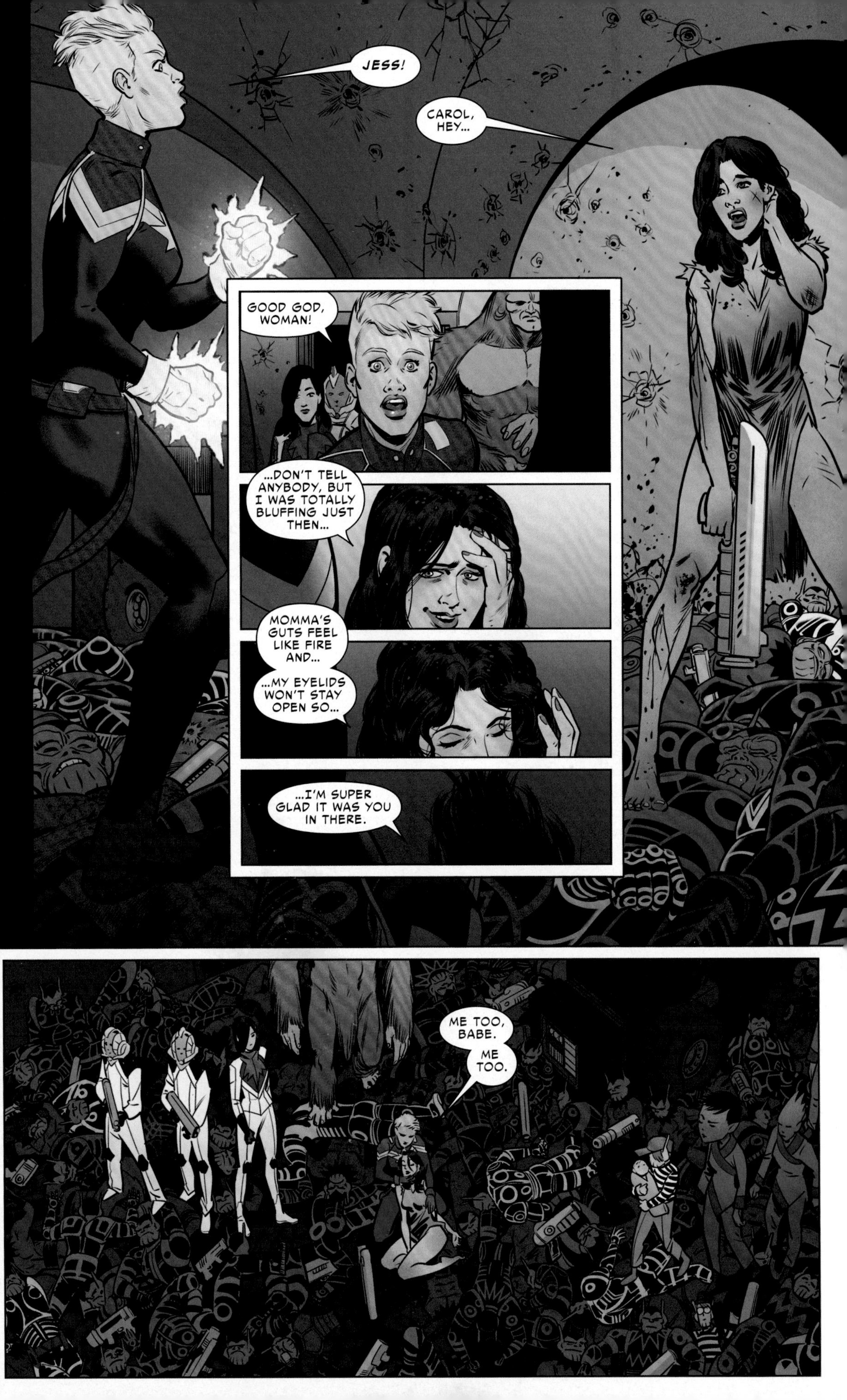
JESS!
CAROL, HEY...
GOOD GOD, WOMAN!
...DON'T TELL ANYBODY, BUT I WAS TOTALLY BLUFFING JUST THEN...
MOMMA'S GUTS FEEL LIKE FIRE AND...
...MY EYELIDS WON'T STAY OPEN SO...
...I'M SUPER GLAD IT WAS YOU IN THERE.
ME TOO, BABE.
ME TOO.

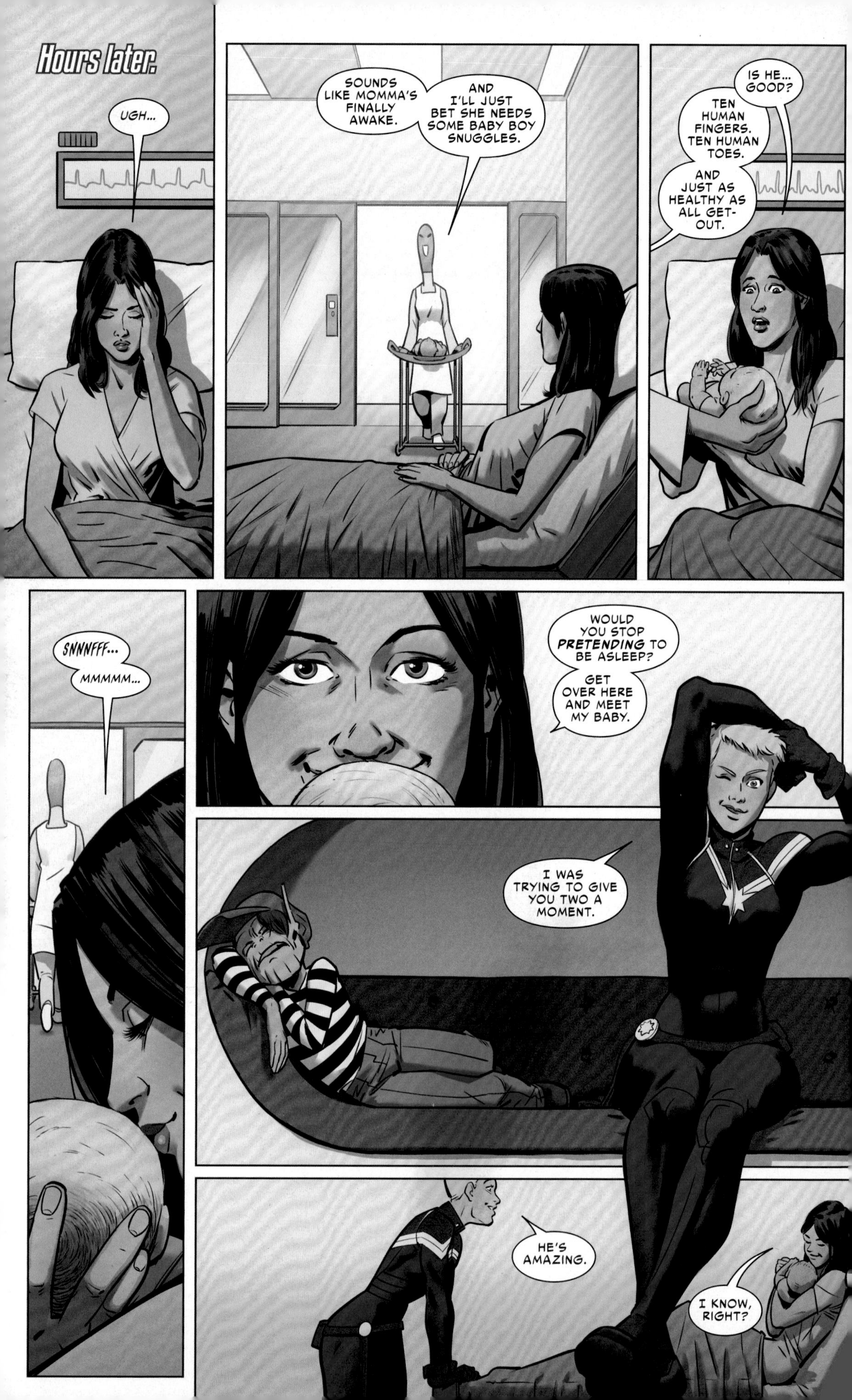
Hours later.
UGH...
SOUNDS LIKE MOMMA'S FINALLY AWAKE.
AND I'LL JUST BET SHE NEEDS SOME BABY BOY SNUGGLES.
IS HE... GOOD?
TEN HUMAN FINGERS. TEN HUMAN TOES.
AND JUST AS HEALTHY AS ALL GET-OUT.
SNNNFFF...
MMMMM...
WOULD YOU STOP PRETENDING TO BE ASLEEP?
GET OVER HERE AND MEET MY BABY.
I WAS TRYING TO GIVE YOU TWO A MOMENT.
HE'S AMAZING.
I KNOW, RIGHT?

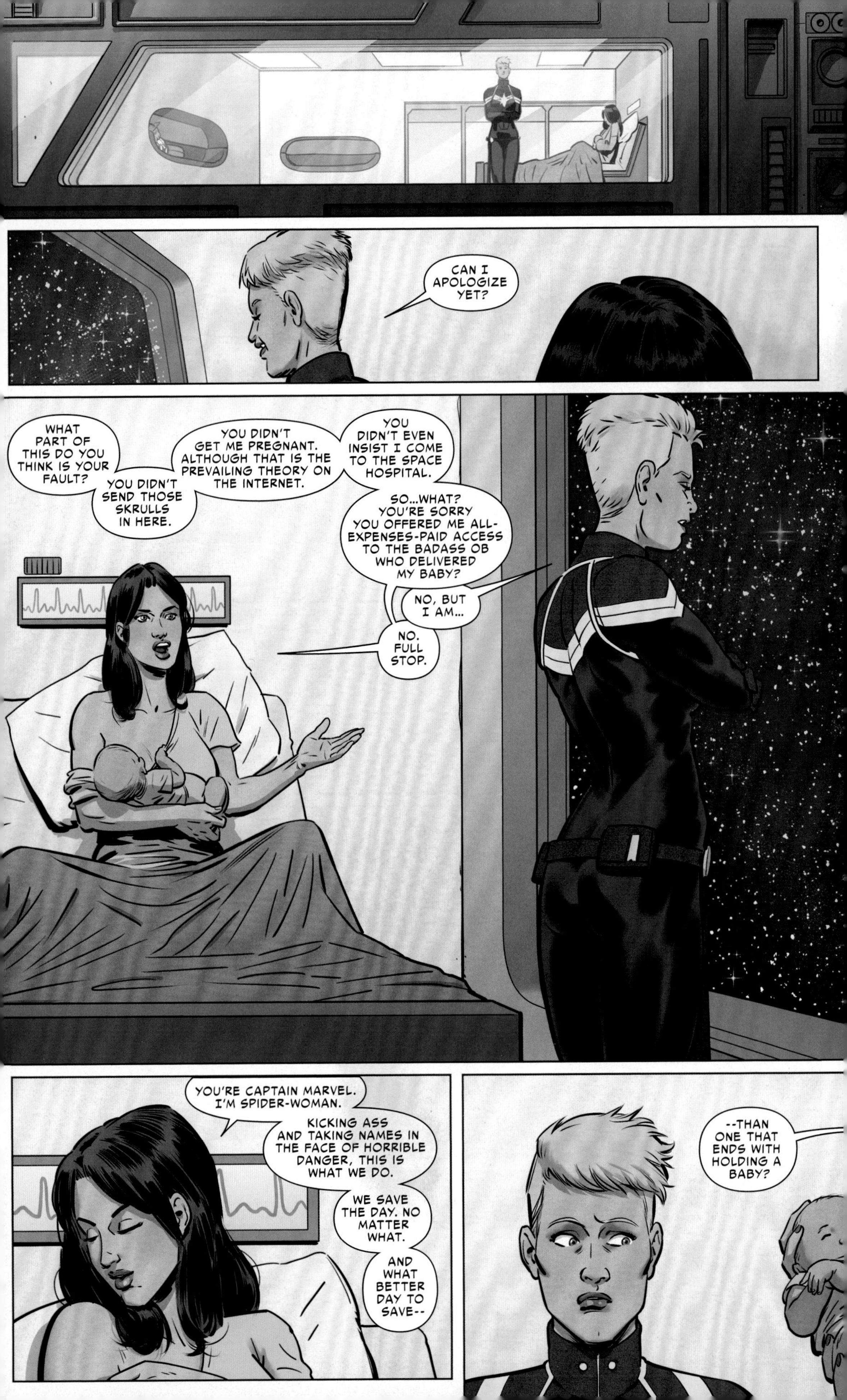
CAN I APOLOGIZE YET?
WHAT PART OF THIS DO YOU THINK IS YOUR FAULT?
YOU DIDN'T SEND THOSE SKRULLS IN HERE.
YOU DIDN'T GET ME PREGNANT. ALTHOUGH THAT IS THE PREVAILING THEORY ON THE INTERNET.
YOU DIDN'T EVEN INSIST I COME TO THE SPACE HOSPITAL.
SO...WHAT? YOU'RE SORRY YOU OFFERED ME ALL-EXPENSES-PAID ACCESS TO THE BADASS OB WHO DELIVERED MY BABY?
NO, BUT I AM...
NO. FULL STOP.
YOU'RE CAPTAIN MARVEL. I'M SPIDER-WOMAN.
KICKING ASS AND TAKING NAMES IN THE FACE OF HORRIBLE DANGER, THIS IS WHAT WE DO.
WE SAVE THE DAY. NO MATTER WHAT.
AND WHAT BETTER DAY TO SAVE--
--THAN ONE THAT ENDS WITH HOLDING A BABY?

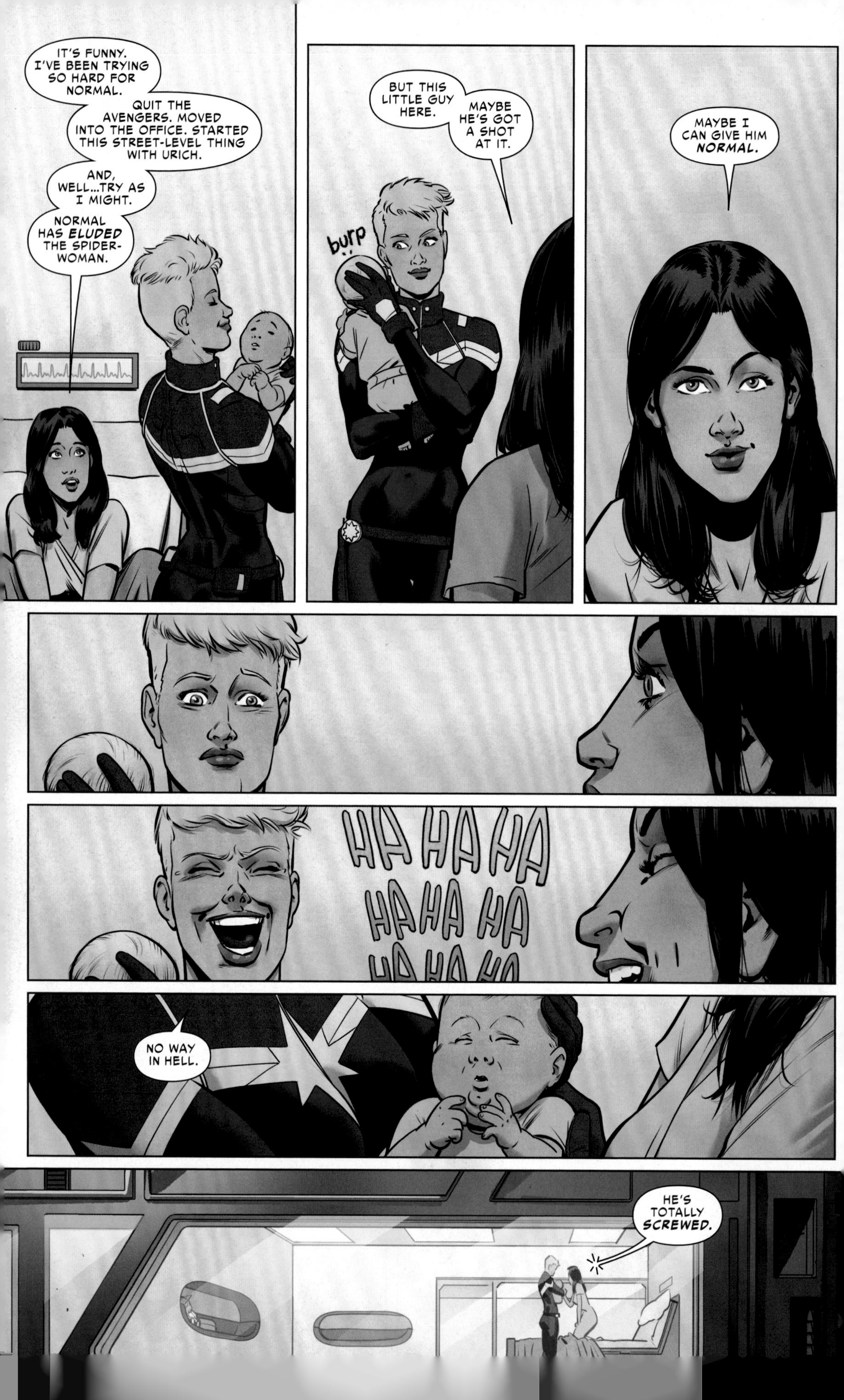
IT'S FUNNY. I'VE BEEN TRYING SO HARD FOR NORMAL.
QUIT THE AVENGERS. MOVED INTO THE OFFICE. STARTED THIS STREET-LEVEL THING WITH URICH.
AND, WELL...TRY AS I MIGHT.
NORMAL HAS ELUDED THE SPIDER-WOMAN.
burp
BUT THIS LITTLE GUY HERE.
MAYBE HE'S GOT A SHOT AT IT.
MAYBE I CAN GIVE HIM NORMAL.
HA HA HA HA HA HA HA HA
NO WAY IN HELL.
HE'S TOTALLY SCREWED.

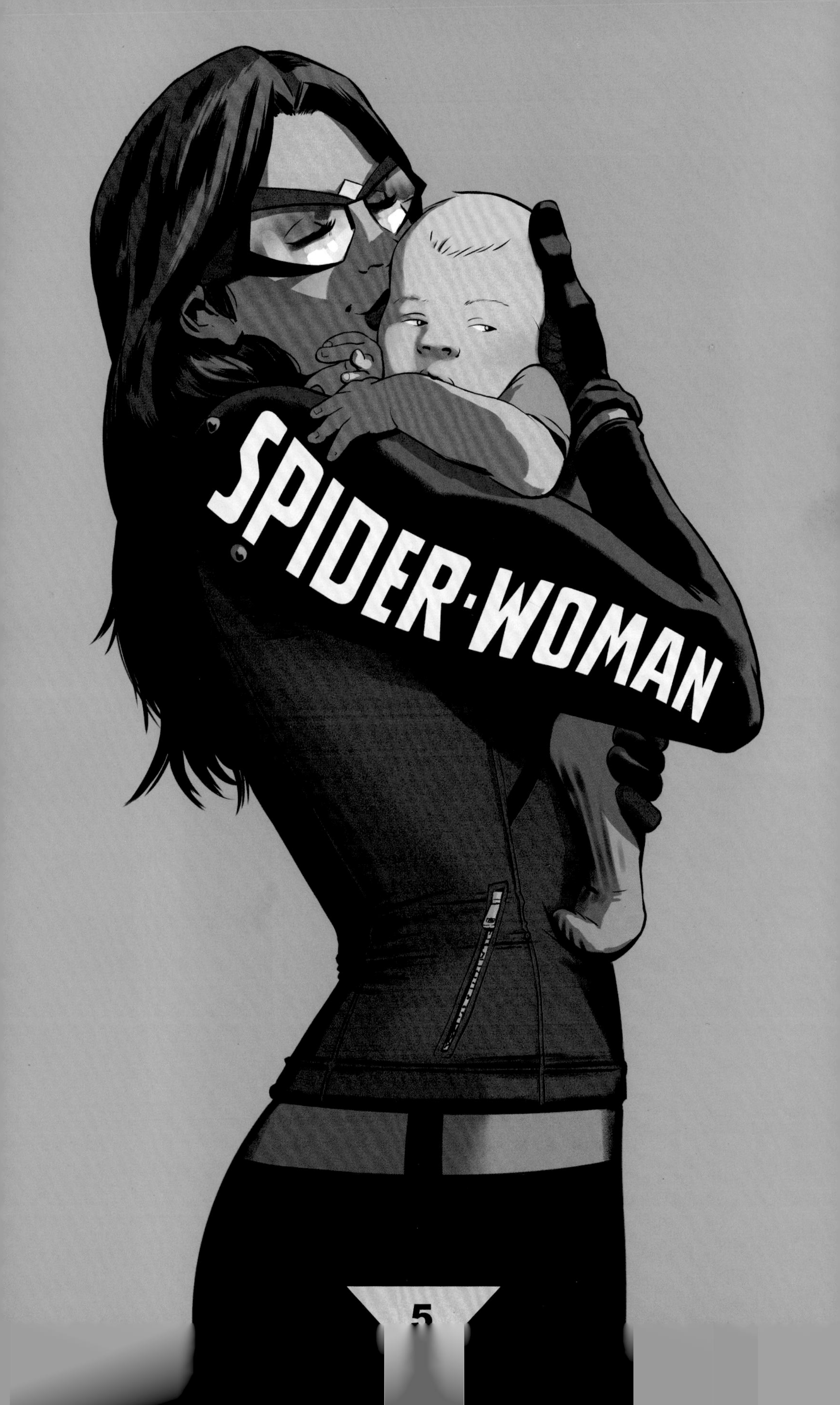
SPIDER-WOMAN
5

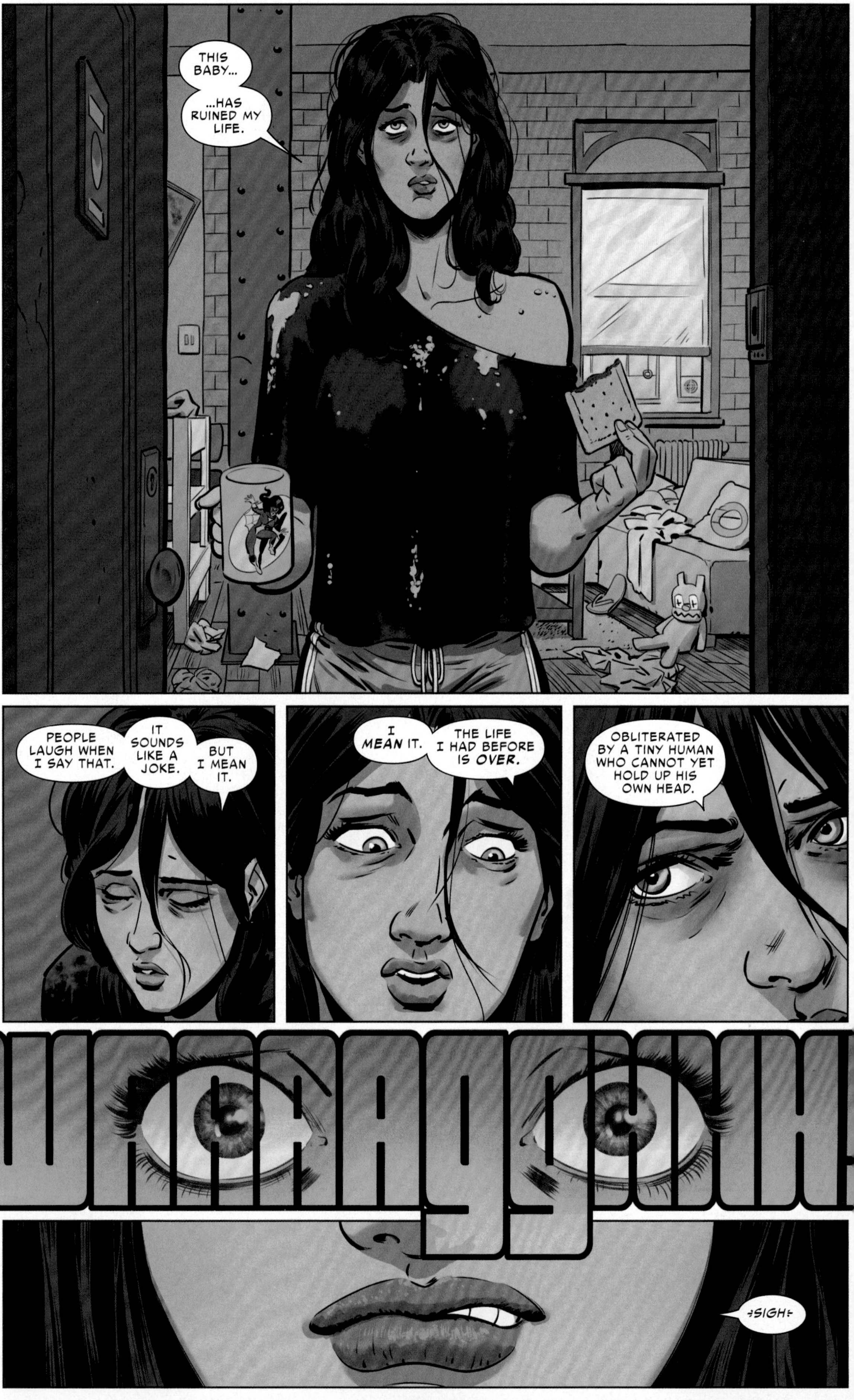
THIS BABY...
...HAS RUINED MY LIFE.
PEOPLE LAUGH WHEN I SAY THAT.
IT SOUNDS LIKE A JOKE.
BUT I MEAN IT.
I *MEAN* IT.
THE LIFE I HAD BEFORE IS *OVER.*
OBLITERATED BY A TINY HUMAN WHO CANNOT YET HOLD UP HIS OWN HEAD.
SIGH

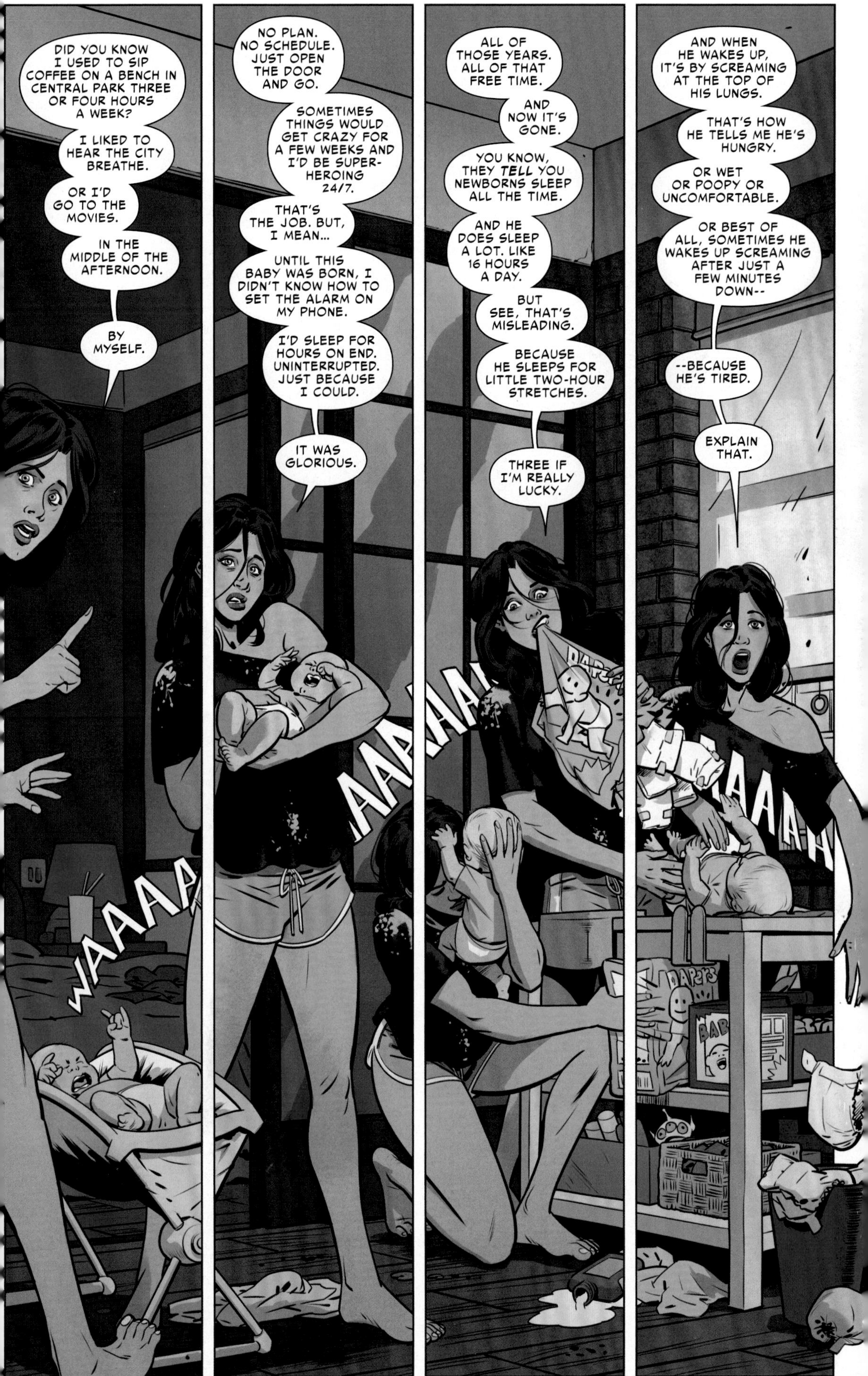
DID YOU KNOW I USED TO SIP COFFEE ON A BENCH IN CENTRAL PARK THREE OR FOUR HOURS A WEEK?
I LIKED TO HEAR THE CITY BREATHE.
OR I'D GO TO THE MOVIES.
IN THE MIDDLE OF THE AFTERNOON.
BY MYSELF.
WAAAA
NO PLAN. NO SCHEDULE. JUST OPEN THE DOOR AND GO.
SOMETIMES THINGS WOULD GET CRAZY FOR A FEW WEEKS AND I'D BE SUPER-HEROING 24/7.
THAT'S THE JOB. BUT, I MEAN...
UNTIL THIS BABY WAS BORN, I DIDN'T KNOW HOW TO SET THE ALARM ON MY PHONE.
I'D SLEEP FOR HOURS ON END. UNINTERRUPTED. JUST BECAUSE I COULD.
IT WAS GLORIOUS.
AAAHAA
ALL OF THOSE YEARS. ALL OF THAT FREE TIME.
AND NOW IT'S GONE.
YOU KNOW, THEY *TELL* YOU NEWBORNS SLEEP ALL THE TIME.
AND HE DOES SLEEP A LOT. LIKE 16 HOURS A DAY.
BUT SEE, THAT'S MISLEADING.
BECAUSE HE SLEEPS FOR LITTLE TWO-HOUR STRETCHES.
THREE IF I'M REALLY LUCKY.
AND WHEN HE WAKES UP, IT'S BY SCREAMING AT THE TOP OF HIS LUNGS.
THAT'S HOW HE TELLS ME HE'S HUNGRY.
OR WET OR POOPY OR UNCOMFORTABLE.
OR BEST OF ALL, SOMETIMES HE WAKES UP SCREAMING AFTER JUST A FEW MINUTES DOWN--
--BECAUSE HE'S TIRED.
EXPLAIN THAT.
AAAAH

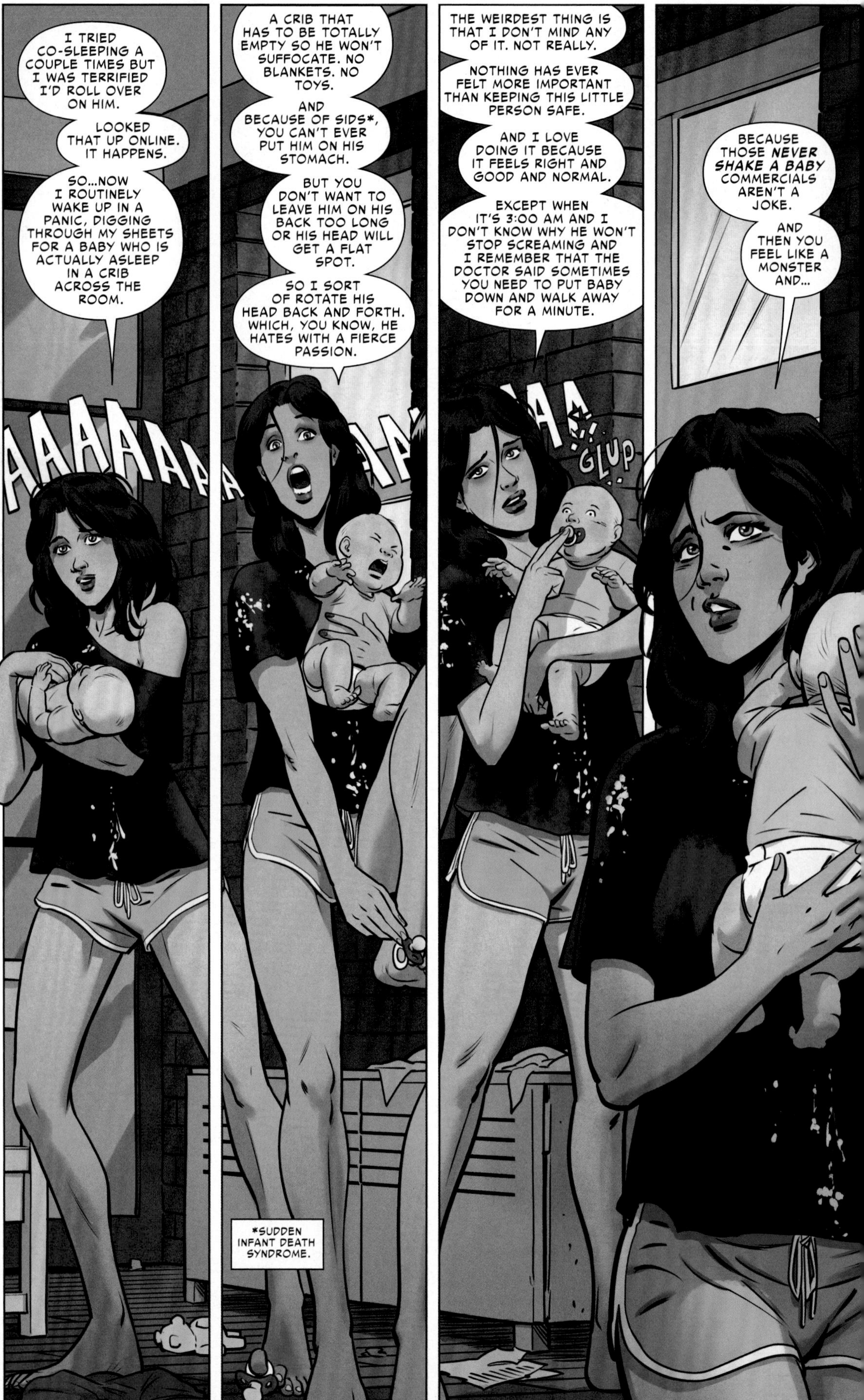

I TRIED CO-SLEEPING A COUPLE TIMES BUT I WAS TERRIFIED I'D ROLL OVER ON HIM.
LOOKED THAT UP ONLINE. IT HAPPENS.
SO...NOW I ROUTINELY WAKE UP IN A PANIC, DIGGING THROUGH MY SHEETS FOR A BABY WHO IS ACTUALLY ASLEEP IN A CRIB ACROSS THE ROOM.
AAAAAAA
A CRIB THAT HAS TO BE TOTALLY EMPTY SO HE WON'T SUFFOCATE. NO BLANKETS. NO TOYS.
AND BECAUSE OF SIDS*, YOU CAN'T EVER PUT HIM ON HIS STOMACH.
BUT YOU DON'T WANT TO LEAVE HIM ON HIS BACK TOO LONG OR HIS HEAD WILL GET A FLAT SPOT.
SO I SORT OF ROTATE HIS HEAD BACK AND FORTH. WHICH, YOU KNOW, HE HATES WITH A FIERCE PASSION.
*SUDDEN INFANT DEATH SYNDROME.
THE WEIRDEST THING IS THAT I DON'T MIND ANY OF IT. NOT REALLY.
NOTHING HAS EVER FELT MORE IMPORTANT THAN KEEPING THIS LITTLE PERSON SAFE.
AND I LOVE DOING IT BECAUSE IT FEELS RIGHT AND GOOD AND NORMAL.
EXCEPT WHEN IT'S 3:00 AM AND I DON'T KNOW WHY HE WON'T STOP SCREAMING AND I REMEMBER THAT THE DOCTOR SAID SOMETIMES YOU NEED TO PUT BABY DOWN AND WALK AWAY FOR A MINUTE.
AA
GLUP
BECAUSE THOSE ***NEVER SHAKE A BABY*** COMMERCIALS AREN'T A JOKE.
AND THEN YOU FEEL LIKE A MONSTER AND...

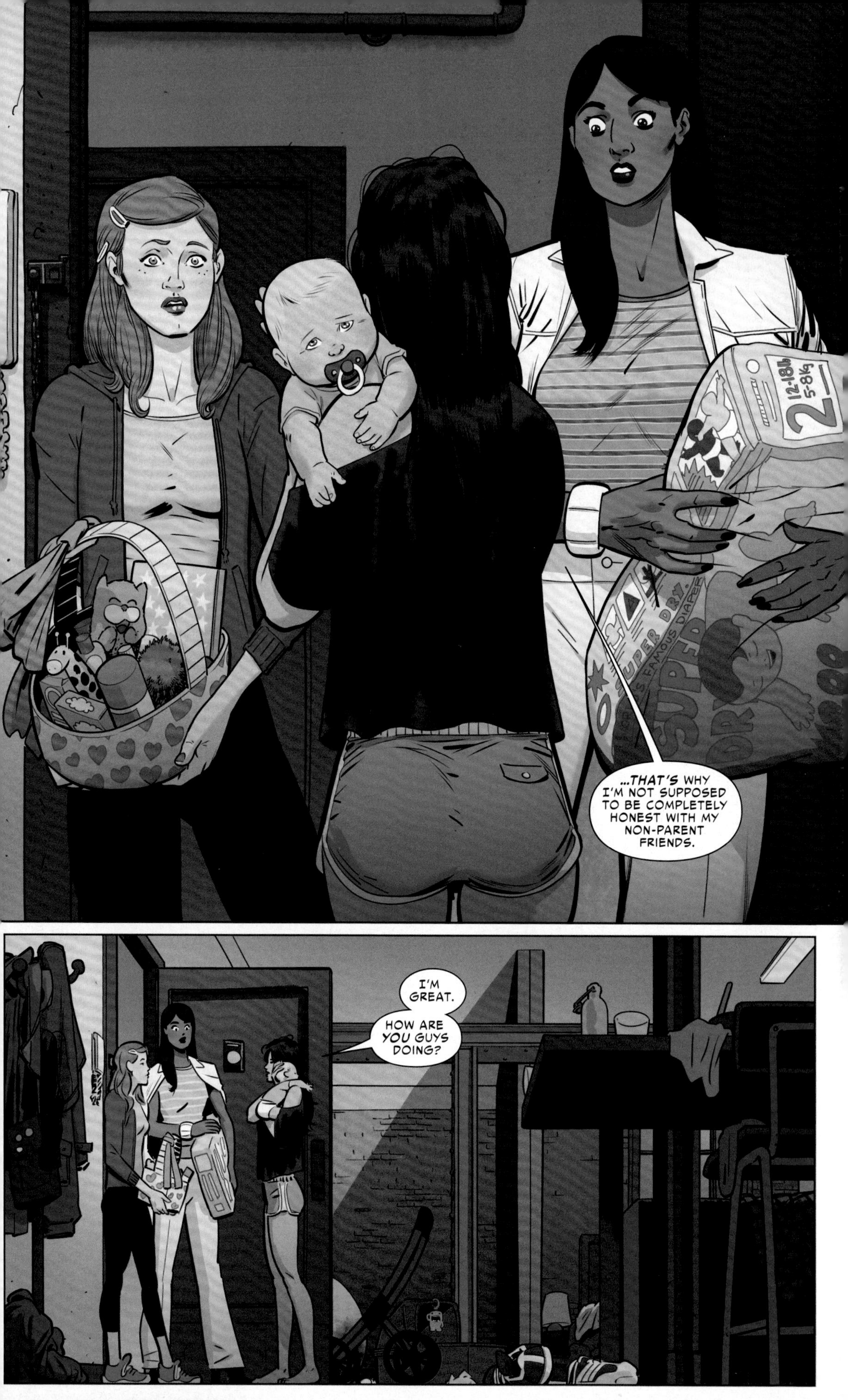
12-18lb
5-8kg
2
SUPER DRY.
...THAT'S WHY I'M NOT SUPPOSED TO BE COMPLETELY HONEST WITH MY NON-PARENT FRIENDS.
I'M GREAT.
HOW ARE YOU GUYS DOING?

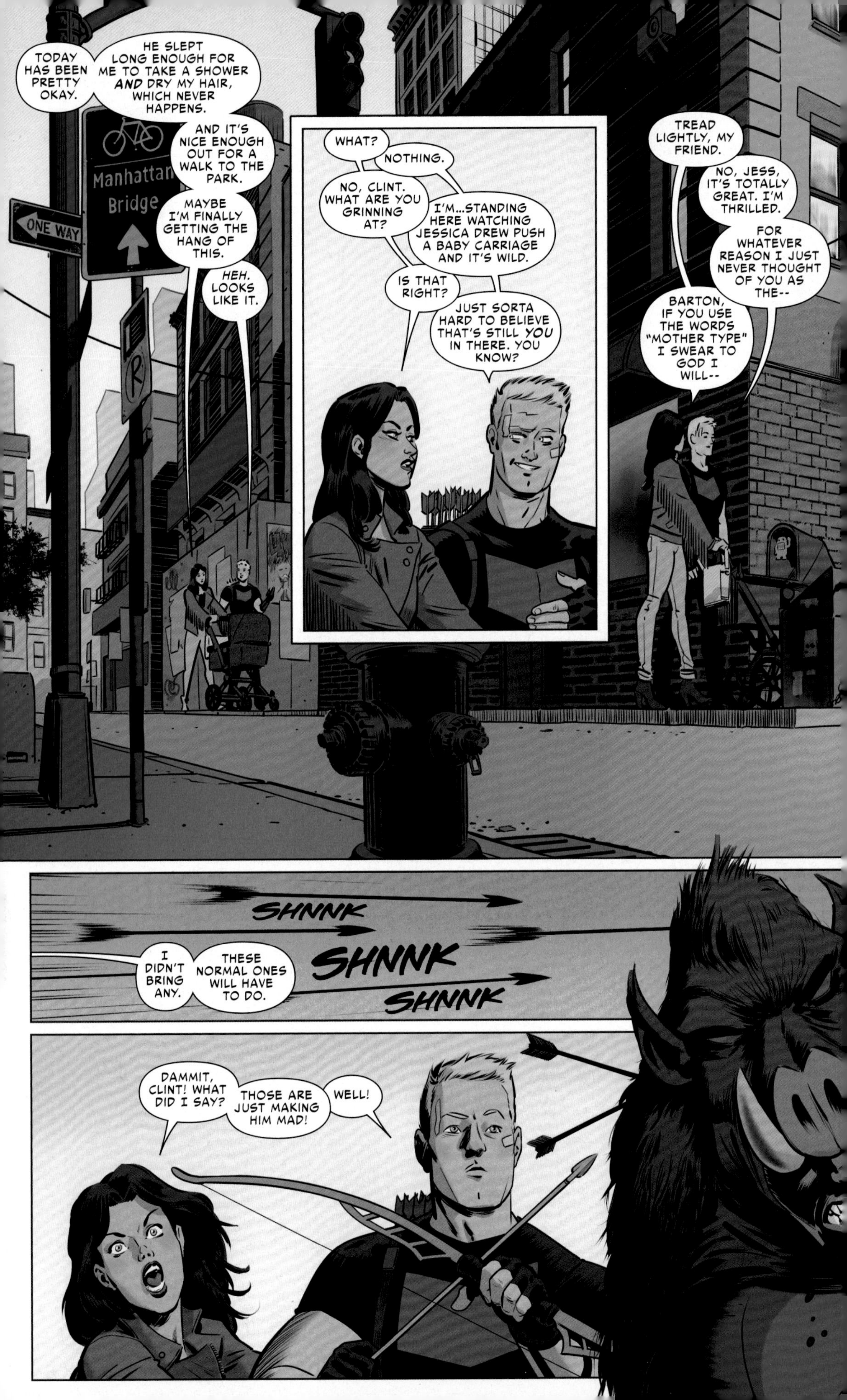
TODAY HAS BEEN PRETTY OKAY.
HE SLEPT LONG ENOUGH FOR ME TO TAKE A SHOWER *AND* DRY MY HAIR, WHICH NEVER HAPPENS.
AND IT'S NICE ENOUGH OUT FOR A WALK TO THE PARK.
MAYBE I'M FINALLY GETTING THE HANG OF THIS.
HEH. LOOKS LIKE IT.
Manhattan Bridge
ONE WAY
WHAT?
NOTHING.
NO, CLINT. WHAT ARE YOU GRINNING AT?
I'M...STANDING HERE WATCHING JESSICA DREW PUSH A BABY CARRIAGE AND IT'S WILD.
IS THAT RIGHT?
JUST SORTA HARD TO BELIEVE THAT'S STILL *YOU* IN THERE. YOU KNOW?
TREAD LIGHTLY, MY FRIEND.
NO, JESS, IT'S TOTALLY GREAT. I'M THRILLED.
FOR WHATEVER REASON I JUST NEVER THOUGHT OF YOU AS THE--
BARTON, IF YOU USE THE WORDS "MOTHER TYPE" I SWEAR TO GOD I WILL--
SHNNK
SHNNK
I DIDN'T BRING ANY.
THESE NORMAL ONES WILL HAVE TO DO.
SHNNK
DAMMIT, CLINT! WHAT DID I SAY?
THOSE ARE JUST MAKING HIM MAD!
WELL!

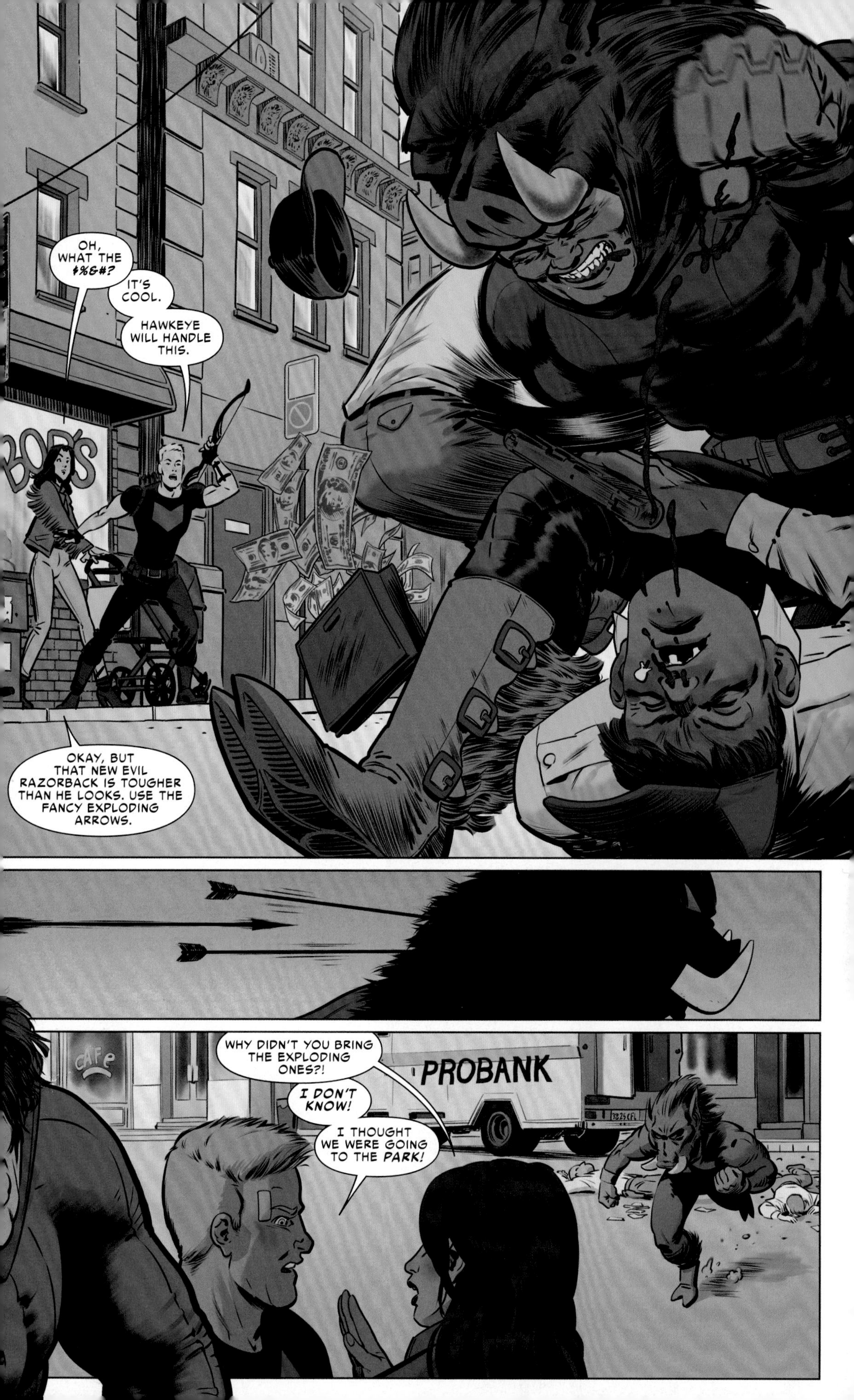
OH, WHAT THE $%&#?
IT'S COOL.
HAWKEYE WILL HANDLE THIS.
BOB'S
OKAY, BUT THAT NEW EVIL RAZORBACK IS TOUGHER THAN HE LOOKS. USE THE FANCY EXPLODING ARROWS.
CAFE
PROBANK
WHY DIDN'T YOU BRING THE EXPLODING ONES?!
I DON'T KNOW!
I THOUGHT WE WERE GOING TO THE PARK!

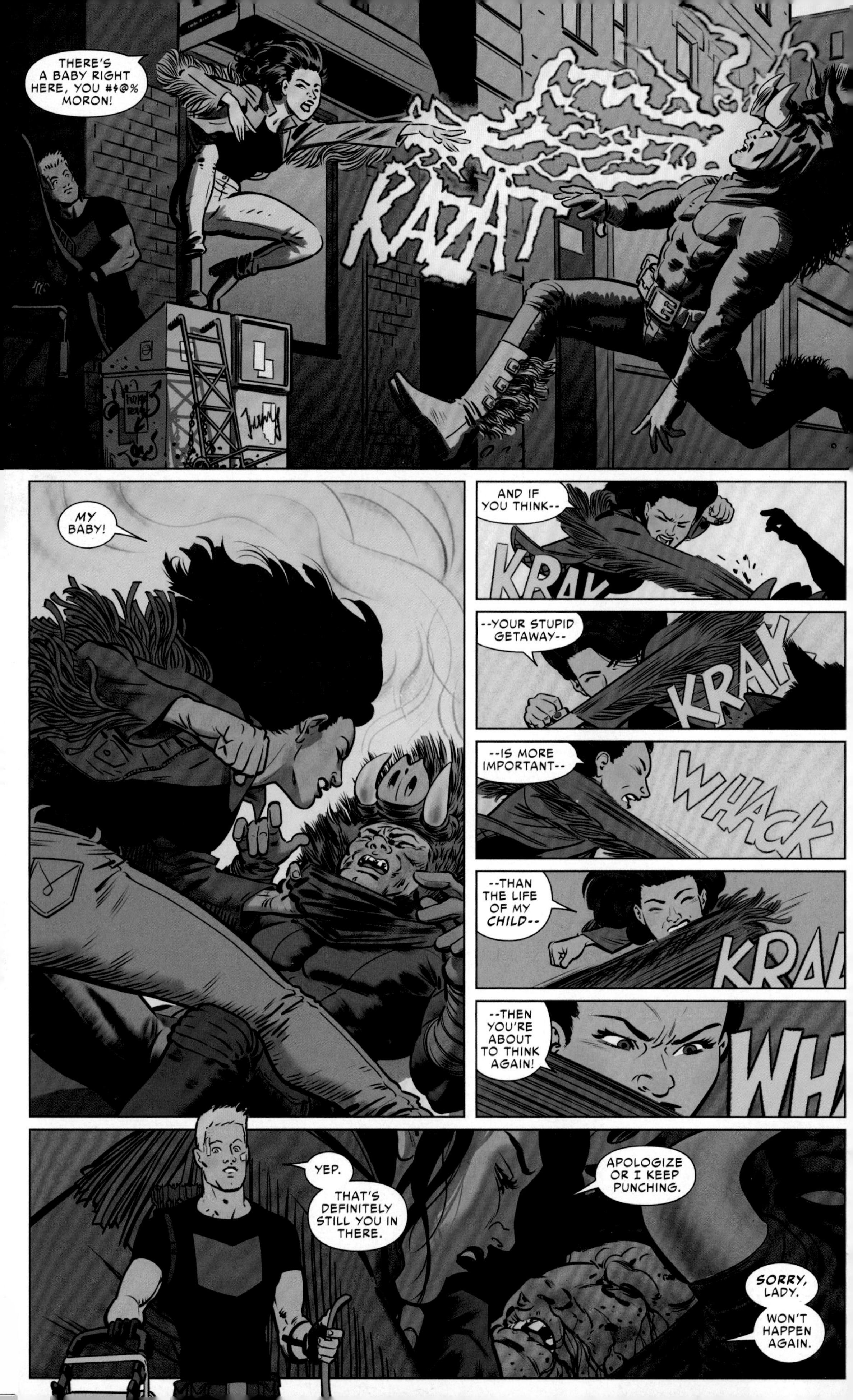
THERE'S A BABY RIGHT HERE, YOU #$@% MORON!
RAZAT
MY BABY!
AND IF YOU THINK--
KRAK
--YOUR STUPID GETAWAY--
KRAK
--IS MORE IMPORTANT--
WHACK
--THAN THE LIFE OF MY *CHILD*--
--THEN YOU'RE ABOUT TO THINK AGAIN!
YEP.
THAT'S DEFINITELY STILL YOU IN THERE.
APOLOGIZE OR I KEEP PUNCHING.
SORRY, LADY.
WON'T HAPPEN AGAIN.

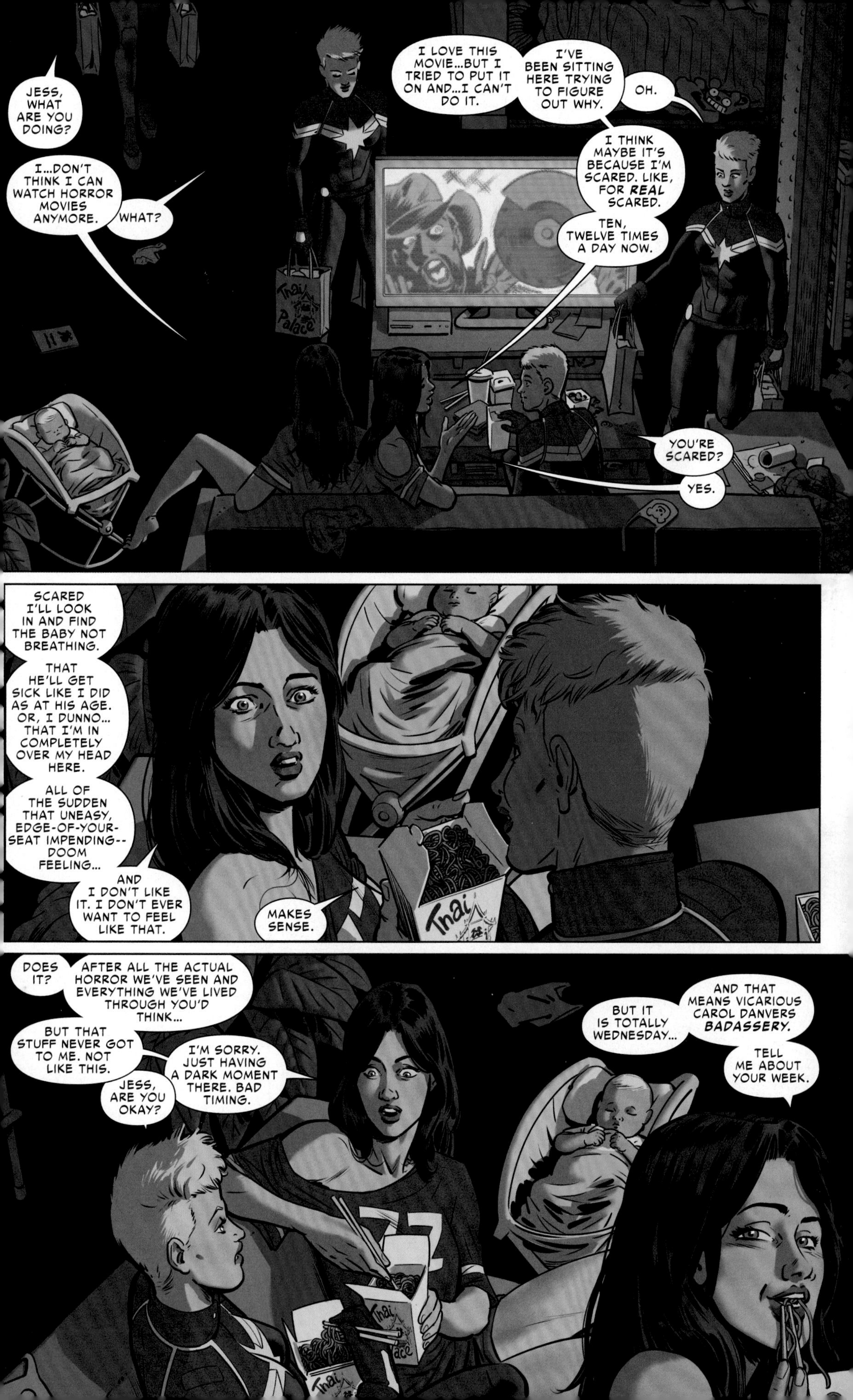
JESS, WHAT ARE YOU DOING?
I...DON'T THINK I CAN WATCH HORROR MOVIES ANYMORE.
WHAT?
I LOVE THIS MOVIE...BUT I TRIED TO PUT IT ON AND...I CAN'T DO IT.
I'VE BEEN SITTING HERE TRYING TO FIGURE OUT WHY.
OH.
I THINK MAYBE IT'S BECAUSE I'M SCARED. LIKE, FOR REAL SCARED.
TEN, TWELVE TIMES A DAY NOW.
YOU'RE SCARED?
YES.
SCARED I'LL LOOK IN AND FIND THE BABY NOT BREATHING.
THAT HE'LL GET SICK LIKE I DID AS AT HIS AGE. OR, I DUNNO... THAT I'M IN COMPLETELY OVER MY HEAD HERE.
ALL OF THE SUDDEN THAT UNEASY, EDGE-OF-YOUR-SEAT IMPENDING--DOOM FEELING...
AND I DON'T LIKE IT. I DON'T EVER WANT TO FEEL LIKE THAT.
MAKES SENSE.
DOES IT?
AFTER ALL THE ACTUAL HORROR WE'VE SEEN AND EVERYTHING WE'VE LIVED THROUGH YOU'D THINK...
BUT THAT STUFF NEVER GOT TO ME. NOT LIKE THIS.
JESS, ARE YOU OKAY?
I'M SORRY. JUST HAVING A DARK MOMENT THERE. BAD TIMING.
BUT IT IS TOTALLY WEDNESDAY...
AND THAT MEANS VICARIOUS CAROL DANVERS BADASSERY.
TELL ME ABOUT YOUR WEEK.

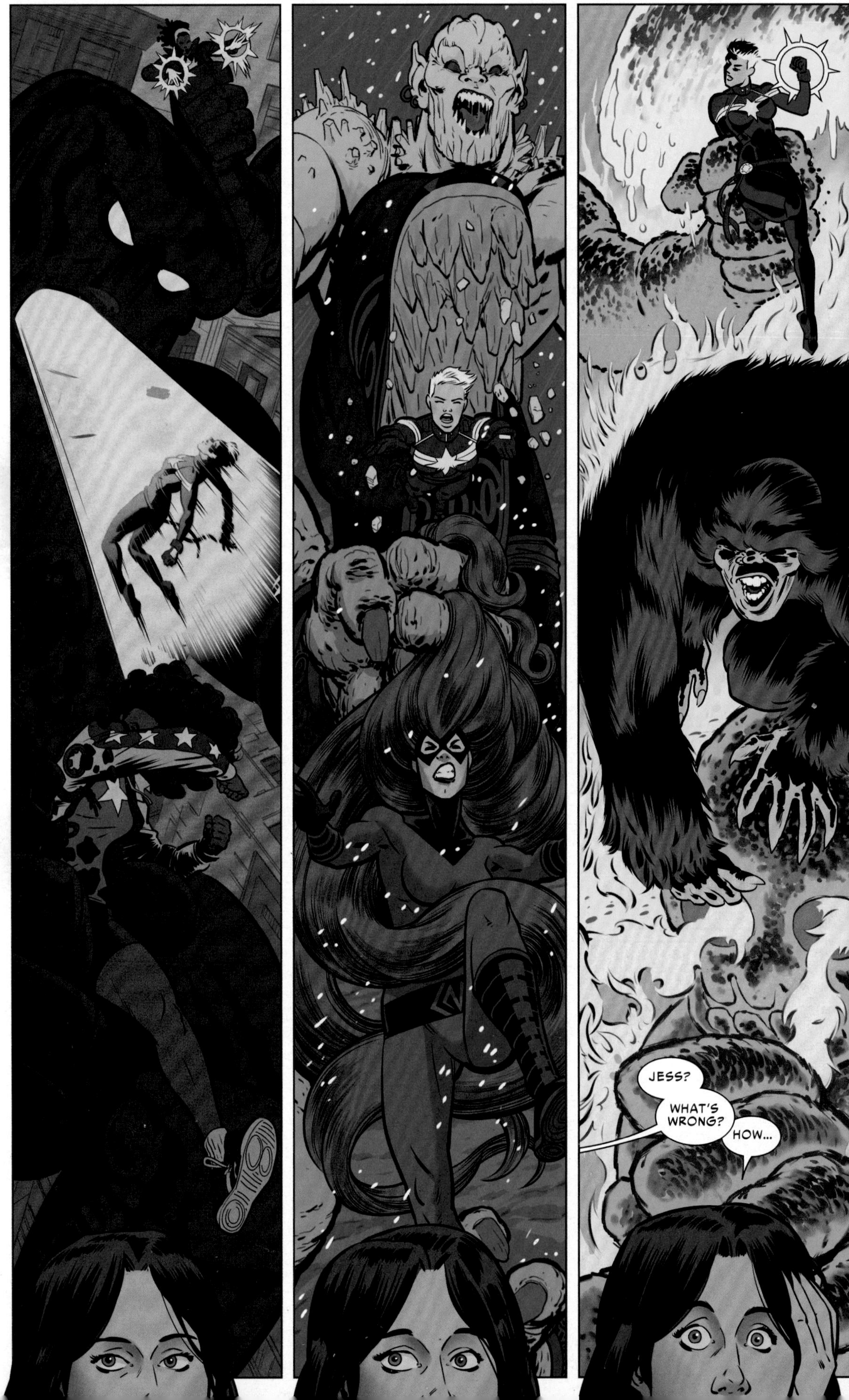
JESS?
WHAT'S WRONG?
HOW...

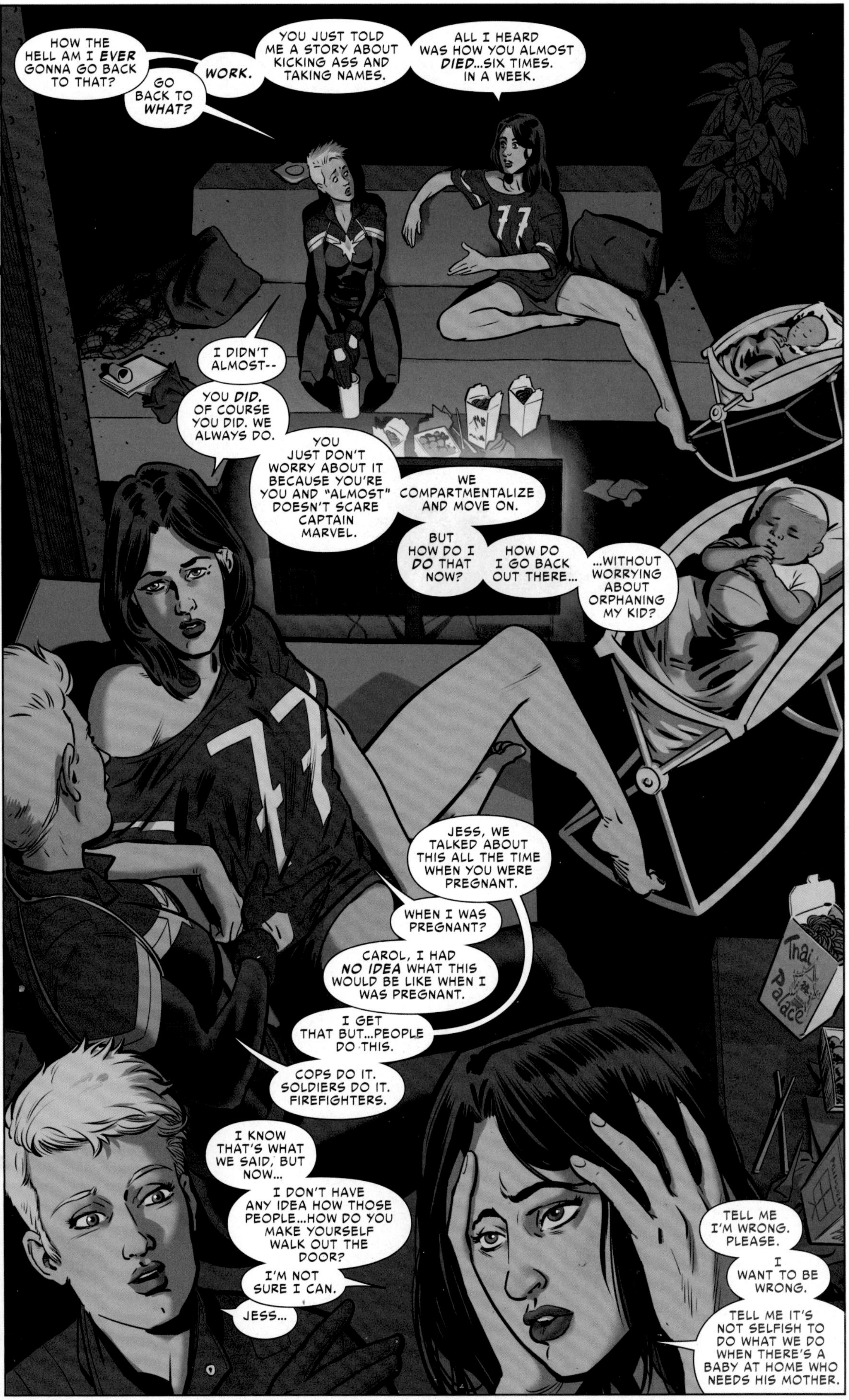
HOW THE HELL AM I **EVER** GONNA GO BACK TO THAT?
GO BACK TO **WHAT?**
WORK.
YOU JUST TOLD ME A STORY ABOUT KICKING ASS AND TAKING NAMES.
ALL I HEARD WAS HOW YOU ALMOST **DIED**...SIX TIMES. IN A WEEK.
I DIDN'T ALMOST--
YOU **DID.** OF COURSE YOU DID. WE ALWAYS DO.
YOU JUST DON'T WORRY ABOUT IT BECAUSE YOU'RE YOU AND "ALMOST" DOESN'T SCARE CAPTAIN MARVEL.
WE COMPARTMENTALIZE AND MOVE ON.
BUT HOW DO I **DO** THAT NOW?
HOW DO I GO BACK OUT THERE...
...WITHOUT WORRYING ABOUT ORPHANING MY KID?
JESS, WE TALKED ABOUT THIS ALL THE TIME WHEN YOU WERE PREGNANT.
WHEN I WAS PREGNANT?
CAROL, I HAD **NO IDEA** WHAT THIS WOULD BE LIKE WHEN I WAS PREGNANT.
I GET THAT BUT...PEOPLE DO THIS.
COPS DO IT. SOLDIERS DO IT. FIREFIGHTERS.
Thai Palace
I KNOW THAT'S WHAT WE SAID, BUT NOW...
I DON'T HAVE ANY IDEA HOW THOSE PEOPLE...HOW DO YOU MAKE YOURSELF WALK OUT THE DOOR?
I'M NOT SURE I CAN.
JESS...
TELL ME I'M WRONG. PLEASE.
I WANT TO BE WRONG.
TELL ME IT'S NOT SELFISH TO DO WHAT WE DO WHEN THERE'S A BABY AT HOME WHO NEEDS HIS MOTHER.

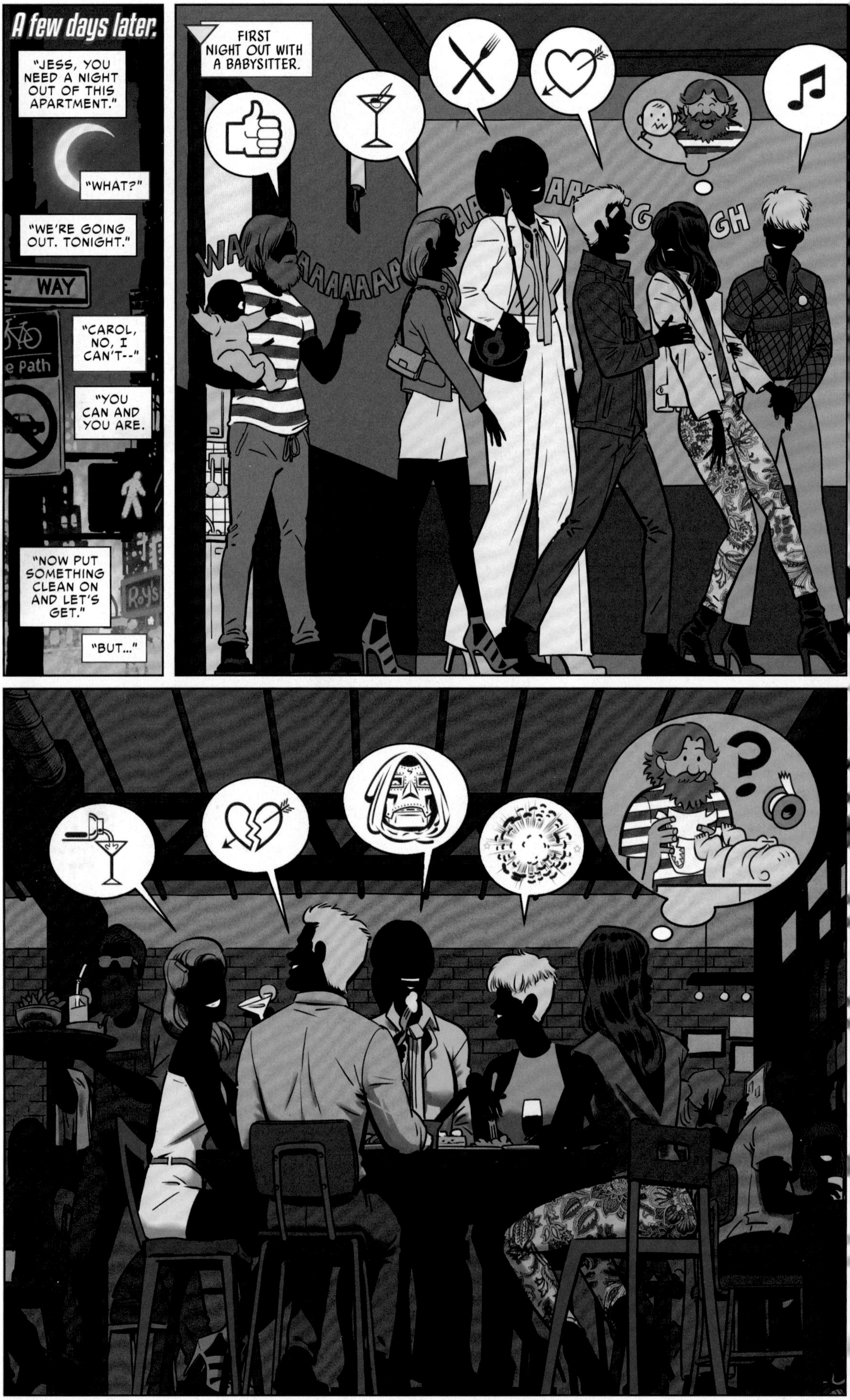

A few days later.
"JESS, YOU NEED A NIGHT OUT OF THIS APARTMENT."
"WHAT?"
"WE'RE GOING OUT. TONIGHT."
"CAROL, NO, I CAN'T--"
"YOU CAN AND YOU ARE.
"NOW PUT SOMETHING CLEAN ON AND LET'S GET."
"BUT..."
FIRST NIGHT OUT WITH A BABYSITTER.

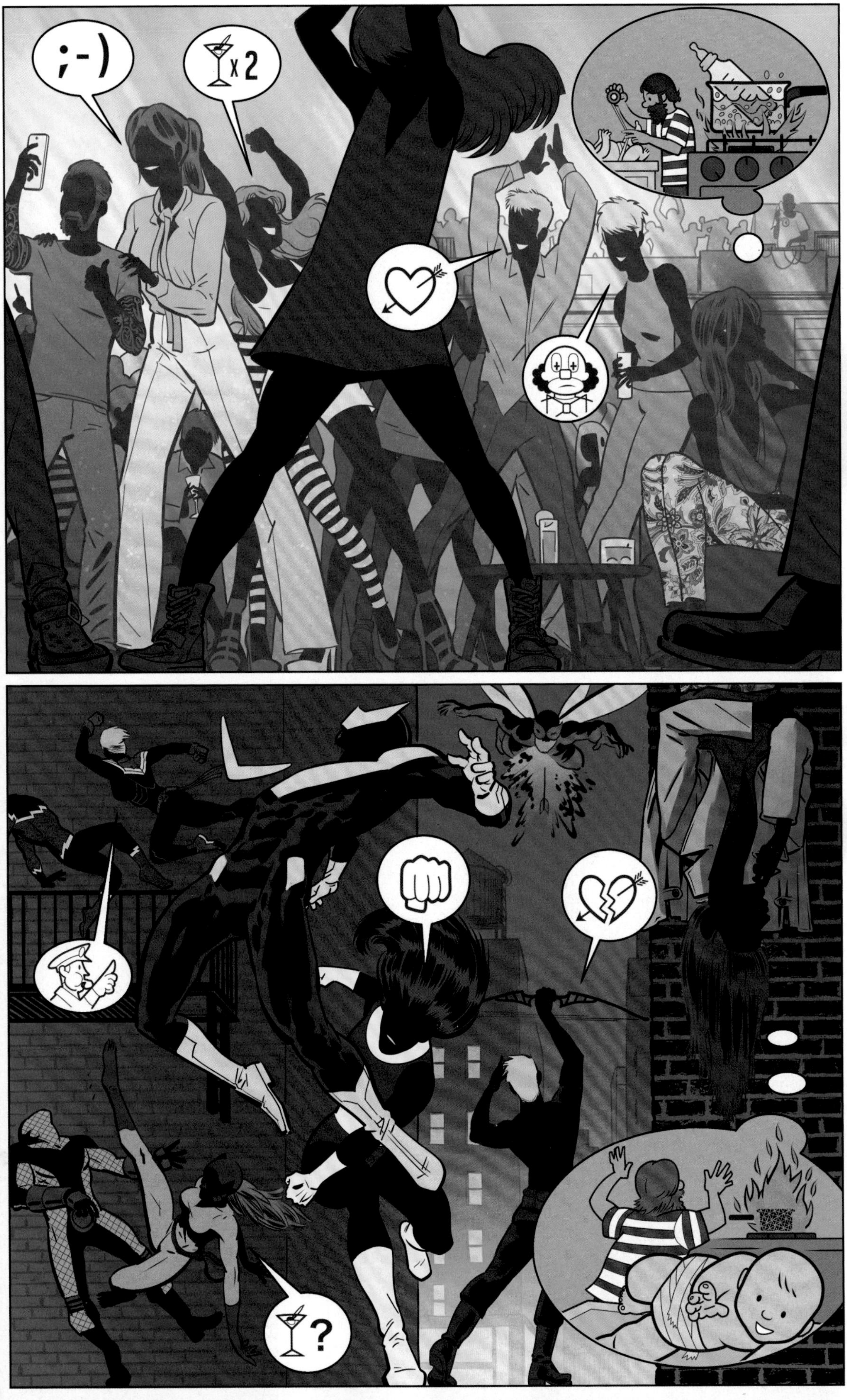
;-)
x 2
?

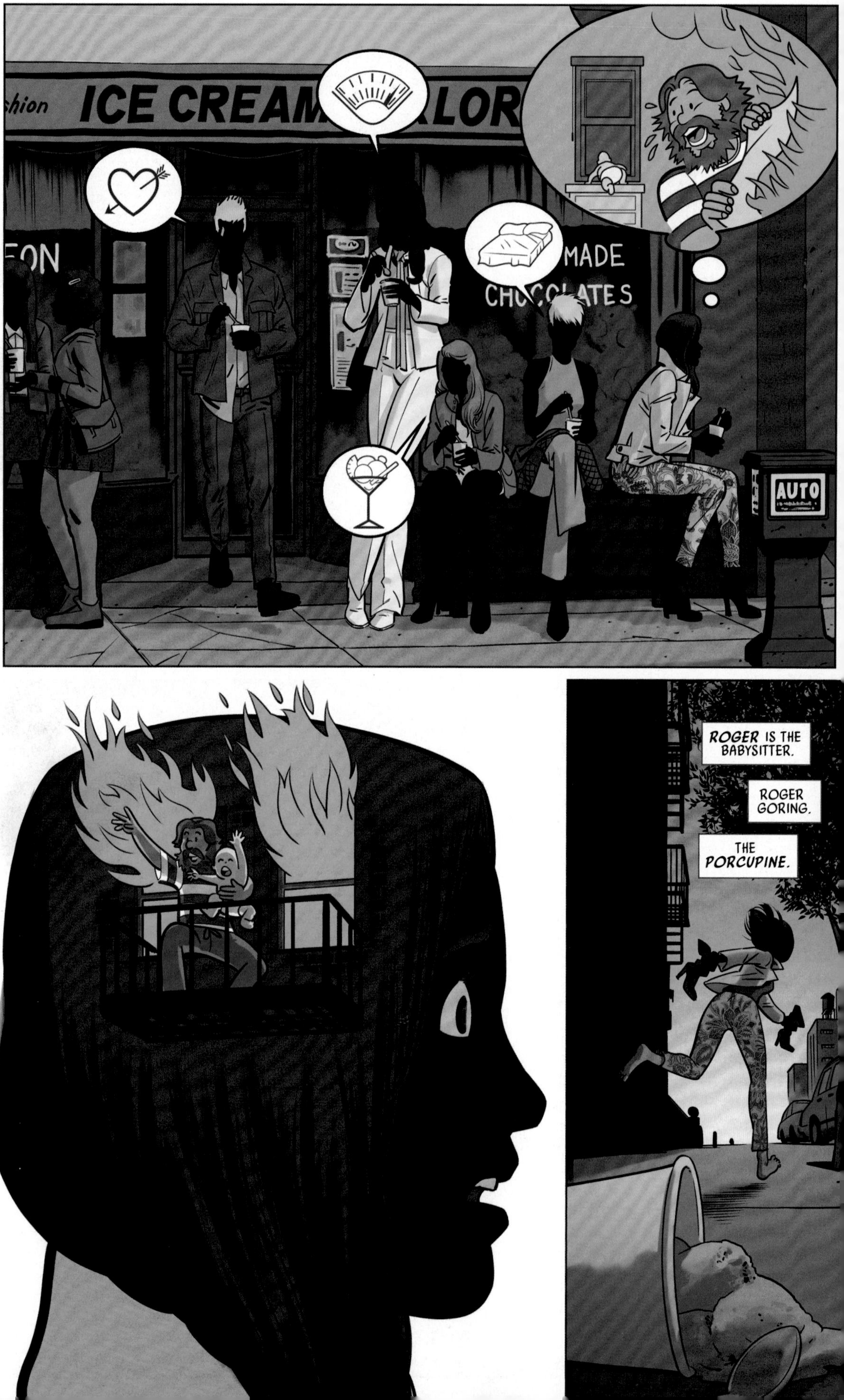

ICE CREAM PARLOR
MADE
CHOCOLATES
AUTO
ROGER IS THE BABYSITTER.
ROGER GORING.
THE PORCUPINE.

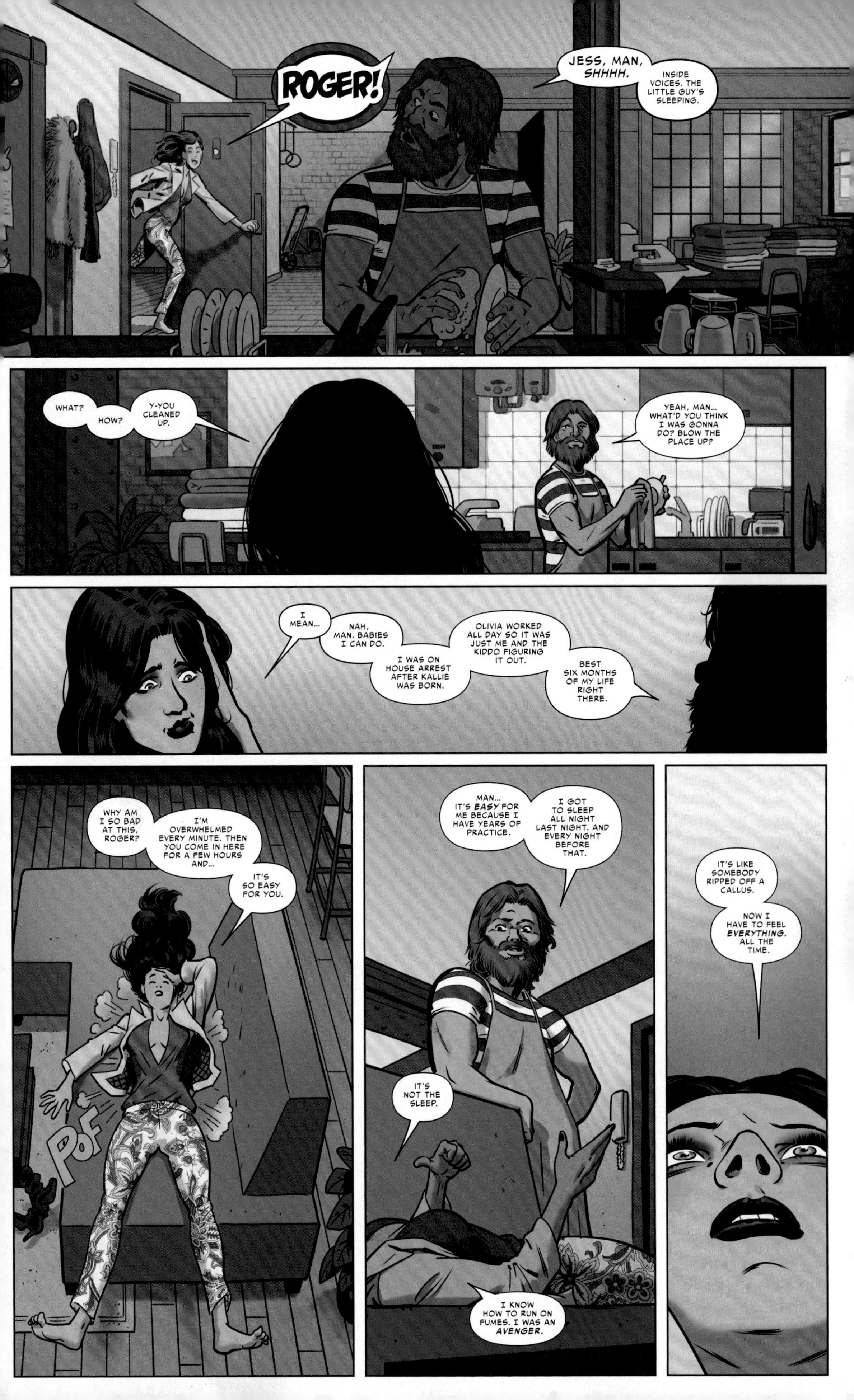
ROGER!
JESS, MAN, SHHHH.
INSIDE VOICES. THE LITTLE GUY'S SLEEPING.
WHAT?
HOW?
Y-YOU CLEANED UP.
YEAH, MAN... WHAT'D YOU THINK I WAS GONNA DO? BLOW THE PLACE UP?
I MEAN...
NAH, MAN. BABIES I CAN DO.
I WAS ON HOUSE ARREST AFTER KALLIE WAS BORN.
OLIVIA WORKED ALL DAY SO IT WAS JUST ME AND THE KIDDO FIGURING IT OUT.
BEST SIX MONTHS OF MY LIFE RIGHT THERE.
WHY AM I SO BAD AT THIS, ROGER?
I'M OVERWHELMED EVERY MINUTE. THEN YOU COME IN HERE FOR A FEW HOURS AND...
IT'S SO EASY FOR YOU.
POF
MAN... IT'S EASY FOR ME BECAUSE I HAVE YEARS OF PRACTICE.
I GOT TO SLEEP ALL NIGHT LAST NIGHT. AND EVERY NIGHT BEFORE THAT.
IT'S NOT THE SLEEP.
I KNOW HOW TO RUN ON FUMES. I WAS AN AVENGER.
IT'S LIKE SOMEBODY RIPPED OFF A CALLUS.
NOW I HAVE TO FEEL EVERYTHING. ALL THE TIME.

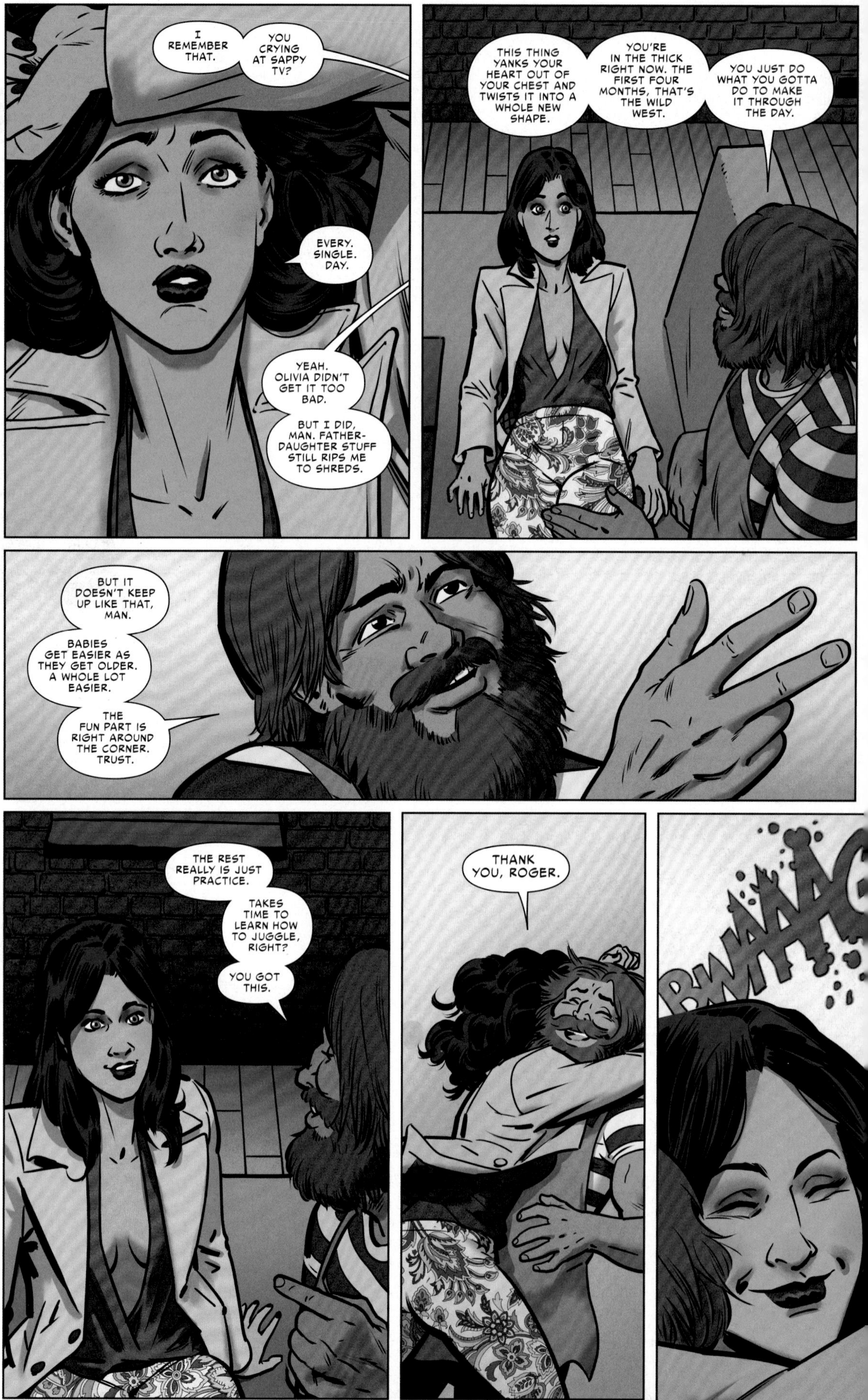
I REMEMBER THAT.
YOU CRYING AT SAPPY TV?
EVERY. SINGLE. DAY.
YEAH. OLIVIA DIDN'T GET IT TOO BAD.
BUT I DID, MAN. FATHER-DAUGHTER STUFF STILL RIPS ME TO SHREDS.
THIS THING YANKS YOUR HEART OUT OF YOUR CHEST AND TWISTS IT INTO A WHOLE NEW SHAPE.
YOU'RE IN THE THICK RIGHT NOW. THE FIRST FOUR MONTHS, THAT'S THE WILD WEST.
YOU JUST DO WHAT YOU GOTTA DO TO MAKE IT THROUGH THE DAY.
BUT IT DOESN'T KEEP UP LIKE THAT, MAN.
BABIES GET EASIER AS THEY GET OLDER. A WHOLE LOT EASIER.
THE FUN PART IS RIGHT AROUND THE CORNER. TRUST.
THE REST REALLY IS JUST PRACTICE.
TAKES TIME TO LEARN HOW TO JUGGLE, RIGHT?
YOU GOT THIS.
THANK YOU, ROGER.

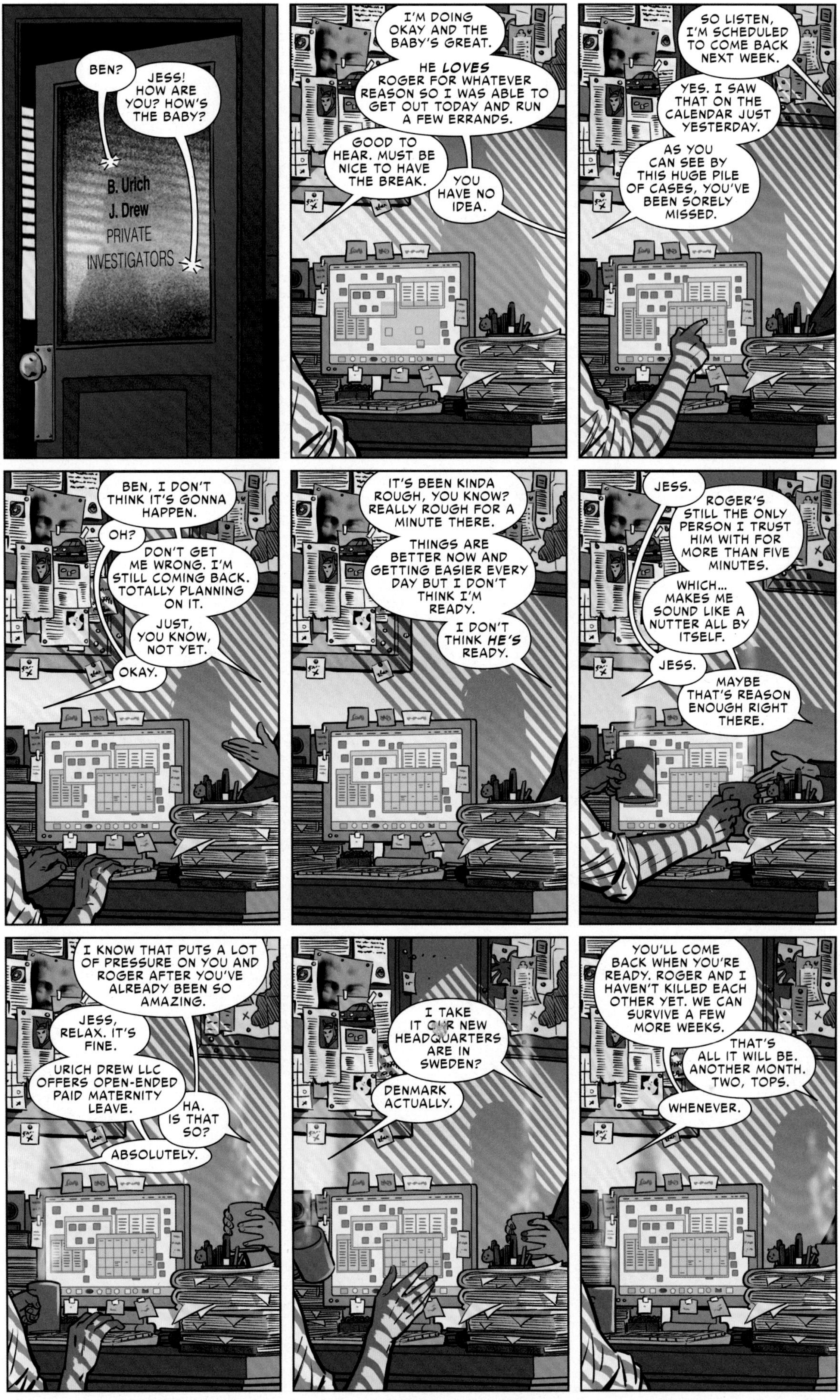
BEN?
JESS! HOW ARE YOU? HOW'S THE BABY?
B. Urich
J. Drew
PRIVATE
INVESTIGATORS
I'M DOING OKAY AND THE BABY'S GREAT.
HE LOVES ROGER FOR WHATEVER REASON SO I WAS ABLE TO GET OUT TODAY AND RUN A FEW ERRANDS.
GOOD TO HEAR. MUST BE NICE TO HAVE THE BREAK.
YOU HAVE NO IDEA.
SO LISTEN, I'M SCHEDULED TO COME BACK NEXT WEEK.
YES. I SAW THAT ON THE CALENDAR JUST YESTERDAY.
AS YOU CAN SEE BY THIS HUGE PILE OF CASES, YOU'VE BEEN SORELY MISSED.
BEN, I DON'T THINK IT'S GONNA HAPPEN.
OH?
DON'T GET ME WRONG. I'M STILL COMING BACK. TOTALLY PLANNING ON IT.
JUST, YOU KNOW, NOT YET.
OKAY.
IT'S BEEN KINDA ROUGH, YOU KNOW? REALLY ROUGH FOR A MINUTE THERE.
THINGS ARE BETTER NOW AND GETTING EASIER EVERY DAY BUT I DON'T THINK I'M READY.
I DON'T THINK HE'S READY.
JESS.
ROGER'S STILL THE ONLY PERSON I TRUST HIM WITH FOR MORE THAN FIVE MINUTES.
WHICH... MAKES ME SOUND LIKE A NUTTER ALL BY ITSELF.
JESS.
MAYBE THAT'S REASON ENOUGH RIGHT THERE.
I KNOW THAT PUTS A LOT OF PRESSURE ON YOU AND ROGER AFTER YOU'VE ALREADY BEEN SO AMAZING.
JESS, RELAX. IT'S FINE.
URICH DREW LLC OFFERS OPEN-ENDED PAID MATERNITY LEAVE.
HA. IS THAT SO?
ABSOLUTELY.
I TAKE IT OUR NEW HEADQUARTERS ARE IN SWEDEN?
DENMARK ACTUALLY.
YOU'LL COME BACK WHEN YOU'RE READY. ROGER AND I HAVEN'T KILLED EACH OTHER YET. WE CAN SURVIVE A FEW MORE WEEKS.
THAT'S ALL IT WILL BE. ANOTHER MONTH. TWO, TOPS.
WHENEVER.

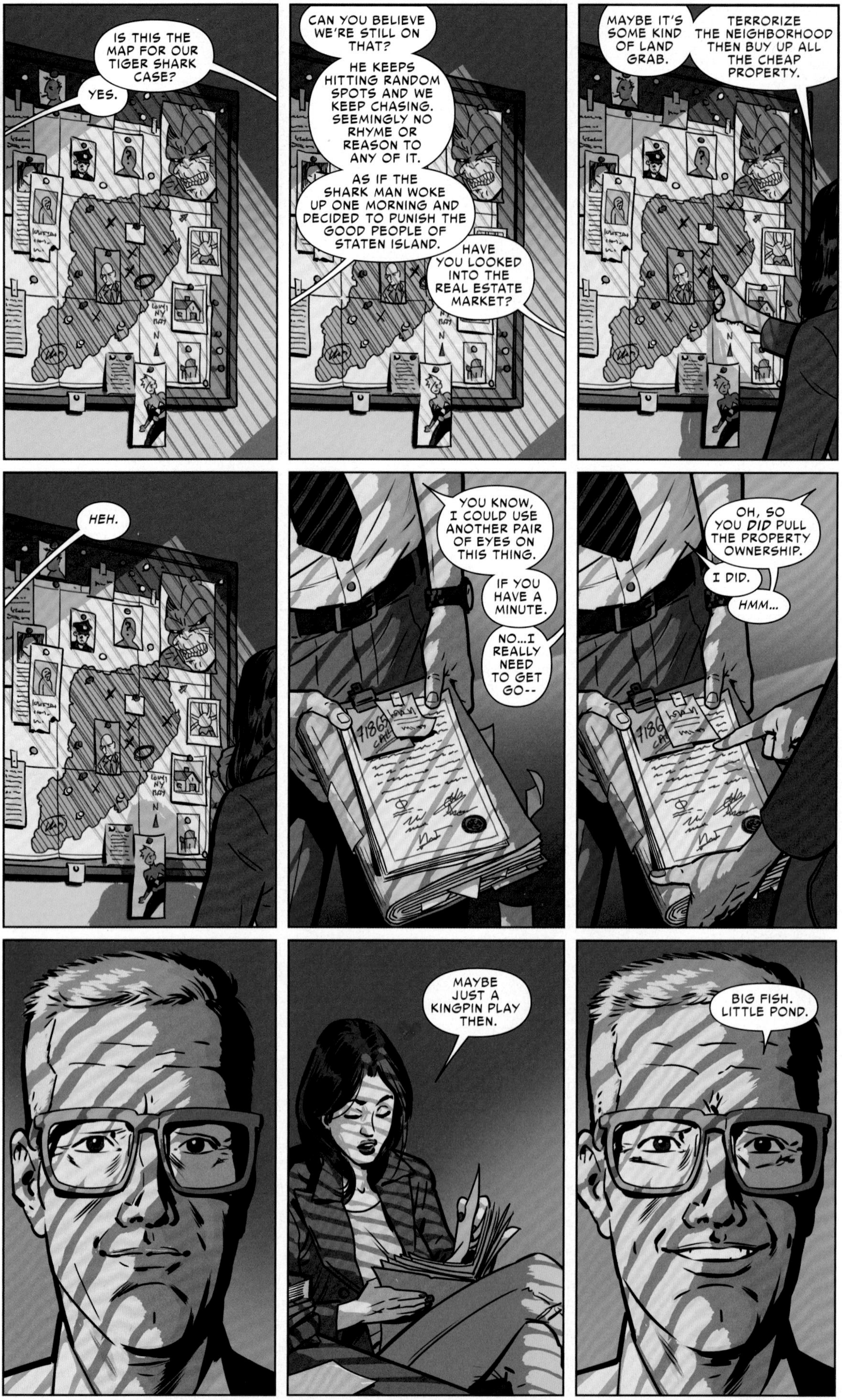

IS THIS THE MAP FOR OUR TIGER SHARK CASE?
YES.
CAN YOU BELIEVE WE'RE STILL ON THAT?
HE KEEPS HITTING RANDOM SPOTS AND WE KEEP CHASING. SEEMINGLY NO RHYME OR REASON TO ANY OF IT.
AS IF THE SHARK MAN WOKE UP ONE MORNING AND DECIDED TO PUNISH THE GOOD PEOPLE OF STATEN ISLAND.
HAVE YOU LOOKED INTO THE REAL ESTATE MARKET?
MAYBE IT'S SOME KIND OF LAND GRAB.
TERRORIZE THE NEIGHBORHOOD THEN BUY UP ALL THE CHEAP PROPERTY.
HEH.
YOU KNOW, I COULD USE ANOTHER PAIR OF EYES ON THIS THING.
IF YOU HAVE A MINUTE.
NO...I REALLY NEED TO GET GO--
OH, SO YOU DID PULL THE PROPERTY OWNERSHIP.
I DID.
HMM...
MAYBE JUST A KINGPIN PLAY THEN.
BIG FISH. LITTLE POND.

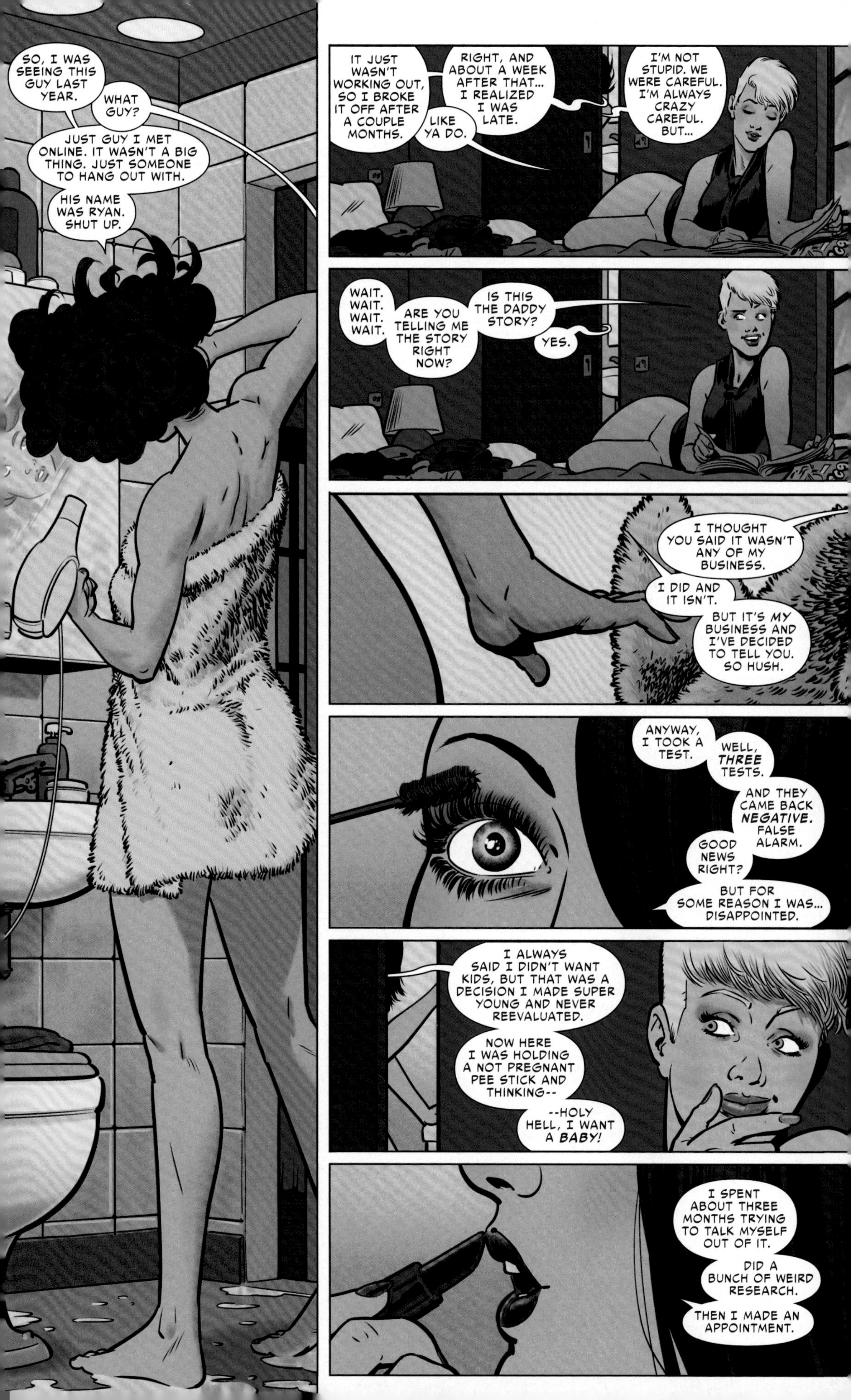
SO, I WAS SEEING THIS GUY LAST YEAR.
WHAT GUY?
JUST GUY I MET ONLINE. IT WASN'T A BIG THING. JUST SOMEONE TO HANG OUT WITH.
HIS NAME WAS RYAN. SHUT UP.
IT JUST WASN'T WORKING OUT, SO I BROKE IT OFF AFTER A COUPLE MONTHS.
LIKE YA DO.
RIGHT, AND ABOUT A WEEK AFTER THAT... I REALIZED I WAS LATE.
I'M NOT STUPID. WE WERE CAREFUL. I'M ALWAYS CRAZY CAREFUL. BUT...
WAIT. WAIT. WAIT. WAIT.
ARE YOU TELLING ME THE STORY RIGHT NOW?
IS THIS THE DADDY STORY?
YES.
I THOUGHT YOU SAID IT WASN'T ANY OF MY BUSINESS.
I DID AND IT ISN'T.
BUT IT'S *MY* BUSINESS AND I'VE DECIDED TO TELL YOU. SO HUSH.
ANYWAY, I TOOK A TEST.
WELL, ***THREE*** TESTS.
AND THEY CAME BACK ***NEGATIVE.*** FALSE ALARM.
GOOD NEWS RIGHT?
BUT FOR SOME REASON I WAS... DISAPPOINTED.
I ALWAYS SAID I DIDN'T WANT KIDS, BUT THAT WAS A DECISION I MADE SUPER YOUNG AND NEVER REEVALUATED.
NOW HERE I WAS HOLDING A NOT PREGNANT PEE STICK AND THINKING--
--HOLY HELL, I WANT A *BABY!*
I SPENT ABOUT THREE MONTHS TRYING TO TALK MYSELF OUT OF IT.
DID A BUNCH OF WEIRD RESEARCH.
THEN I MADE AN APPOINTMENT.

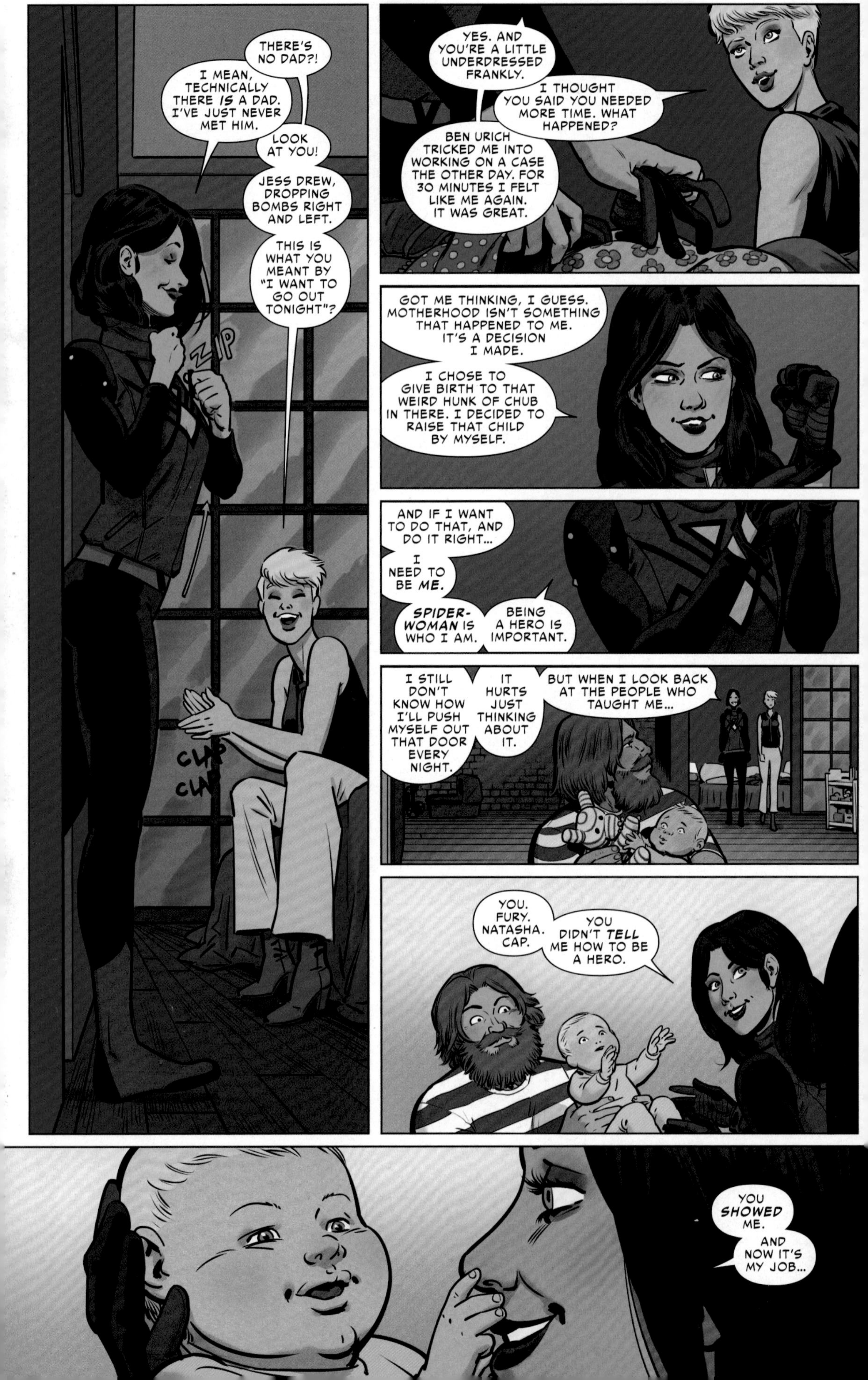
THERE'S NO DAD?!
I MEAN, TECHNICALLY THERE *IS* A DAD. I'VE JUST NEVER MET HIM.
LOOK AT YOU!
JESS DREW, DROPPING BOMBS RIGHT AND LEFT.
THIS IS WHAT YOU MEANT BY "I WANT TO GO OUT TONIGHT"?
ZIP
CLAP
CLAP
YES. AND YOU'RE A LITTLE UNDERDRESSED FRANKLY.
I THOUGHT YOU SAID YOU NEEDED MORE TIME. WHAT HAPPENED?
BEN URICH TRICKED ME INTO WORKING ON A CASE THE OTHER DAY. FOR 30 MINUTES I FELT LIKE ME AGAIN. IT WAS GREAT.
GOT ME THINKING, I GUESS. MOTHERHOOD ISN'T SOMETHING THAT HAPPENED TO ME. IT'S A DECISION I MADE.
I CHOSE TO GIVE BIRTH TO THAT WEIRD HUNK OF CHUB IN THERE. I DECIDED TO RAISE THAT CHILD BY MYSELF.
AND IF I WANT TO DO THAT, AND DO IT RIGHT...
I NEED TO BE *ME.*
SPIDER-WOMAN IS WHO I AM.
BEING A HERO IS IMPORTANT.
I STILL DON'T KNOW HOW I'LL PUSH MYSELF OUT THAT DOOR EVERY NIGHT.
IT HURTS JUST THINKING ABOUT IT.
BUT WHEN I LOOK BACK AT THE PEOPLE WHO TAUGHT ME...
YOU. FURY. NATASHA. CAP.
YOU DIDN'T *TELL* ME HOW TO BE A HERO.
YOU *SHOWED* ME.
AND NOW IT'S MY JOB...

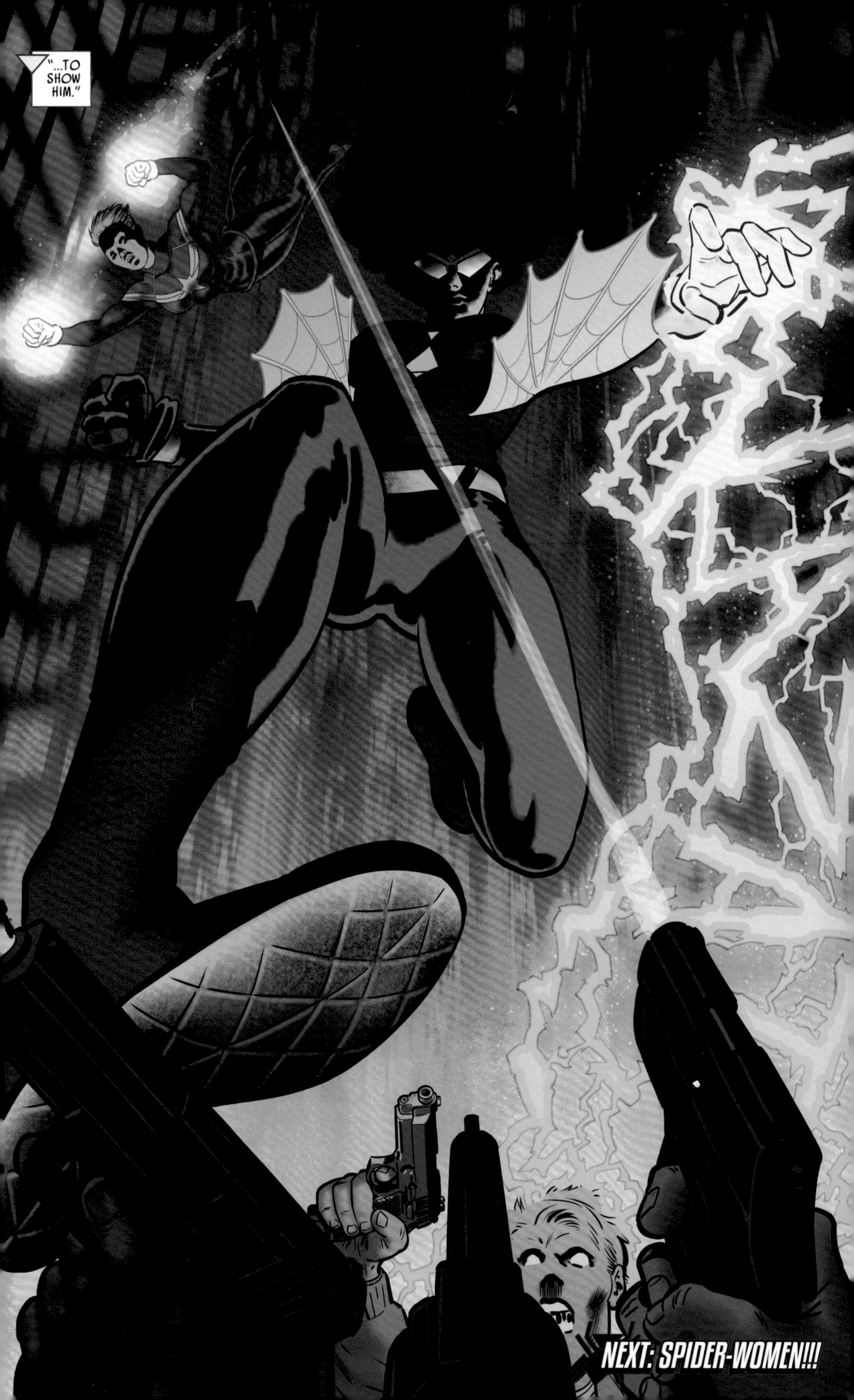
"...TO SHOW HIM."
NEXT: SPIDER-WOMEN!!!

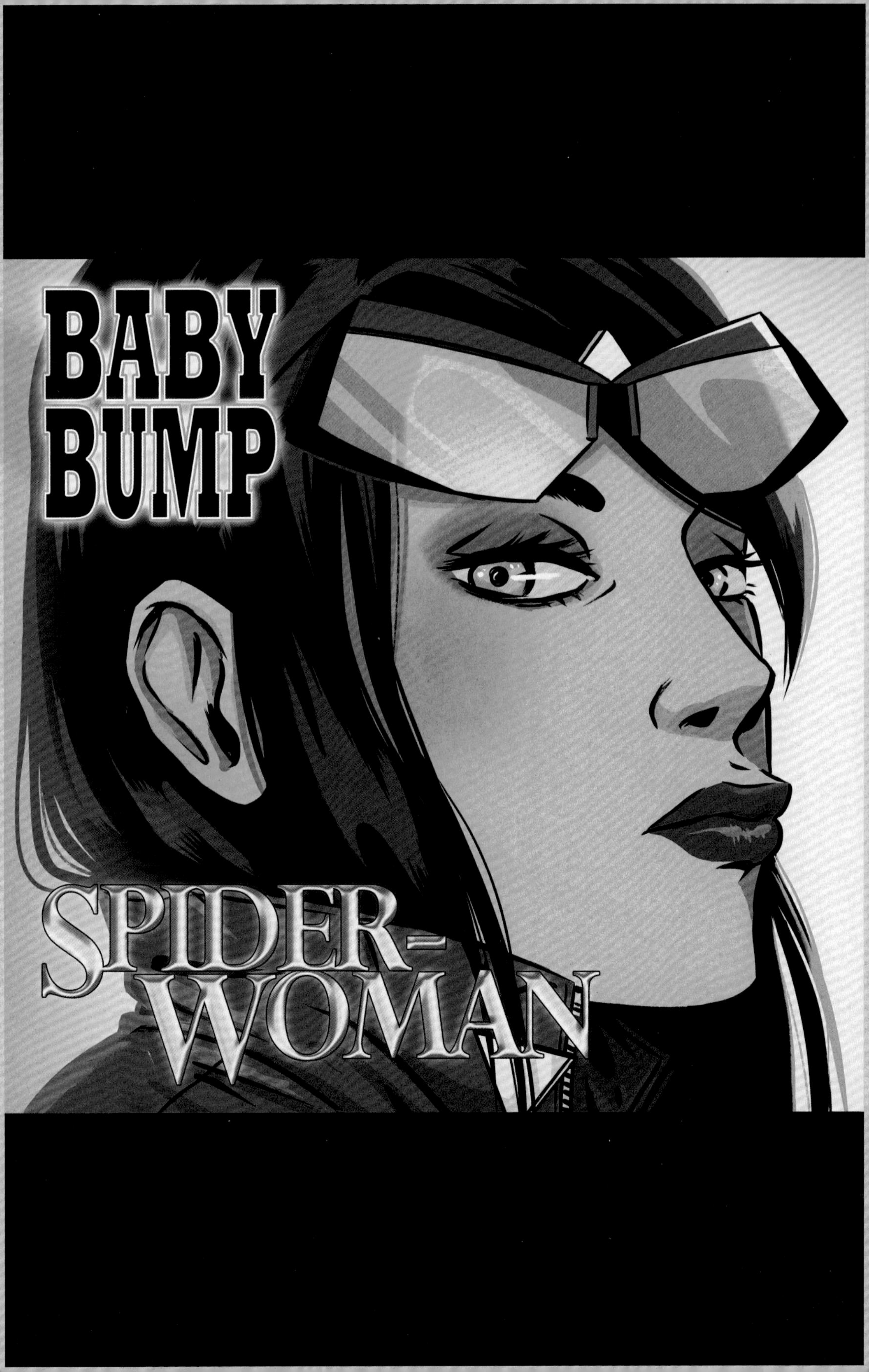
BABY BUMP
SPIDER-WOMAN

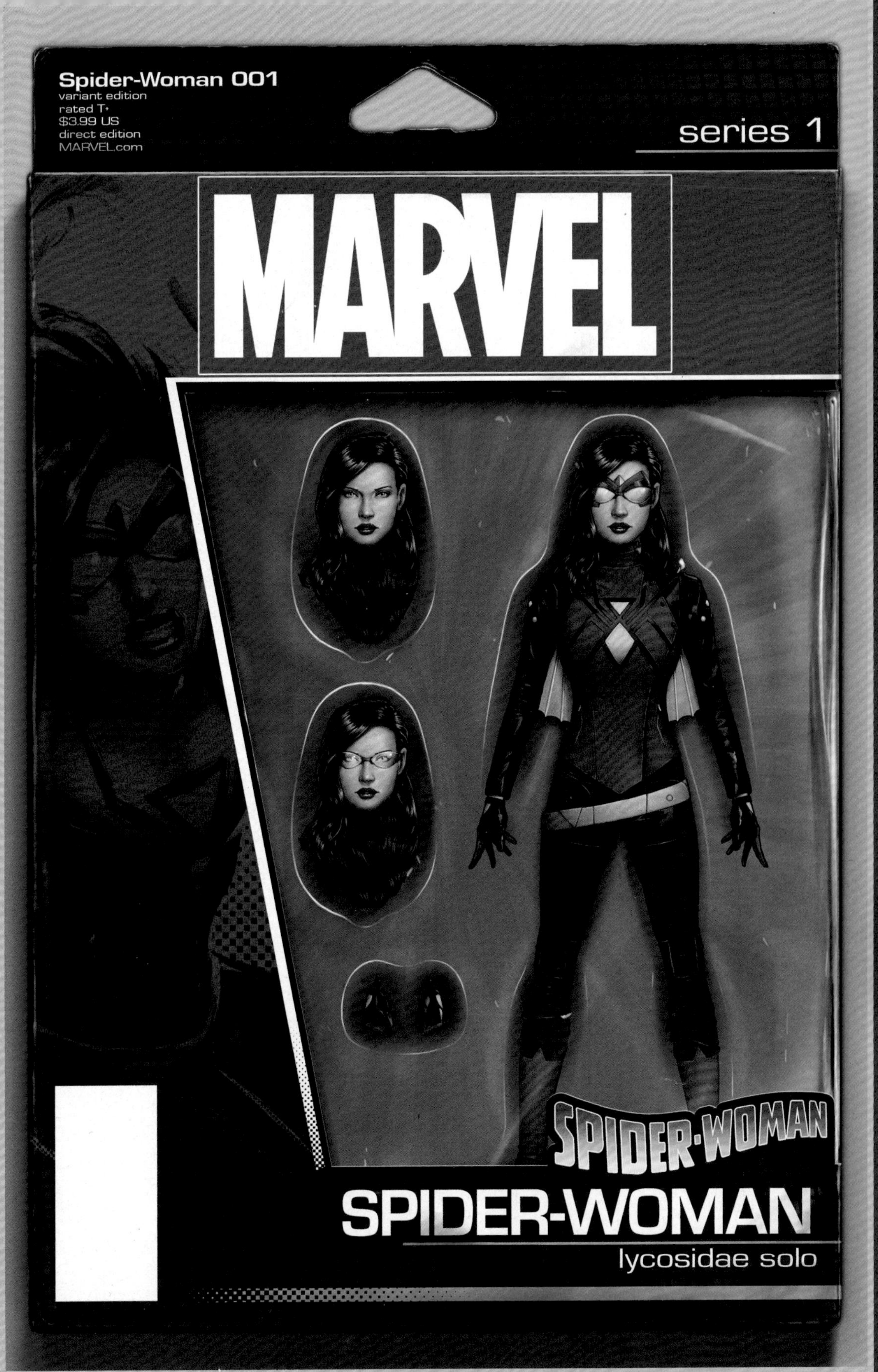
Spider-Woman 001
variant edition
rated T+
$3.99 US
direct edition
MARVEL.com
series 1
MARVEL
SPIDER-WOMAN
SPIDER-WOMAN
lycosidae solo

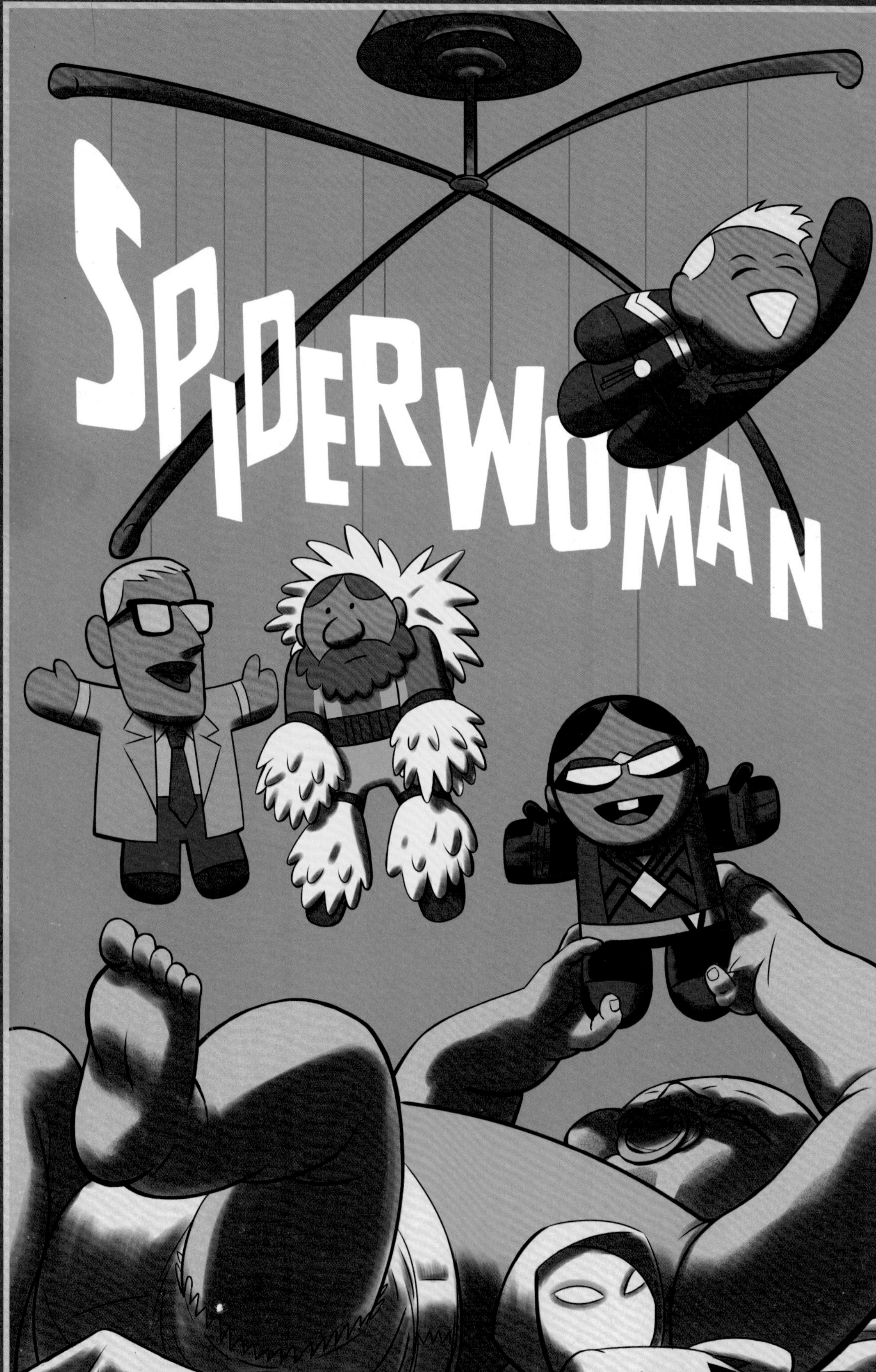
SPIDER WOMAN